'What is the use of a book,' thought Alice,
'without pictures or conversations?'

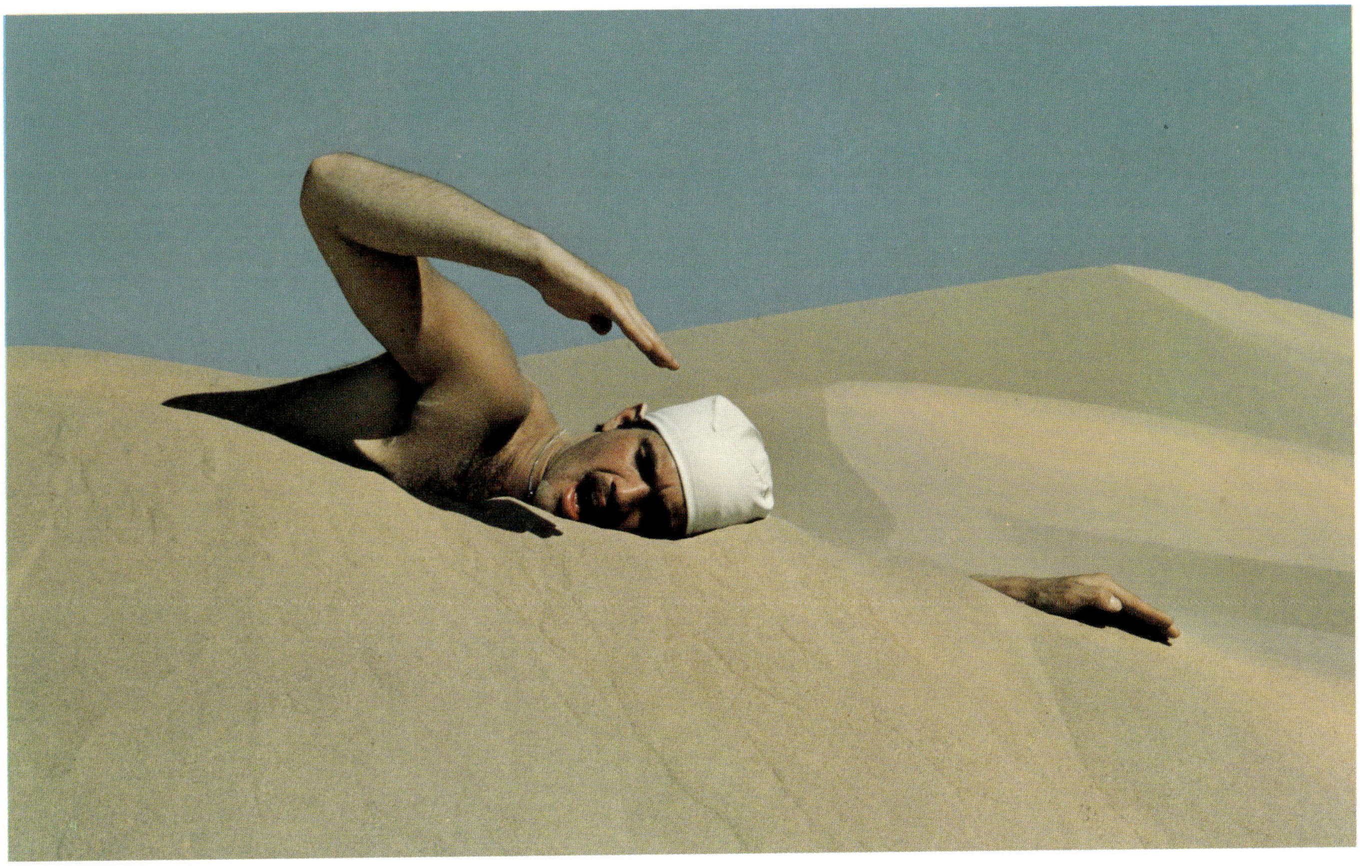

The Meaning of Life

Swimmer in the Desert

Shot with 35-mm Nikomat with W/A lens; f16 at 1/125th. Straight photography taken in daylight with Kodachrome X. The location is the Yuma desert, Southern California. It's morning.

This was photographed whilst we were shooting the cover of 'Wish You Were Here' for the Pink Floyd. It was an idea that was only half related to the rest of the package but we decided to shoot it anyway. It was used as a very small throwaway at the end of the Pink Floyd songbook and similarly at the end of our last book 'Walk Away René'. It was most gainfully employed as a greeting card for Heroes Card Company, in conjunction with Miss Deidre Morrow. For this purpose it was entitled 'The Meaning of Life'.

While we were working on 'Wish You Were Here', there was a lot of discussion about the nature of absence. A friend, Nod Brown, suggested that 'absence' might be embodied in the notion of a swimmer crawling through the desert towards a hamburger restaurant. He arrives at the door, utterly exhausted, to find a note saying 'Out to Lunch'. This struck us as too involved for a still picture, but a man crawling, or rather swimming, through the desert, was something different.

It's the simplicity that works for me. And the crazy optimism. The swimmer looks unperturbed as he struggles onward. But it's all so useless: how is he going to get anywhere? The image is a comment on the futility of life. On the other hand, perhaps this picture is only about a very speedy swimmer who swam so fast out of the sea that he just kept on going, up the beach and over the dunes.

the photoDesigns of

HIPGNOSIS

THE GOODBYE LOOK

Selected by Peter Christopherson, Aubrey Powell and Storm Thorgerson
Designed by Neville Brody and Hipgnosis
Text by Storm Thorgerson
Edited by Nick Sedgwick

VERMILION

By the same authors

Album Cover Album I

Hands Across the Water
(Wings tour America)

Walk Away René

Album Cover Album II

For Donald and Rosie

Vermilion and Company

An imprint of the Hutchinson Publishing Group

17–21 Conway Street, London W1P 6JD

Hutchinson Group (Australia) Pty Ltd
30–32 Cremorne Street, Richmond South, Victoria 3121
PO Box 151, Broadway, New South Wales 2007

Hutchinson Group (NZ) Ltd
32–34 View Road, PO Box 40–086, Glenfield, Auckland 10

Hutchinson Group (SA) Pty Ltd
PO Box 337, Bergvlei 2012, South Africa

First published 1982

Printed and bound in Great Britain by W. S. Cowell Ltd,
London and Ipswich

British Library Cataloguing in Publication Data
Thorgerson, Storm.
The goodbye look
1. Commercial art
2. Rock music – Miscellanea
659.13'23 NC1000
ISBN 0 09 150641 7

Introduction

Come a little closer, for I have a confession. The preferred practice is to get sombody famous to write one's introduction. Or, at the very least, a so-called expert in the field. We thought of a variety of people, from the Pope to Marilyn Chambers, from Mrs Bandaranaike to Johnny Rotten, but in the final analysis none of them seemed to fit the bill. Or our rampant egos. It is down, I'm afraid, to the trumpet syndrome: not voluntarily, I assure you.

This book is a collection of pictures by the design studio of Hipgnosis. The pictures were originally posters, record sleeves or pieces of editorial and advertising. We have included what we think is our best work from the last five years. No other connection between the separate images is intended. Likewise there are no general themes or ideas we wish to expound, nor a chronology which seems imperative. Thus the order of the book has evolved spontaneously from the chosen material. When arranging it we bore in mind two things: the visual continuity and the realization that this book may be read many ways: forwards, backwards or from the middle. It can be dipped into, idly thumbed or carefully scrutinized. Alternatively it can be used as a doorstop.

Picture books can sometimes be too rich, image following hard upon image. We decided therefore to intersperse ours with text to provide visual relief and some, though not much, intellectual stimulation. The writing is an attempt to illuminate the illustrations in the belief that although pictures can 'stand on their own', they can also be talked about in such a way as to increase the enjoyment of looking at them. Then again, written explanations may occasionally become too prescriptive, restricting the viewer's ability to think what he likes about what he sees. Consequently we have omitted some of our own interpretations. And for those of you currently squinting uncomfortably at this writing, the typeface is small so as to encourage you to look first at the images and secondly at the text. This text has been divided into categories.Those of you interested in, say, the technical aspects, may easily identify which bits to concentrate on. The coding system is for you to work out. It's not difficult; even I can do it.

The layout is as simple as we could make it. We decided upon one image per spread, though a few black and white rough illustrations are included to augment the text. The term 'photodesign' refers to the way we produce pictures; images we ourselves have both designed and executed using photography in some form or another, either by itself or in association with anything else we can think of.

Andy Partridge of the band XTC suggested we call the book 'A Voyage of Discovery'. We nearly did, because the cleverness and relevance are so uncannily appropriate, but we decided not to as it might have suggested we were solely in the business of packaging for rock and roll stars. Creative labour is very fulfilling, as Marx pointed out (that's Groucho, of course, not Karl). Whatever it was exactly that we discovered is not easy to describe; but it is here somewhere, immersed in these pages. Enough of this rambling. Enjoy a good look, if only because we think good looks are fundamentally fun.

Hasta la vista

Storm Thorgerson
May 1982

Rainbow Surgeons

Colour photography using daylight Ektachrome. Hasselblad plus 50-mm lens; f16 at 1/60th, flashlit with three overhead soft strip lights and additional light on white cyclorama.

Hired studio (ours was not big enough) and hired surgeons' outfits, including smocks, masks, hats and rubber gloves. The entire cast was made up of friends and ourselves.

Pretty straightforward although it took all day. The main problems involved composition and lighting. The dilemma was to arrive at the right blend of antiseptic and dramatic qualities, and to position the people so that they didn't shadow each other. We avoided overdramatic lighting because we wanted it to look a bit as though it was in a hopsital and not a still from some horror film about gruesome limb transplants.

The artwork is flat art: an R-type print taken from the selected transparency. The front figure is brought forward by spraying back the rest of the group with white paint. The whites of his eyes are bleached a little to make them brighter than normal. We tried lighting them separately with a snoot but this was too noticeable, as well as a trifle ghoulish.

This was a poster for shop display. It was used by Rainbow to promote their album 'Difficult to Cure'. Their engaging and utterly charming manager, Bruce Payne (and he's not paying us for this plug), told us to do as we pleased and not to feel restricted. Something 'strong', relating to the title.

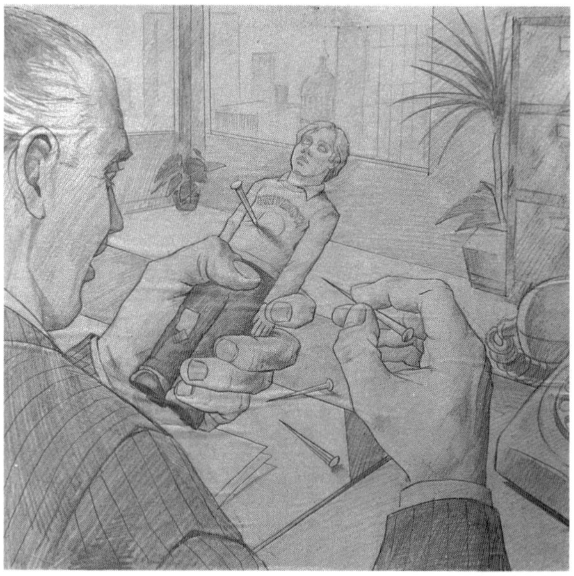

Although we submitted more esoteric designs, including a voodoo doll, this one was immediately accepted for its directness and, I think, its slightly sinister quality – both of which presumably appealed to Ritchie Blackmore and the band. Simple the picture may be, but its origins are not. The group of surgeons is posing for a team photograph, rather like those school rugby jobs. The class of '57. 'Here we are, just prior to that disastrous transplant.' Serious countenances, professional postures. Team pride.

I don't wholly trust the medical profession: doctors, surgeons and consultants. A cabal of mystification and doubletalk. Do we know what they do? They are protected by their institutions and by their arcane knowledge. 'Can't operate on Thursday, I'm playing golf.' Prescribe tranquillizers and lessen the load. Curative, but not preventive. Concerned with illness, but not with health. Hippocrates or hypocrisies? In China, patients only pay doctors when they are well.

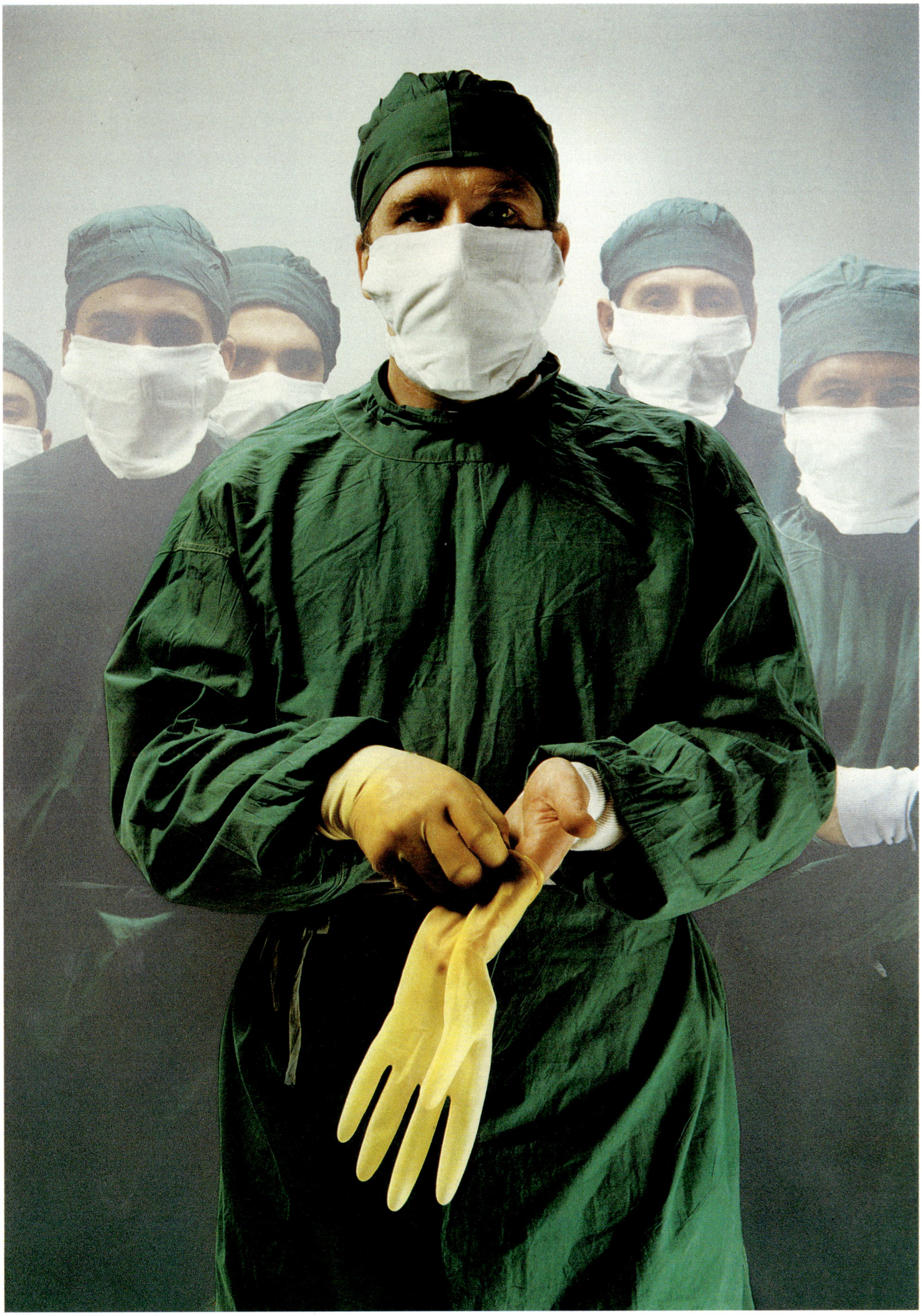

Baby and Gangsters

Hasselblad with 50-mm W/A lens using Tri-X, f16 at 1/60th, processed normally. Flashlit from the side and the back with minimal front reflector fills. The greatest problem was trying to isolate the baby in light whilst at the same time keeping the men shaded and menacing. In the end we cheated by bleaching back the B/W print to make it lighter, before applying a dash of hand-colouring.

This is a rough but unused design for The Police. It was submitted as a potential picture bag for a single called 'De Do Do Do, De Da Da Da'. It was rejected, by Sting in particular, who thought it too threatening. The song was also the inspiration for the optical design on page 27. I took verbal duplicity as the theme, and in this instance tried to suggest that noises such as de do do do de da da da might be preferable (i.e. more honest or more emotionally meaningful) to spoken words. The idea came from my feeling that the sounds a baby makes are the purest and least misleading of all human noises.

In this design the baby and the gangsters are part of a hallowing ceremony, a formal ritual, which embodies respect for the truth and innocence inherent in young children. The baby is being officially welcomed into the world of human affairs. And I thought it would be more weighty and bizarre if the initiation was performed by very sinister members of an adult fraternity, a criminal fraternity, whose moral code is strict where its own people are concerned, but loose in terms of the rest of society. They are, perhaps, the last people one would expect to be so respectful, loving and protective of children. They would as soon shoot your grandmother . . . I find this irony adds substance to the threatening air of the picture. I also sense another ambiguity about this picture. The hoods could as easily be malevolent, about to drop the baby into the murky depths of the local river.

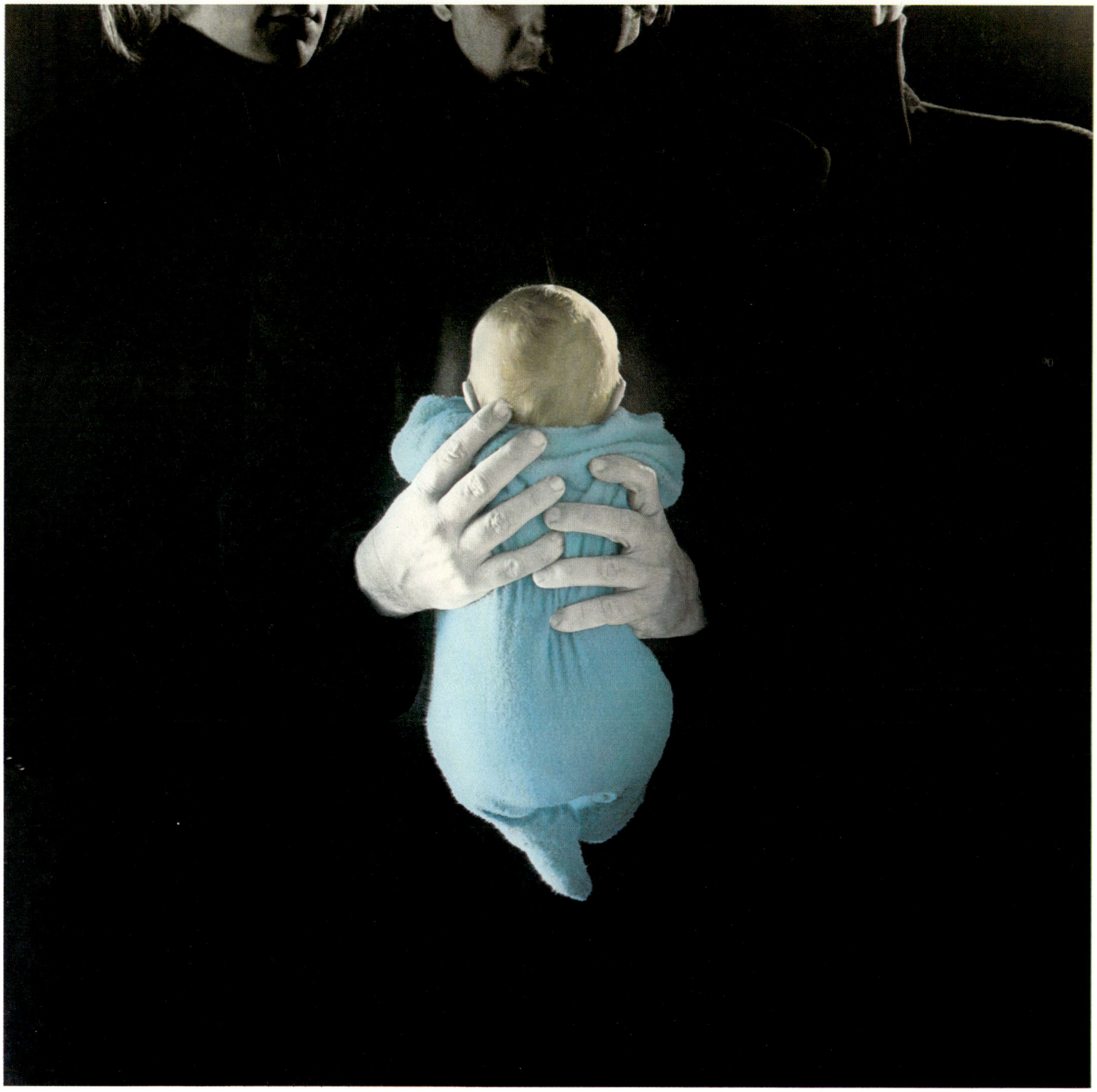

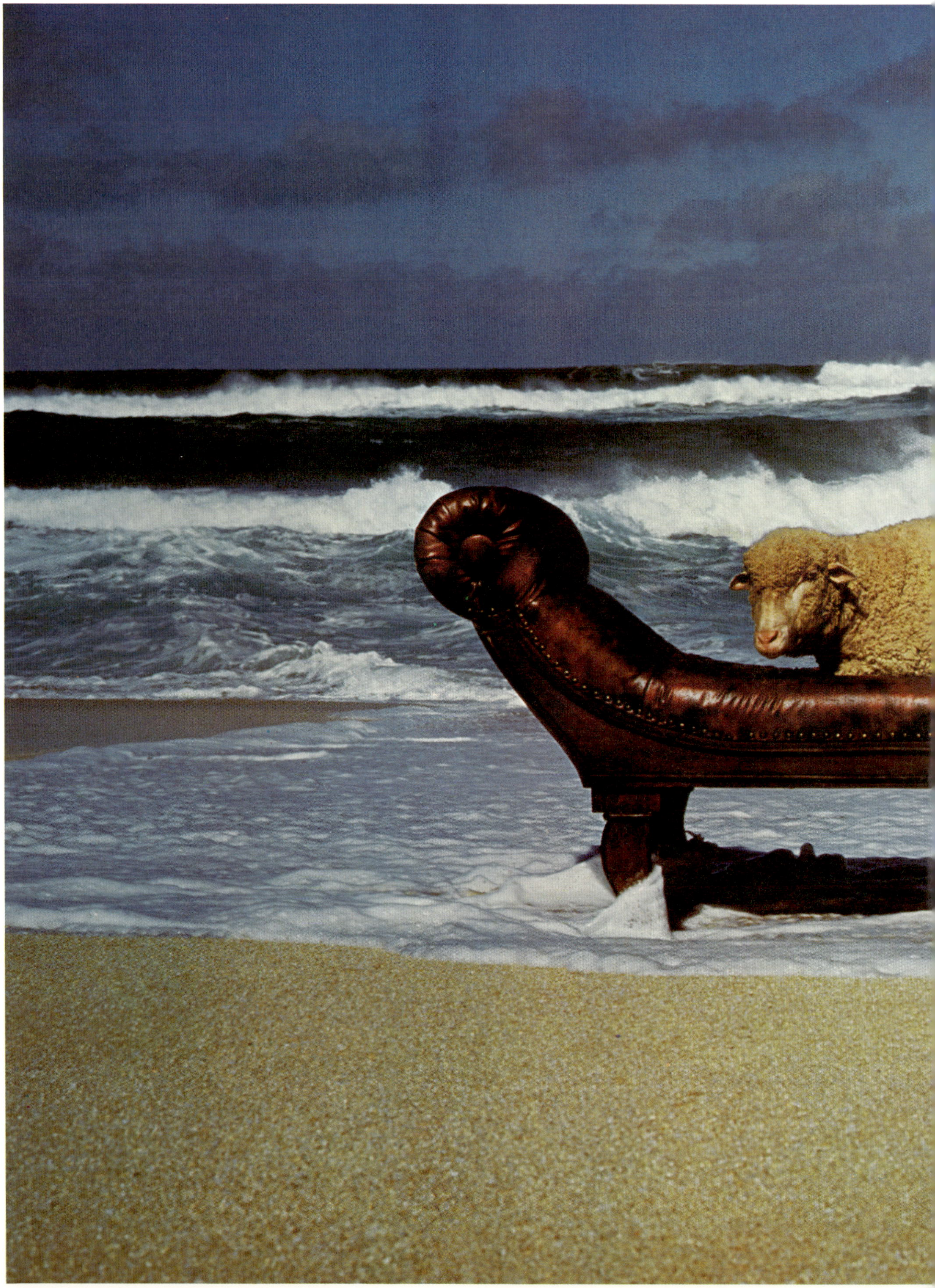

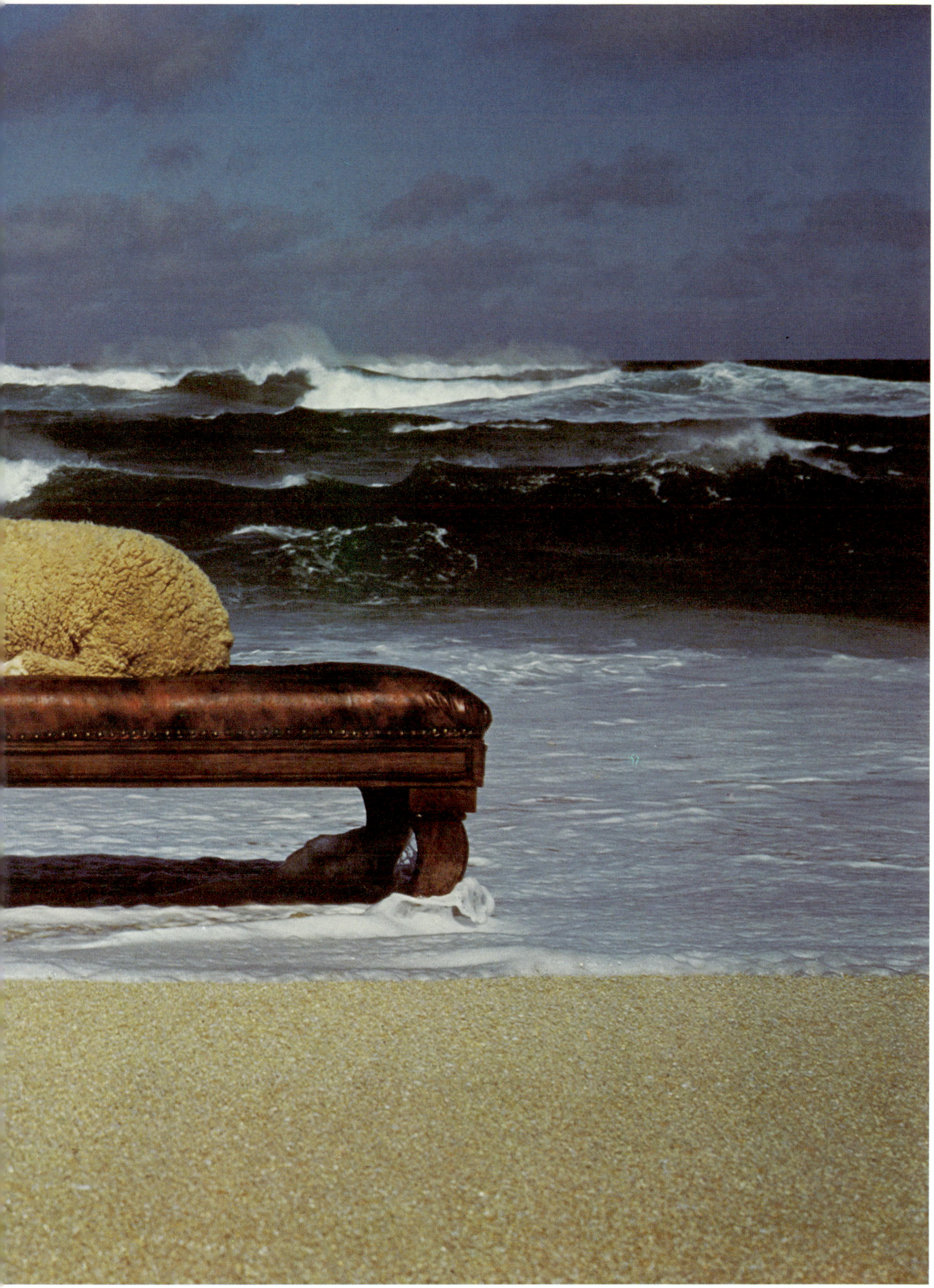

Are You Normal

Hasselblad Aloha with normal lens and daylight Ektachrome uprated half a stop to enrich the colour; f22 at 1/125th. No filters.

Where can you be sure of decent-sized waves in winter? And reasonable light? Not Brighton or Biarritz. Hawaii, of course. So Po went there whilst Peter and I stayed at home and had fish fingers. All he needed was a sheep, a psychiatrist's leather couch and a nice day.

Po was very far-sighted – he rang Hawaii first to see if they had sheep. They did. The couch had to be specially made in Honolulu. Maybe they don't have shrinks in Hawaii, or nutters.

The A/W is an R-type print. There is a little retouching to remove blemishes and extend the crest of one of the waves, but no collage or trickery in this one.

This was a poster for 10cc, included in the package of the album 'Look Hear' and used for shop display. A brief didn't really exist. The idea emerged from the album cover which incorporated words with large letters. On the front was 'Are You Normal', but with no question mark. It didn't work so well because everyone thought this was the title of the record. But it wasn't; it was the cover design.

Normality means different things to different people. The question 'Are you normal?' elicits a variety of responses. Some people say they are in order to appear inconspicuous. Others say they aren't just to be perverse or interestingly 'different'. For our purposes, 'normality' was bound up with doing the things most people do, i.e. doing what is allowed. Doing only what is permitted rather than what is possible could indicate a state of repression. Perhaps being normal is really being mad. Thus we juxtapose the images: one representing normality, the other representing madness. The sheep seemed a good symbol for nomality: sheep follow other sheep and have little will or individuality of their own. The psychiatric couch is an obvious symbol for madness. The great normal/abnormal, sane/insane debate involves the unconscious, so our little tableau is set against rolling waves which we hoped would suggest the depths of the psyche.

The sheep stayed put, not because it was docile by nature, nor because Po had pumped it full of Valium, but because there were crashing rollers on one side and three snarling dogs on the other.

'What turns me on most about this one are the irrefutable facts: Po had to fly to Hawaii, find a suitable sheep (did he audition?), get the beast shampooed, and hoist it onto a specially made settee. What on earth did the locals make of it . . . truly, are you normal?' (Jill Furmanovsky – Photographer)

'I don't know what it means but it's a great photo. Three unconnected elements. It's very abnormal. I've seen it on a lot of record company walls. I know . . . it's about a guy who thinks he's a sheep . . .' (Graham Gouldman – 10cc)

Sad Café

This is shot with a Hasselblad plus normal lens, using Tri-X, f11 at 1/60th. Flashlit with bounced light from the right-hand side, reflector on left.

The man behind the mask is not the Count of Monte Cristo but Mr Paul Young, lead singer for a band called Sad Café. The mask was made by make-up expert Tom Smith. First Paul had to have a face mould taken so that the inside of the mask would fit his face properly. The outer part of the mask was made some time later, fashioned in latex and based on a drawing we submitted. It includes stretched skin, finger holes and glass eyes. When we did the session, the mask fitted snugly over Paul's face and was then joined at the forehead and round the eyes with liquid latex, and smoothed over with make-up. Some water was dropped onto the eyes to give them a little more life. The A/W was a B/W print with just a little retouching to improve the join between the mask and the real face.

Sad Café used this for the cover of their album 'Misplaced Ideals' in 1979. They didn't, however, use it for long. The management and record company thought it far too heavy and changed the cover later. Why people get *so* worried escapes me. Why do so many managers and record companies continually tread the middle ground and choose the safe solution? Probably because of their own misplaced ideals. It's just a picture. Although as a street poster, seen from across the road, it was very powerful.

Do you remember a film called 'The List Of Adrian Messenger' by John Huston? Not a great film. One of those troughs that Huston seems to hit every now and then. Kirk Douglas was in this one and he played the villain. He adopts various disguises when committing murder. Near the beginning he is disguised as an aged vicar. You don't know it's Kirk until he goes into an airport loo and takes off his latex mask. I've obviously never forgotten the moment when he pulls it from his face: the latex stretching and clinging to his cheeks (and that wonderful chin), Kirk grimacing as he peels it off his skin like rapidly torn Elastoplast.

Our model is not into crime. It is metaphor. It's about how people say one thing out loud, when their eyes say something completely different.

All I really know is that the image is a little like a mask itself – ripped off.

'I think the Sad Café sleeve is good because it immediately attracts your attention because it's so gross.' (Steve Kincaid – Manager, Our Price Records, London)

'I think most people would be put off buying Sad Café because of its sleeve. If I was a punter, I'd think Sad Café was a heavy metal band, judging by the sleeve.' (Phil Stoker – Manager, Virgin Megastore, London)

'Although I wasn't at RCA when the Sad Café album was released, I was there about six months later when it was decided to redesign the sleeve as it was obvious that both the sales team and the dealers were visually turned-off by it and didn't feel com-

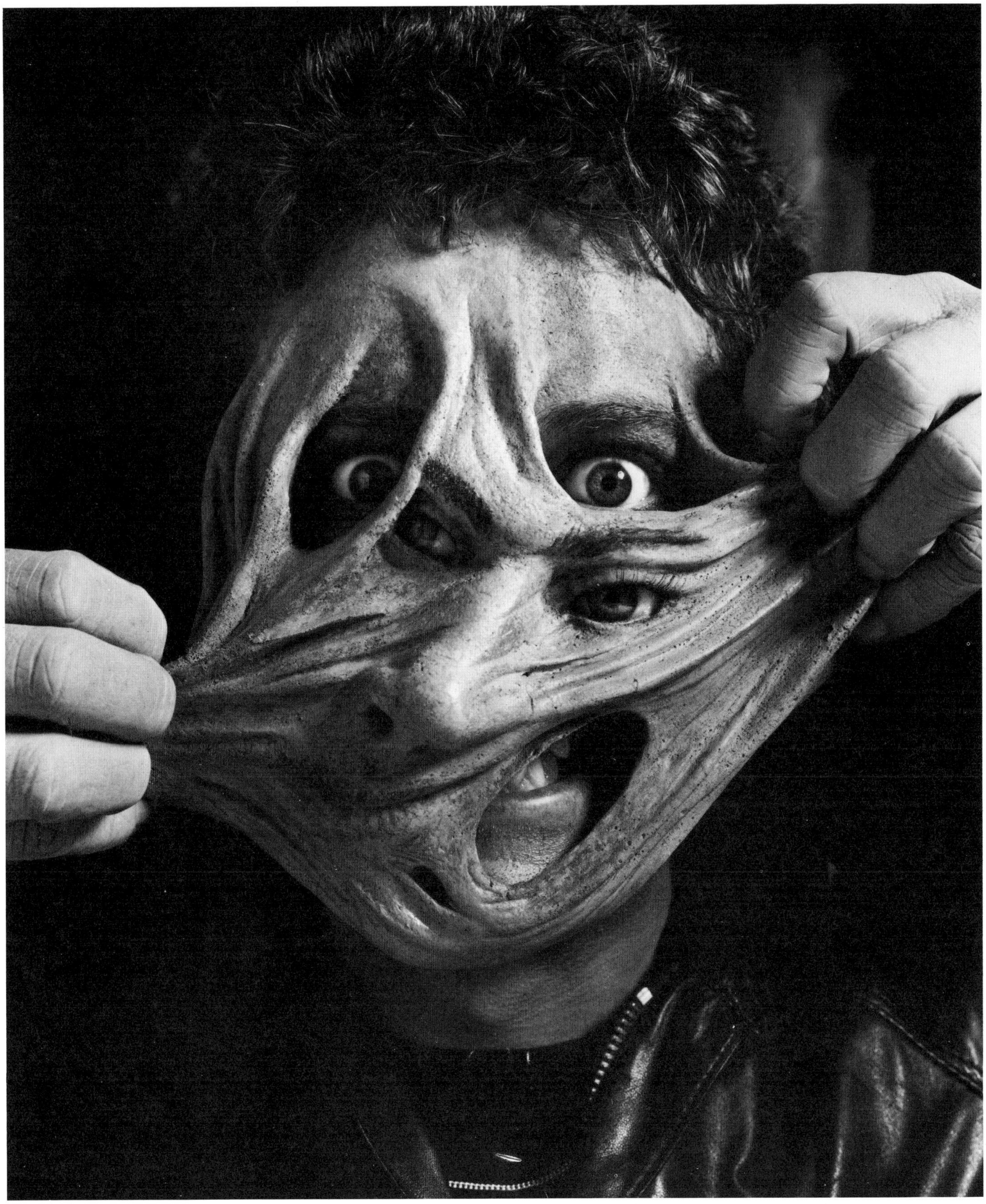

fortable about stocking it. They thought it was vulgar and unpleasant.' (Andrew Christian – RCA)

'This is probably my favourite Sad Café album sleeve. I got a great buzz out of meeting and working with Tom Smith, and I felt more involved personally with this one (that's me behind the mask). The concept seemed to me to express the ambiguity of the Sad Café situation at that time (music, image, business, etc.) but, unfortunately, few people seemed to grasp the intention and when released the reaction was, to say the least, schizophrenic.

'Stories abounded in the sales department. Little old ladies were fainting in horror and refusing to stock it (a poster was used on "Coronation Street" to illustrate Mavis's apprehension at the prospect of selling pop records to degenerate teenagers). Eventually, the company replaced the sleeve with a paradoxically idealistic one. Ironically, this original sleeve is now a rare collector's item. Oh well, most Geminis are unemployed. Now, let me see, how about "Façades"?' (Paul Young – Sad Café)

Forks in the Back

Hasselblad 500C and 80-mm normal lens, Tri-X. Flashlit, two heads (4000 joules), and reflector fills. Slightly backlit. Balanced exposure with daylight outside and flash inside, f11 at 1/8th.

Shot in our studio using our assistant, Lindsey Redding, and a lot of cutlery.

This was a piece of editorial in 'The Creative Handbook Diary 1980'. It was one of twelve dividing pictures prefacing each month. This was for November. The client said he wanted something to illustrate each month appropriately and at the same time explore the world of illusion.

We often use free association, especially when we're stuck. We asked ourselves what came to mind when we thought of November. Autumn is on the wane, winter is yet to begin. That seemed to exclude anything environmental or climatic. But there was Fireworks Night, Guy Fawkes and the Gunpowder Plot. Guy Forks. A guy with a lot of forks. Plots, treason, betrayal; knives (or forks) in the back. Silly really. There would, of course, be some difficulty in persuading anyone to have forks actually implanted in his back. We also bore in mind that the brief involved the idea of illusion, of things not being what they seem. We therefore *created* an illusion. The illusion is called 'A Penny for Your Forks'.

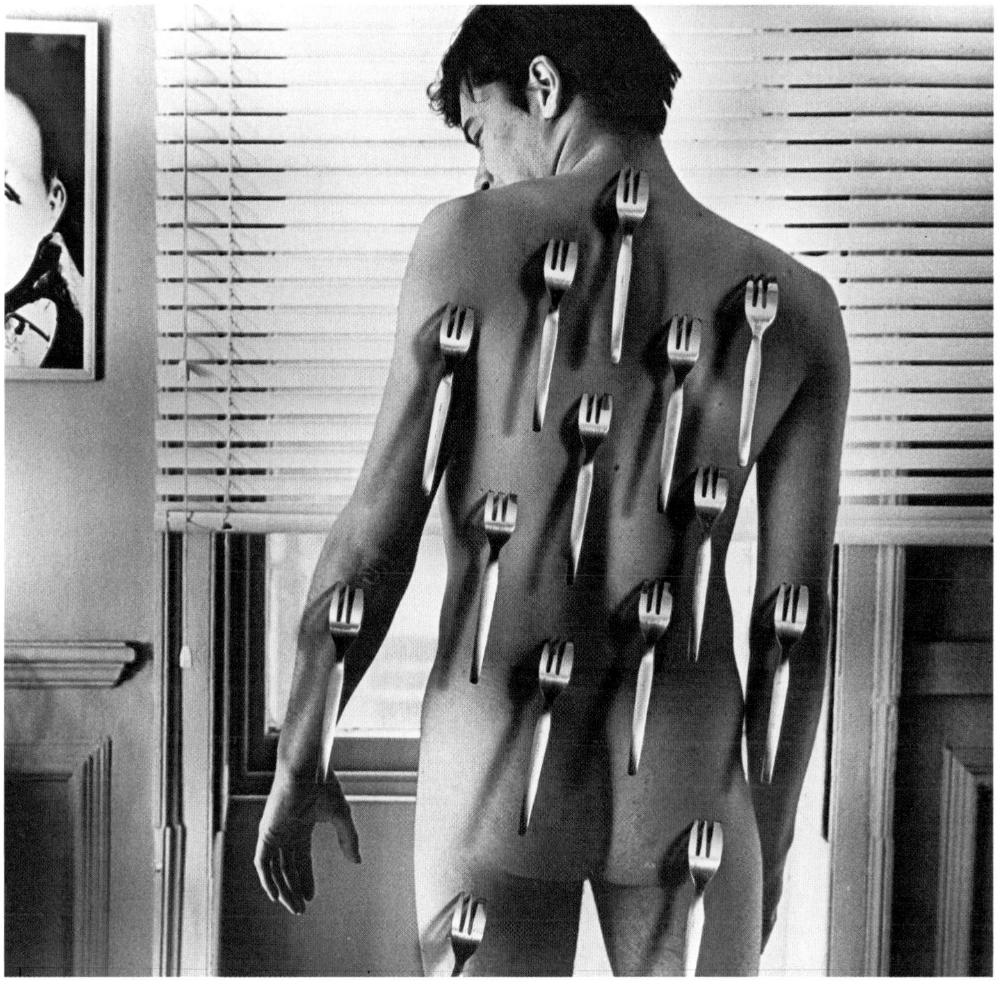

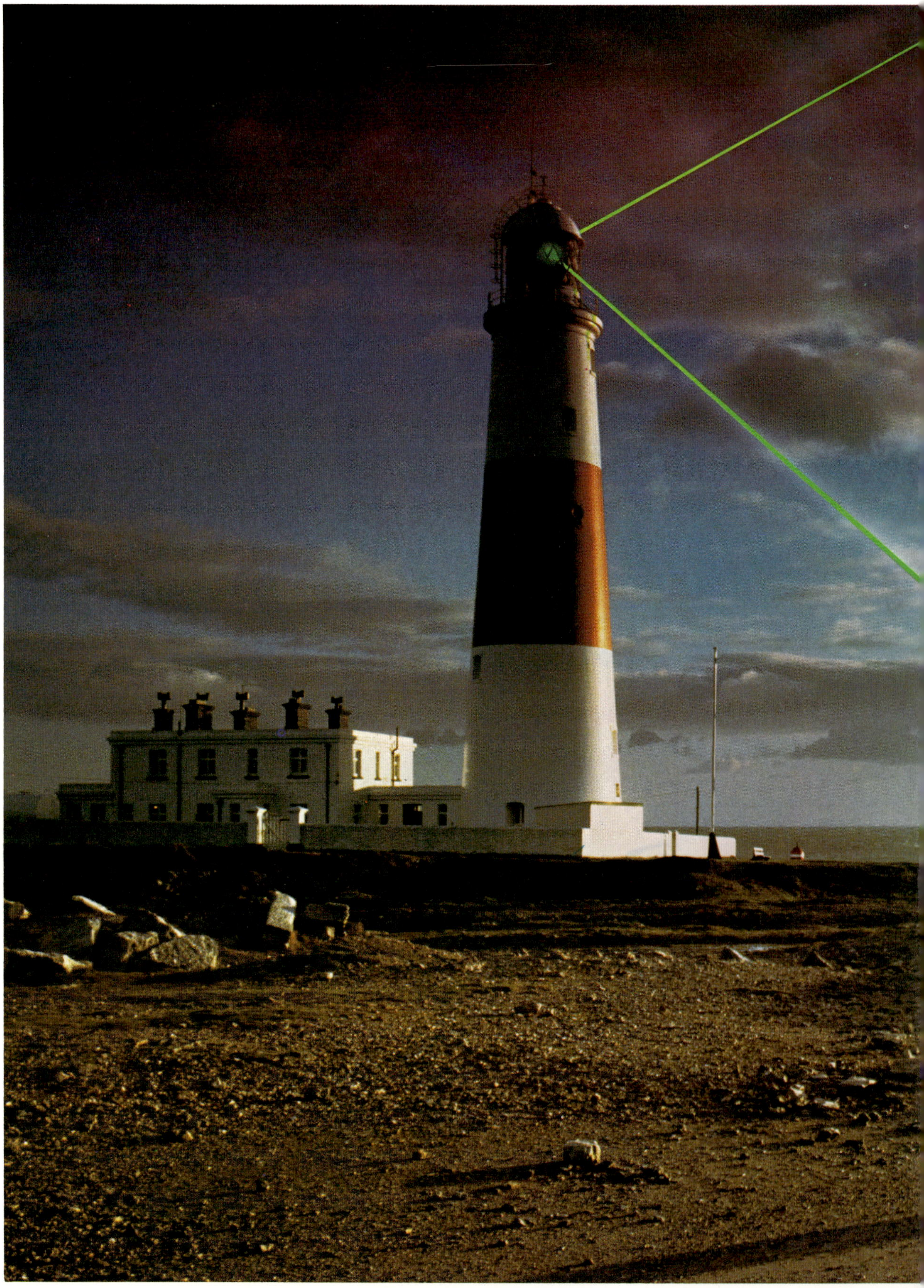

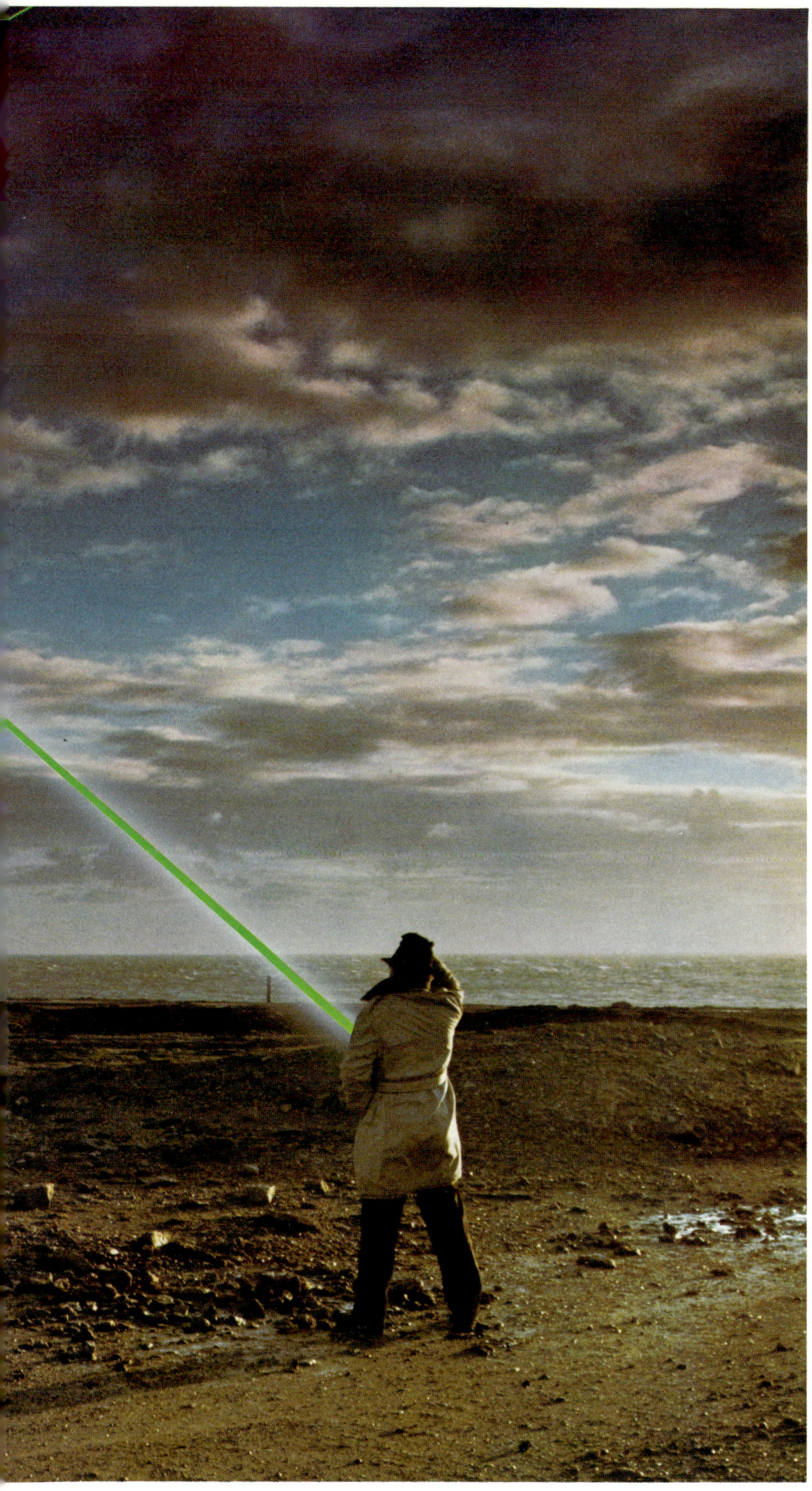

GGK England

× Hasselblad with W/A lens and daylight Ektachrome, f16 at 1/15th.

This is a lighthouse on the south coast of England, near Portland Bill. It is early morning.

⊕ This is a colour print made from a transparency. The selection of the final transparency from the many shots taken is assisted by making several small test prints and then experimenting with strips of coloured paper masquerading as the energy beam. On the A/W this beam was applied to the flat print by first bleaching away the area to be occupied by the beam (using frisk film), and then spraying green dye in its place. The edge of this line is lost in a soft glow achieved by spraying on white paint.

◻ Polygram's advertising agency GGK in New York asked us to devise several images for a campaign loosely called 'A World Atlas of Music' (see also pages 42–3, 89 and 113). The idea was to illustrate the way in which Polygram perceived the musical personality of various countries and how they visualized their own role in its development and promotion. The picture on the preceding page was for England, which Polygram saw as the continuing source and wellspring of all rock music.

O We adapted a very old idea which we had been tossing around for years. It came to light while we were evaluating Led Zeppelin and their role in contemporary music in the early 70s. Whether or not you care for Zeppelin's music, there's no question but that they were a power, a source of great energy. This seemed to tie in nicely with the client's vision of music in England, and since we had to design fifteen separate pictures for the campaign, we were tempted to plunder our past to make the task easier.

Think of life on a lighthouse. I wonder how the guys in there keep themselves entertained, let alone how they manage to sleep as the beams rotate. I wonder if lighthouses are what they appear to be. Tall, phallic-shaped totem poles, emitting vast energy or light from their tips – the cosmic cock. Imagine if a primitive tribe came across one without knowing what it was. They might take it as an emblem of man's great powers. Perhaps a lighthouse is not solely an aid to navigation. It might radiate energy, sustaining us; if we were able to bask in the glow of its ethereal rays, we would not even have to eat. The top of the lighthouse absorbs energy from the stars, restructures it, and then beams it out to us. Maybe this is a load of rubbish. Either way, the hypothesis is very similar to the idea behind the black object used on Zeppelin's cover for 'Presence'. Ironically this lighthouse was a rejected design at that time.

In 'The Separate Reality' by Carlos Castenada, Don Genero, a teacher of Yaqui sorcery, climbs a waterfall by emitting some form of ray from his solar plexus – he throws it forward and curls it round a rock, hauling himself up like a mountaineer. Except that his rope is a beam of mystic energy which, it is implied, we could all learn to develop if only we believed in ourselves as 'warriors', or self-seekers. Or if we believed in the Yaqui way of knowledge. Or in Castenada.

< 'There's a rich visual language that has hardly been used in advertising circles: the imagery of rock music. To study the best album covers is so much more refreshing and stimulating than looking at the clichés or packaged goods or corporate visuals.

'We thought: why not introduce this visual language into advertising for our client, an entertainment conglomerate? And why not with the best? The result: a campaign of startling images. The audience: no one unfortunately. Once the production was finished, the music business recession stripped away the funds for the insertion.' (Wolf Rogotsky – GGK Agency, New York)

MSG

× This photograph is taken on 10/8 Sinar with a normal lens using tungsten film, f16 at ⅛th. The tungsten lighting is arranged like a scene from a film. There is a 2k top light, to simulate the lamp in the picture. There is one spotlight backlighting the nurse at the door, large front reflectors for fill, and one floodlight to illuminate the back wall. Photographed with Rob Brimson.

We were making a film at the same time as this shoot, so we used the back end of a video studio and dressed it up as a laboratory. The chair and light are dentist's equipment, the other bits and pieces are medical. All were hired from a props company. The wire and electrodes are from the electrical shop near our studio.

◻ Michael Schenker, heavy metal/hard rock guitarist who used to be with UFO and occasionally the Scorpions, and whose inclination has been to disappear from time to time, was the unsuspecting client and victim of the experiment. And that's the way to treat a client: 'give us the job, you schwein, or else it's another 100 volts'.

This is a poster for his first solo album, released in 1980. I don't recall getting a brief from him or his manager Peter Mensch, so we just suggested ideas we liked; as opposed, that is, to ones we didn't like.

O There's a touch of the horror film in this one. The devilish experiment performed on the unblemished mind and body of an Aryan youth, conducted by a cunning and totally amoral scientist. There are references to coercion and brainwashing. Our hero is being wired up so that his mind can be tapped and reprogrammed to suit the whims of the authorities. Or is it a lie-detector test? Is he seeking political asylum? Michael Schenker is an unknown force. The wires and electrodes are part of an attempt to understand what makes him tick. How do his brainwaves scan? What biochemical phenomena account for his (electric) music? Where does the driving intensity in his work come from? What is the meaning of Watt?

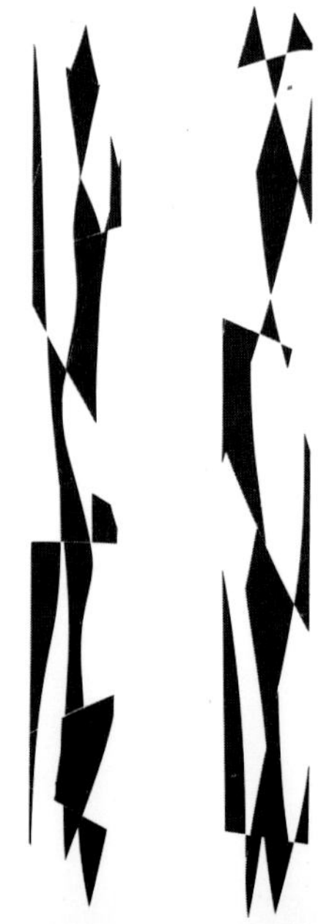

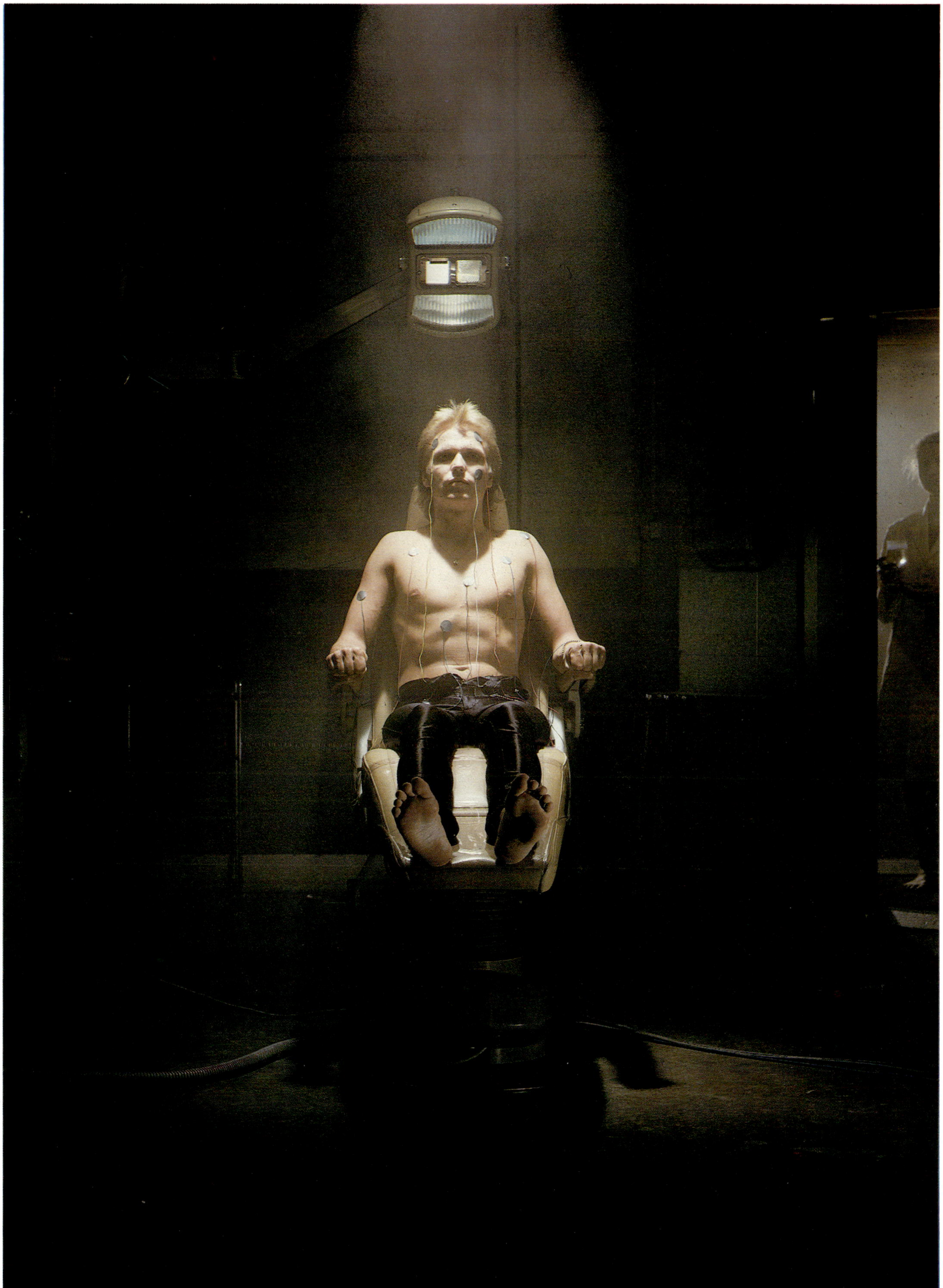

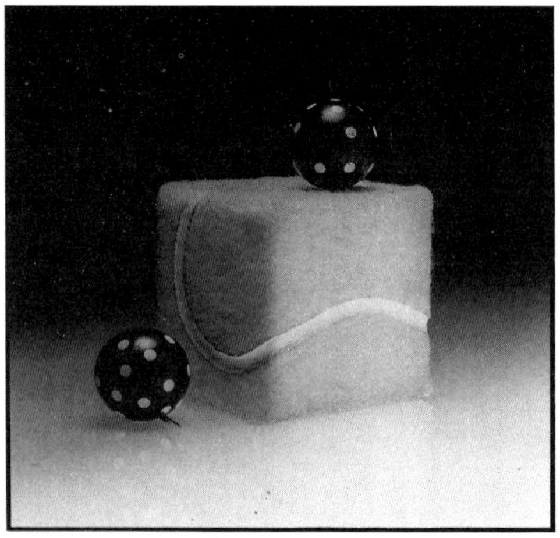

Nick Mason

× Hasselblad plus 50-mm and 80-mm lenses. Daylight Ektachrome uprated half a stop. Ordinary British daylight.

This picture is 95 per cent photographic. It is a composition of four aerial shots taken from a builder's crane. You sit in a bucket at the end of an enormous arm and get raised up into the sky. The hydraulic system levers you up steadily and the arm swings you out into space. Very exhilarating, until you have to lean out of the bucket and twist over to see through the camera clearly. The Hasselblad viewing mirror reverses everything. So there you are, 80 feet in the air, reversed, upside down, hanging from a bucket, shooting the corner of a bowling green in North London. What a life.

Apart from the bowling green, there are other aerial shots of adjacent sandpit and tarmac area and some clay tennis courts near my house.

Did you notice the shoes?

⊕ Our friend Geoff Halpin designed this 'sports pitch' from Peter's original concept and we took these shots to suit it. He made B/W line A/W from which we made four acetate film masks – one for each shot. Each mask is transparent only where the required tennis court, bowling green or whatever is supposed to show. These films are registered to fit each other on a pin bar and are separately laid across the R-type print for each exposure of the appropriate transparency. Each transparency is registered in the carrier of the enlarger so that each exposure prints the required picture in the prescribed area of the final design. In this way there is only the one final print containing all the ingredients, rather than a collage of four different prints. This would have given us edges and forced us to make a copy, losing quality and definition.

□ This was for the first solo album by Nick Mason. He called it 'Fictitious Sports' and wanted a cover to reflect this title. He also said he wanted it to be a little 'arty' and graphically inclined. Not too pretentious or meaningful, but humorous if possible.

○ Peter imagined a sports pitch of the future or for a game from an alien culture. Perhaps it would look like a piece of abstract art, but it would be a photographic design rather than a painting. Nick Mason suggested that it should comprise familiar textures, but in an unlikely combination, and have markings that were half-recognizable as being connected with sport. He argued that if the ingredients were too abstract, the result wouldn't resemble a sports pitch at all, and would be less relevant to the title.

Because the design was short on humour, Nick chose another of our ideas to go on the liner bag: a square tennis ball and round dice. Which is the more disturbing? I think the dice. Tennis with a square ball is just awkward, but round dice are so *wickedly* contrary to the raison d'être of dice that it would drive you mad. It's impossible. Non-dice. No dice. Or rather, very dicey.

< 'The Nick Mason sleeve looks like a Picasso painting and . . . reflects the sort of music it is.' (Steve Kincaid – Manager, Our Price Records, London)

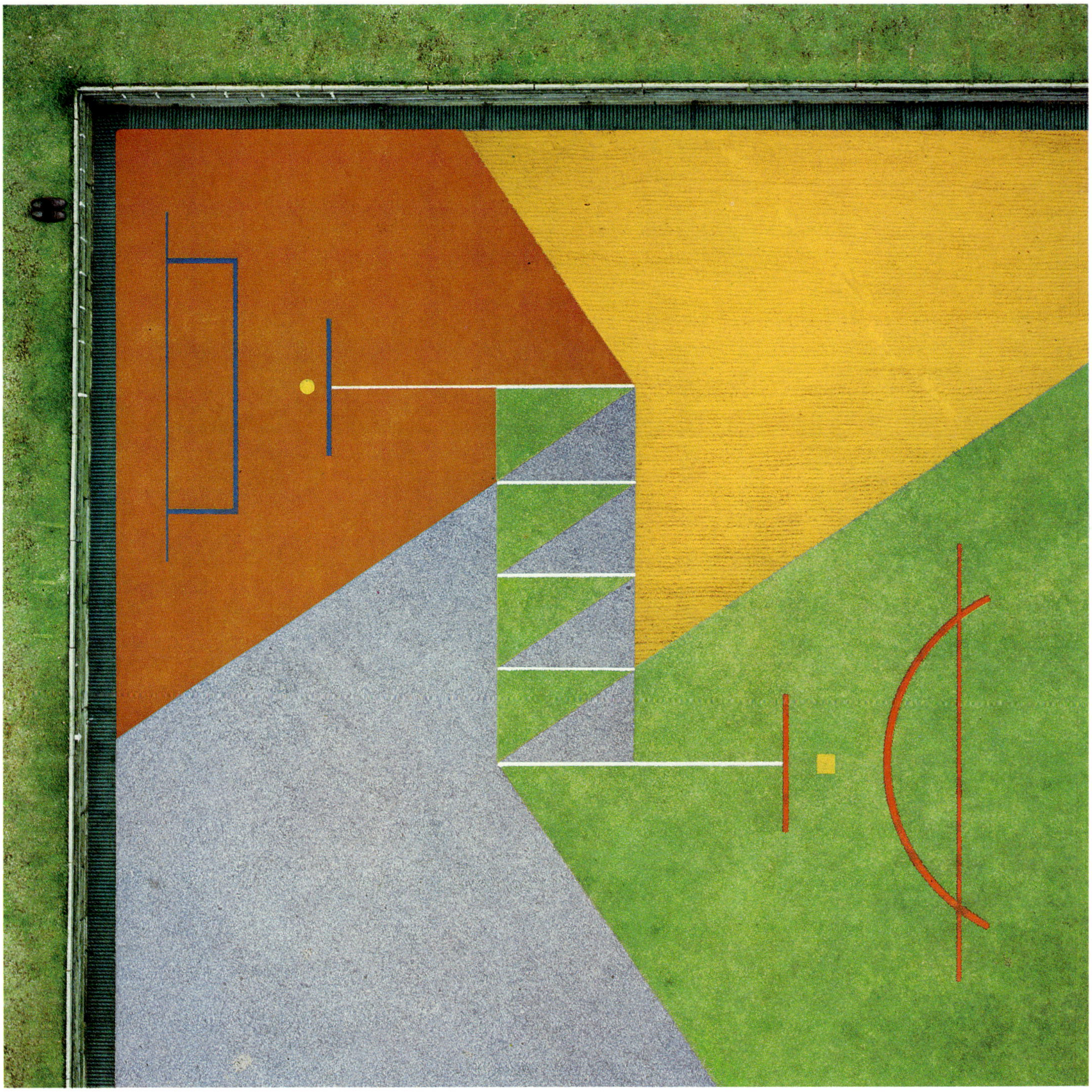

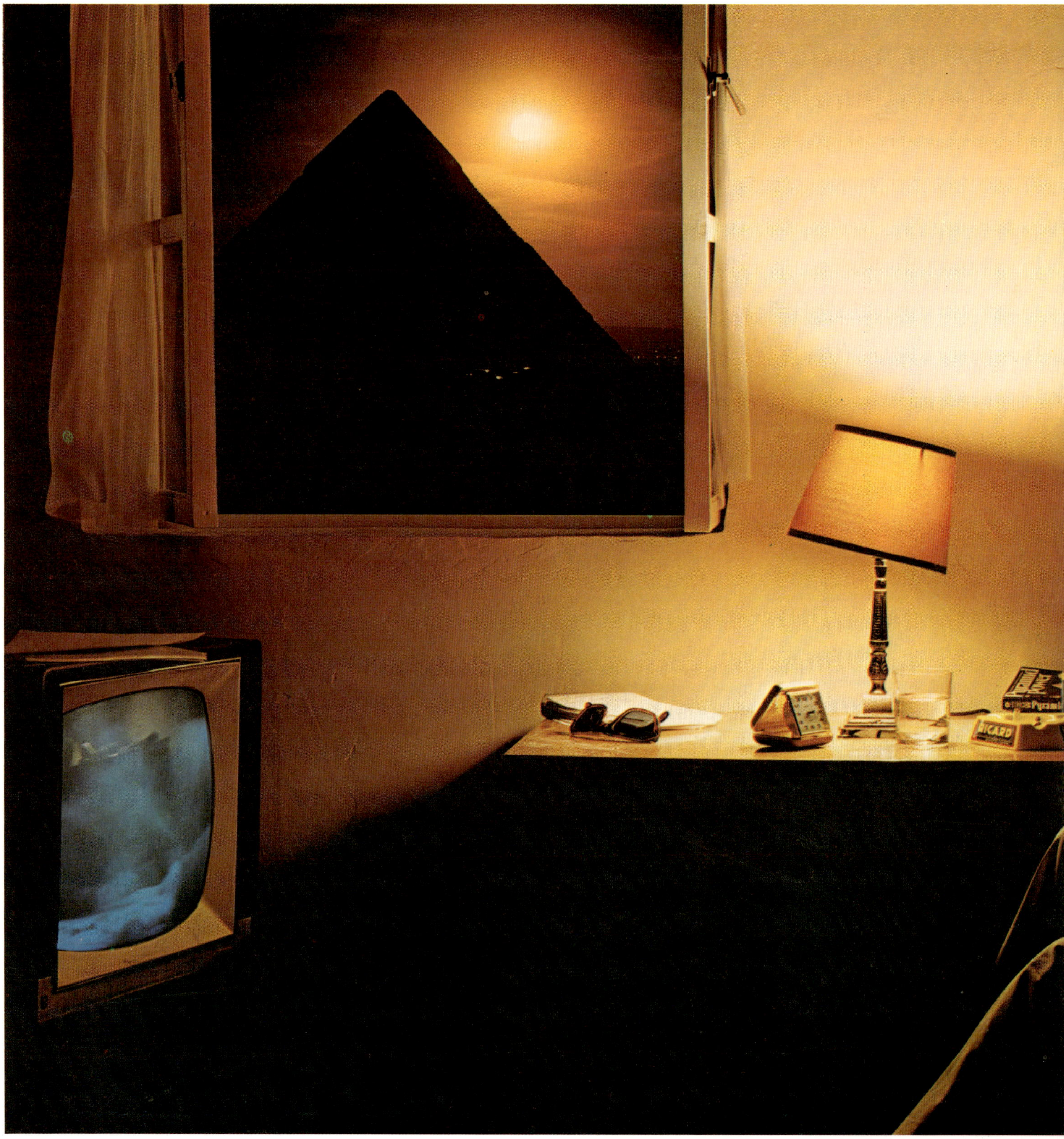
RICARD

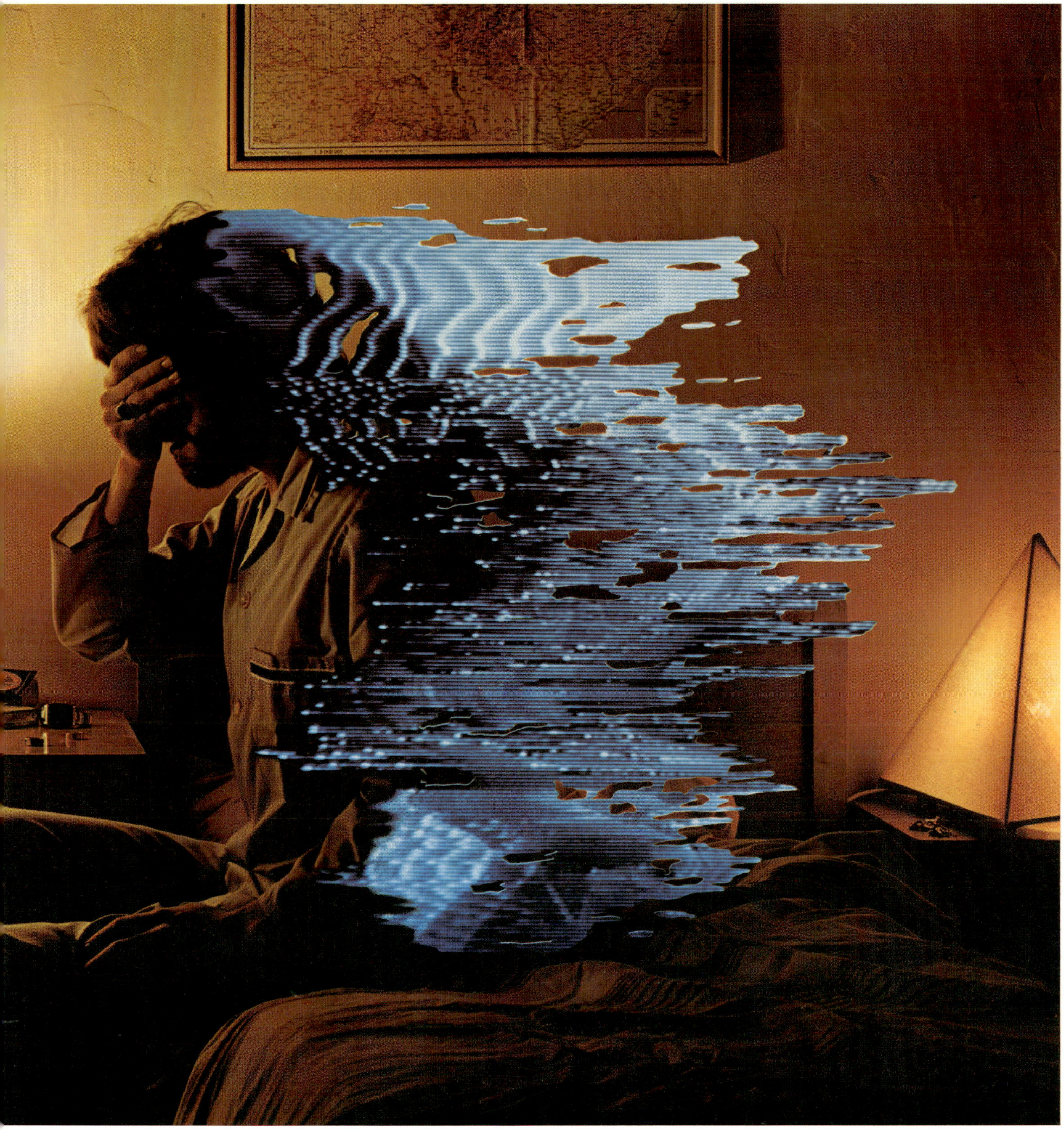

Pyramid

× No Hassel. This time we wanted the delicate tonal properties of a 10/8. We used a Sinar with normal lens. Tungsten lit, longish time exposure, f32 for ¼ of a second. Photofloods in the bedside lamps. TV interference shot on a B/W TV monitor. Photographed with our friend, Rob Brimson.

The location is El Cheapo motel on the edge of Cairo. The walls are recently plastered (like some of the guests, no doubt) and the TV is an imported model from the late 50s. As you can see, the great pyramid of Gîza is close by and, in a gesture of reverence, the motel has provided a pyramidic lamp and pyramid-shaped drawer handles. How thoughtful. Otherwise known as our studio. Set designed by us and built by John Whitely. The model is Alan Parsons, with a headache.

⊕ Dye transfer strip-in of pyramid into the window of the bedroom, and also TV interference onto the back of Alan. The whole thing is retouched in order to remove unwanted strip line, although the TV interference is out of sync anyway: it shows a 'white' shadow top side. This was a mistake made during the process of stripping-in, but we left it there thinking that it might give the interference a certain 3-D quality.

⌑ The Alan Parsons Project used this design for a gatefold album called 'Pyramid' in 1978. Their brief was to design something for the music which they felt was sometimes atmospheric, sometimes electronic, and sometimes straight pop. The theme of the record was, of course, the pyramids.

○ I say in connection with Styx that some years ago the subject of the pyramids often deteriorated into a repository for woolly philosophical thinking. However, another view is that they are indeed fantastic, fascinating and mysterious. They tower into the sky, haunting and magnificent. Strange, still sentinels of the dead.

Po and I photographed them for the Floyd in 1973. Po succumbed to the dreaded Arab tummy and I did a stint alone, through the night of a full moon! It was very beautiful, but very spooky, and it was easy to believe that they had 'magical' powers, or some form of electrical or occult emanations.

In our picture, Alan (or any traveller) is staying near Cairo. He is preoccupied with the pyramids. He reads about them, makes notes, surrounds himself with pyramid-like things. Even the clock has stopped at 3.14 (which is the figure pi, in turn inextricably bound up with numerological properties ascribed to the pyramids). He wakes up, sits on his bed and begins to feel very strange. He holds his face. The emanations from the pyramids, unlocked by an orange moon, begin to take hold of him. They interfere with his sense of reality. He begins to shift; another dimension, another memory.

The TV interference seemed a way of suggesting that Alan was being affected by the pyramid. It also has an electric blue quality which goes well with the orangeness of his room, which in turn was determined by already having the pyramid picture – which was orange. I once had a room that was all orange. But I'm all right now.

< 'A sleeve should be a showcase for the band and its music and, as a marketing device, is very important. The main problem as I see it with this sleeve is that it doesn't promote the right image for the band in the UK market. Although their style has changed, people still see the band as one of those self-important concept bands who are trying to be deep and meaningful in a grandiose way when people are just not interested in that sort of thing any more. Unfortunately, the sleeve reinforces this image. In an age of style and image, concept is a dirty word.' (David Shortt – Ariola Records)

'The theme of the "Pyramid" album, the meeting of worldly and other-worldly forces, is clearly and strikingly presented by the cover art. The blending of photography, video and retouching creates an arresting image that reinforces the album's theme by the very fact that separate elements come together to create their own reality.' (Rick Dobbis – Arista Records)

'I always felt that there was something missing from the "Pyramid" sleeve. Possibly a comic-strip speech balloon with Alan Parsons (for it is he) saying something like, "That's the last time I buy Sainsbury's Egyptian claret." ' (Eric Woolfson – Manager)

Billy Karloff

× We used B/W Plus-X film rated normally. Hasselblad with normal 80-mm lens. Flashlight, two heads (2000 joules), side and front, and suitable reflectors.

The film was developed slowly in ordinary D-163 developer. The A/W is simplicity itself: just a straightforward B/W print. It was tempting to print it in line to maximize the optical effect, but this would have destroyed the few greys in the lapels and in the shirt collar shadowing. It's a very harsh, contrasty print that has been souped up with a little B/W retouching, noticeably on the shirt squares.

This was shot in our studio and took half a day. The only prop was the clobber, worn, I think, by Billy himself.

The greatest difficulty was remembering how to do the tie knot: a bent windsor; a half nelson. . . ?

⌑ Used by Billy Karloff and the Extremes as an LP front cover, released by WEA in 1982. The product was printed in four shades: black, blue, red and green, on white. The title was 'Let Your Fingers Do the Talking'. The Manager, Tony Howard, didn't want to add much to this other than to stress the value of 'strong packaging'. He said he didn't want to restrict us. Although this was the band's first album, Tony wanted to get away from the predictable 'shots of the band' formula. It was his opinion that, given our head, we would either be inspired or calamitous. We submitted three or four designs based on the title and threw this one in as a version of 'strong packaging'. Po was keen to do a range of coloured versions of the cover.

○ This piece was also originally intended for The Police and a single called 'De Do Do Do, De Da Da Da'. The song was about verbal miscommunication. That's what Sting told me – well, at least, I think that's what he told me.

Our purpose was to convey this visually by means of a simple optical device. Unlike Vasarely or Bridget Riley, whose work usually has an abstract basis, this is a slice of reality; an optical in nature as it were, a metropolitan nature, anyway. The retinal disturbance prevents you from identifying it, but I don't expect anyone to be fooled for long; rather, they should enjoy the coincidence of it. And what a natty dresser. About a week later, we really did see an outfit just like this, worn by a gentleman boarding a London omnibus in Acton!

The Police rejected it as too too two-tone. Billy Karloff felt it had relevance, or maybe he just liked it. One rarely knows.

< 'I like it because it's black and white only. Vitality via restraint.' (Malcolm Garrett – Designer)

'This album sleeve almost defeats singlehandedly the modern philosophy of packaging. The sleeve design was compulsive and attracted attention, comments and compliments everywhere. However I can't recall anybody listening to the album. It was a total stiff. Condemned without a trial although everybody was familiar with the artwork, nobody could get past it enough to listen to the music contained therein. Oh well, you win some and lose many.

'A word about Hipgnosis. Well known and established, their work has an instantly recognizable style to those who have been familiar with their stuff over the years – like myself. This particular piece of artwork was so different that I felt that they must have nicked it – and so unlike their usual style that I was obliged to use it on first sight. The concept of the four-colour range of sleeves was quite

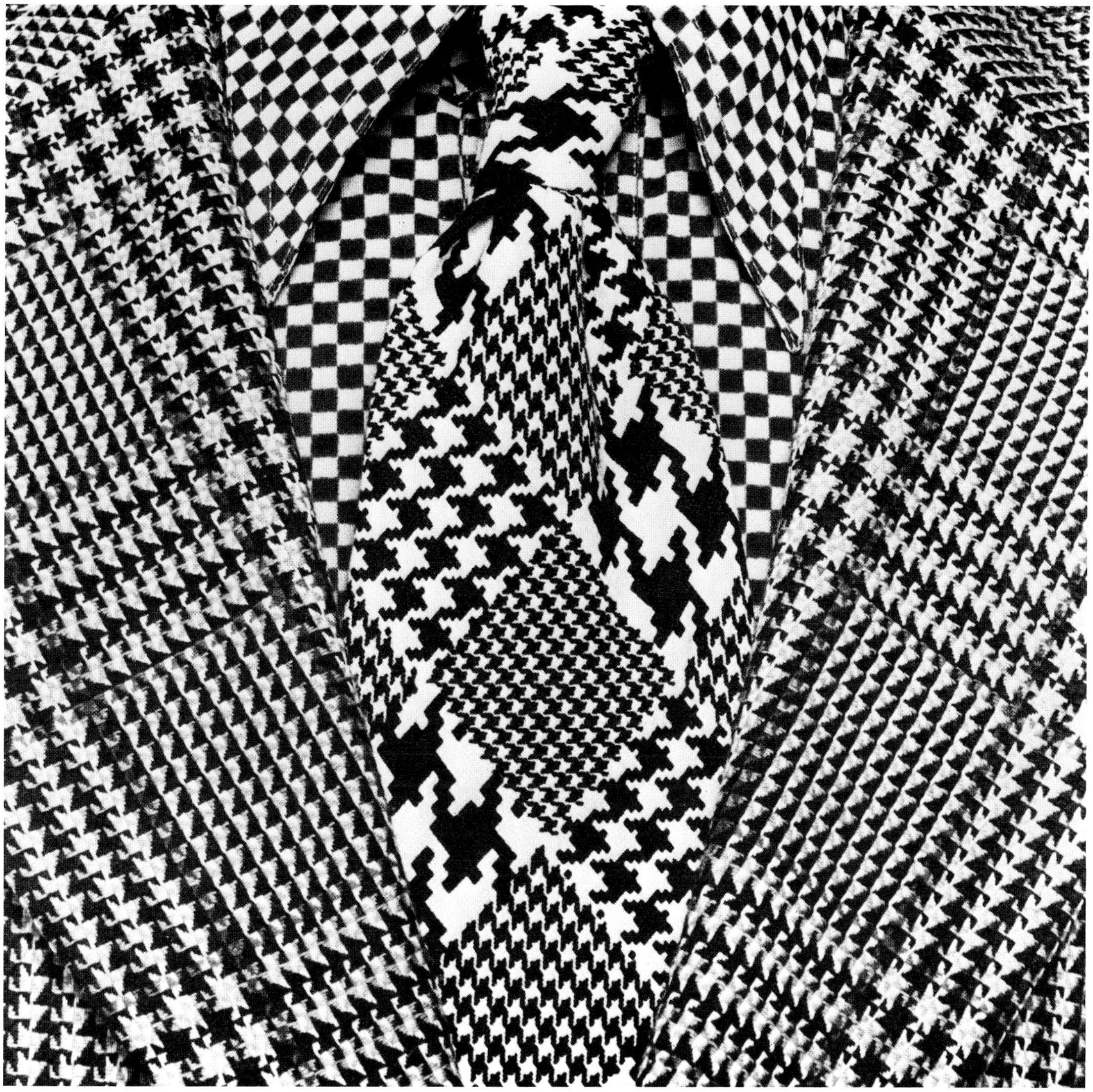

innovative and should really have been used on an artist who can command massive sales in order that the idea could have been exploited to the full.' (Tony Howard – Manager of Billy Karloff)

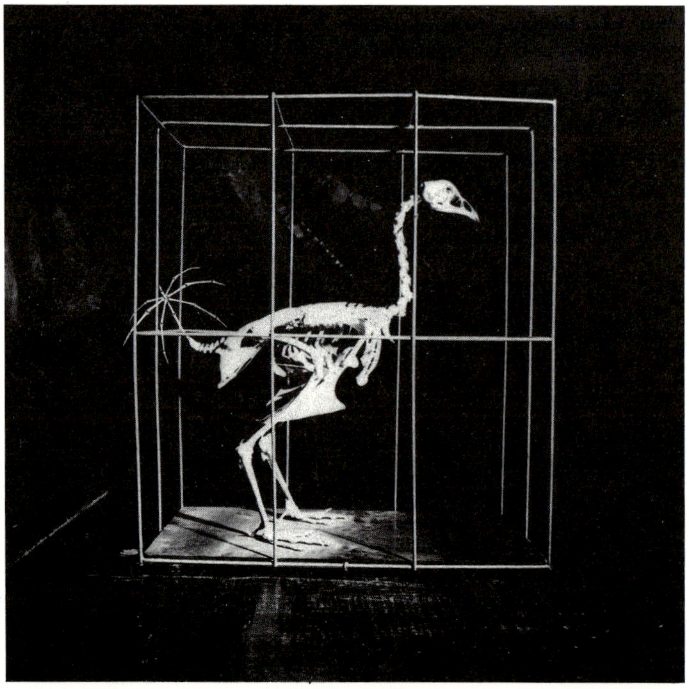

Rialto Calendar

Anarchy, chaos. Enough of these categories. We'll just dive straight into this one. It's a library shot plus lettering. The A/W is a B/W bromide with the Letraset applied directly. Our clients were the brothers Heath of Rialto Records, who decided to put out a promotional calendar to mark their inception and asked us to do the design and pictures. The theme was umbrellas, since at that time an umbrella was their company logo. Typically, we delivered it late, which is hardly appropriate for a calendar.

Different typefaces scattered over pictures tend to add an extra level of interest. The words become part of the design. They also have their own meaning, and these meanings may play games with the object upon which they appear. Sometimes the labelling may go wildly astray, or add an extra dimension, or say the obvious, or redefine a behaviour pattern. As they are placed directly on the photograph, you cannot easily escape them, although you can look 'through' them, readjusting the eyes so that the words nearly disappear and the image jumps towards you. Fun for the eyes: they have to refocus, although everything is on the same surface.

This design was for August. Hence the seaside. The umbrellas are now parasols, protecting people from the sun and not the rain. This picture puts others in the shade. Which is more than you can say for this joke.

'Hipgnosis conceived an innovative and, some would say, amusing little calendar to celebrate the launch of Rialto as a mega-record company with suitably grandiose ideas. Unfortunately the theme was not beautiful girls draped naked in exotic locations. The theme was . . . umbrellas.

'But, as I frequently muse whilst lazing in the office jacuzzi, there's a lot you can do with umbrellas. Storm & Co. agreed and had no shortage of brill ideas. Somewhat quaintly they saw Rialto – despite the origins of the name – as the epitome of upper-crust, honest, diplomatic, dependable, sturdy Britishness (wrong on all counts except one) hence the umbrella.

'August represents Hipgnosis's ability to make people laugh – deliberately in this case.

'Some might say juvenile. Some might say bring on the naked girls. But I liked it, and so did most who had the honour of receiving a copy.' (Nick Heath – Rialto Records)

Brollysaurus

The adjacent design is a very silly picture we took for the same calendar. It shows the skeleton of the very rare *Brollysaurus vulgaris*. We shot it (the picture, not the bird) at the Royal Veterinary College in Camden, whose collection of skeletons is, frankly, unbelievable.

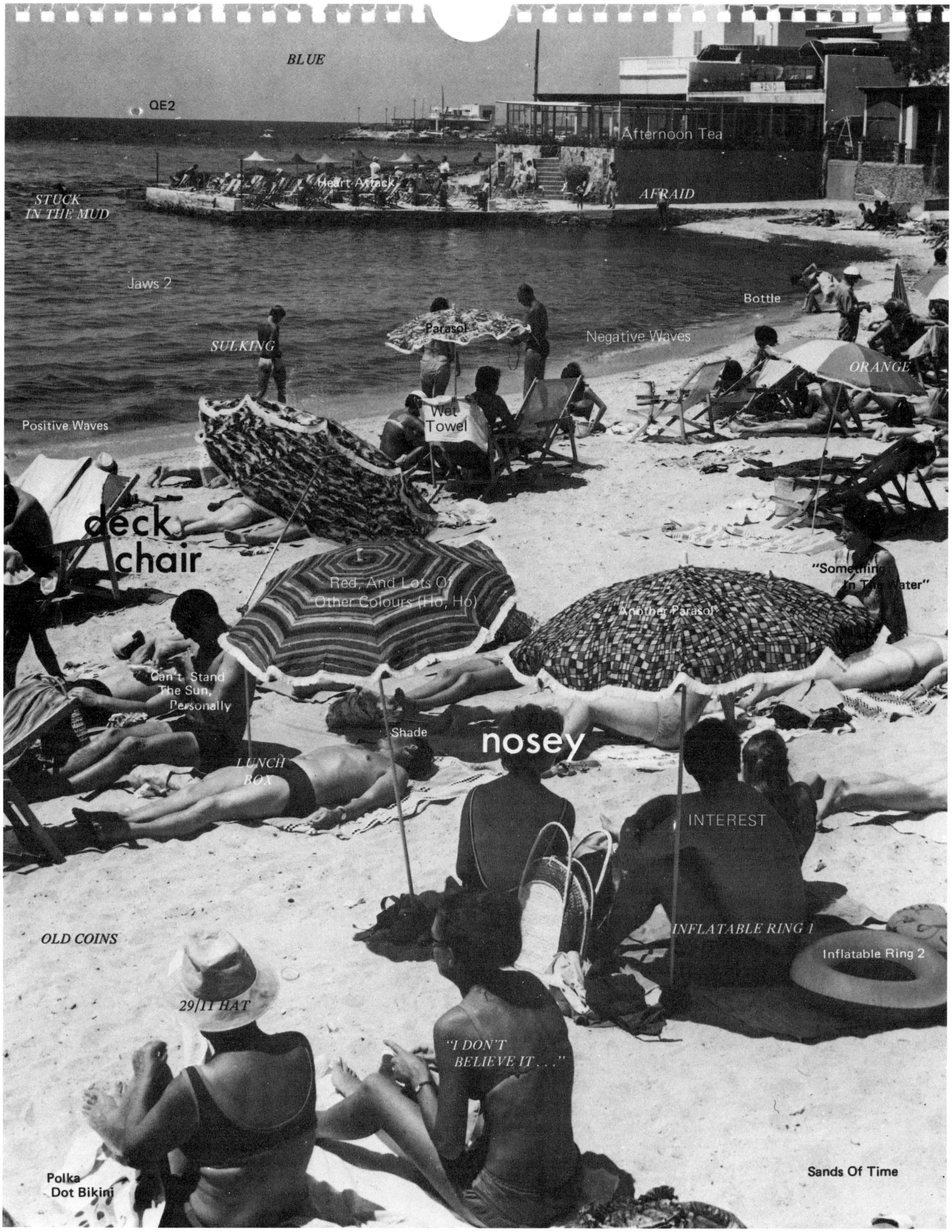
BLUE
QE2
Afternoon Tea
Heart Attack
STUCK IN THE MUD
AFRAID
Jaws 2
Bottle
Parasol
Negative Waves
SULKING
ORANGE
Wet Towel
Positive Waves
deck chair
"Something In The Water"
Red, And Lots Of Other Colours (Ho, Ho)
Another Parasol
Can't Stand The Sun, Personally
Shade
nosey
LUNCH BOX
INTEREST
INFLATABLE RING 1
OLD COINS
Inflatable Ring 2
29/11 HAT
"I DON'T BELIEVE IT . . ."
Polka Dot Bikini
Sands Of Time

1

There was a film by Ralph Nelson called 'Thirty Minutes' which lasted about thirty-eight minutes. It showed lots of pictures of motor boats, speed boats, launches and luxury yachts as if they were slides projected on the wall at a dinner party. Sarcastic guests played a droll game inventing names for each boat, paying particular attention to the kind of people who used them and what they might be doing. The level of invention and humour increased the more the party became inebriated. This game was called 'Out to Launch'.

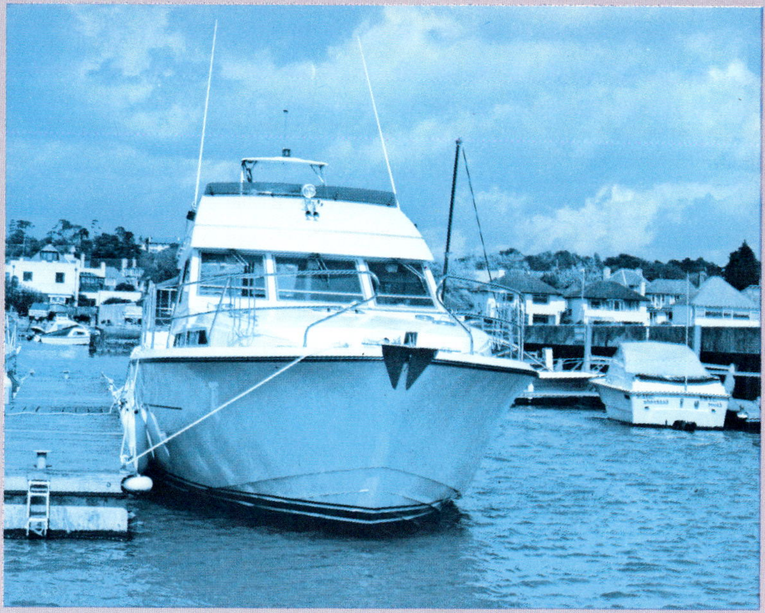

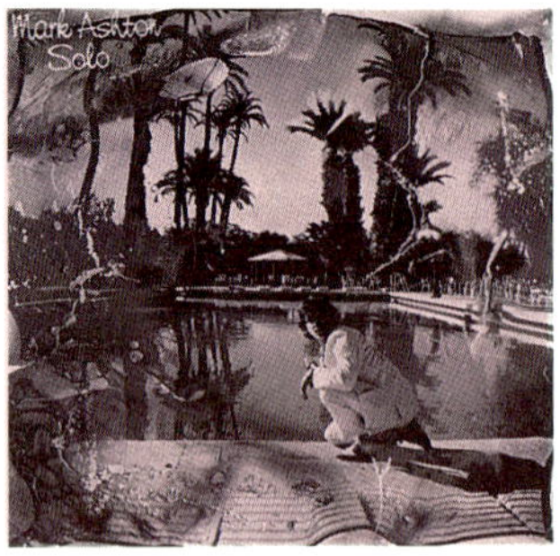

Mark Ashton

A Hasselblad with 50-mm W/A lens, daylight Ektachrome, f22 at 1/125th, using available light. And a small Belling cooker with hotplate.

The model is Mark Ashton and the location is Marrakesh, in Morocco. A long way to go for such a shot you might think, but we really went to Morocco to score a hundredweight of kif and then set up a dope-smuggling ring involving Marrakesh, Rabat, Spokane and Luton, air stewardesses and Berber tribesmen. In truth, we went for the quality of light (which is terrific) – Paul Klee went to Tunisia for the same reason – and for the blueness of the sky, direct or reflected.

The selected transparency is printed as an R-type colour print. This is put into the Belling cooker and roasted at 320° for ten minutes. Or, alternatively, it can be done on the hotplate, backside down.

I kid you not. When we were designing a thing entitled 'No Smoke Without Fire', it was suggested that whatever it was we designed, we should burn it. Set fire to it. Put it in the oven. So we gave it a try and put some old colour prints in the Belling. Lo and behold, it produced an excellent effect. The plastic surface shrank, curled, bubbled, pulled away from the backing and turned bright red. A terrific texture. Every time we did it, it was different, but always red. And red is nice with blue, and blueness is one of the reasons why we went to Marrakesh.

Before they fell to bits, the cooked photos, all charred and gnarled, were carefully copied on 10/8 transparencies for the actual A/W.

Mark Ashton used this process for his solo album, engagingly called 'Solo' (?!?). His brief was to include a picture of him, but not up-front or overposed. He liked the oven technique and the idea of going to Morocco, although his record company were not so keen.

As to the origins and meaning of this design, there are none.

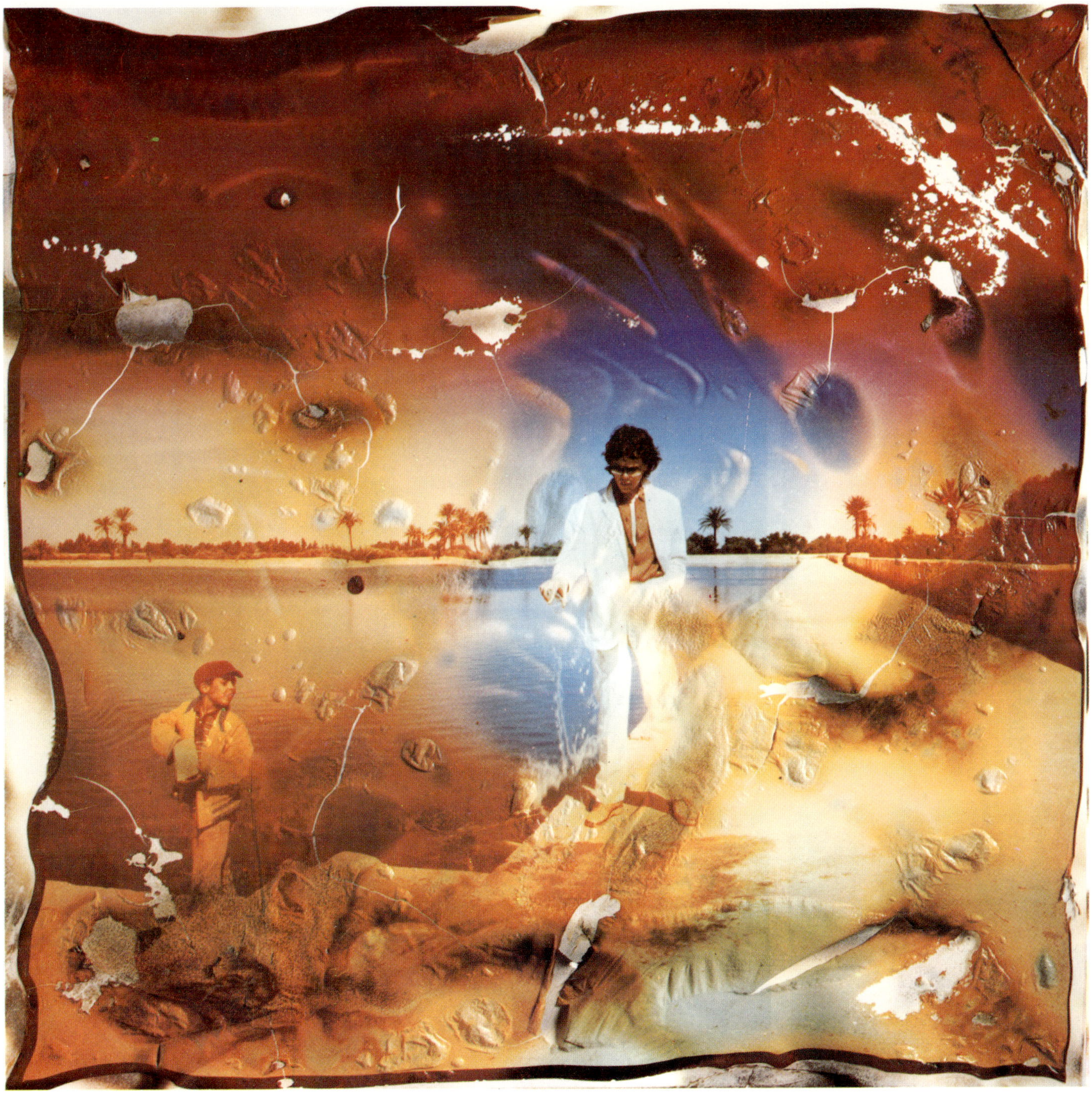

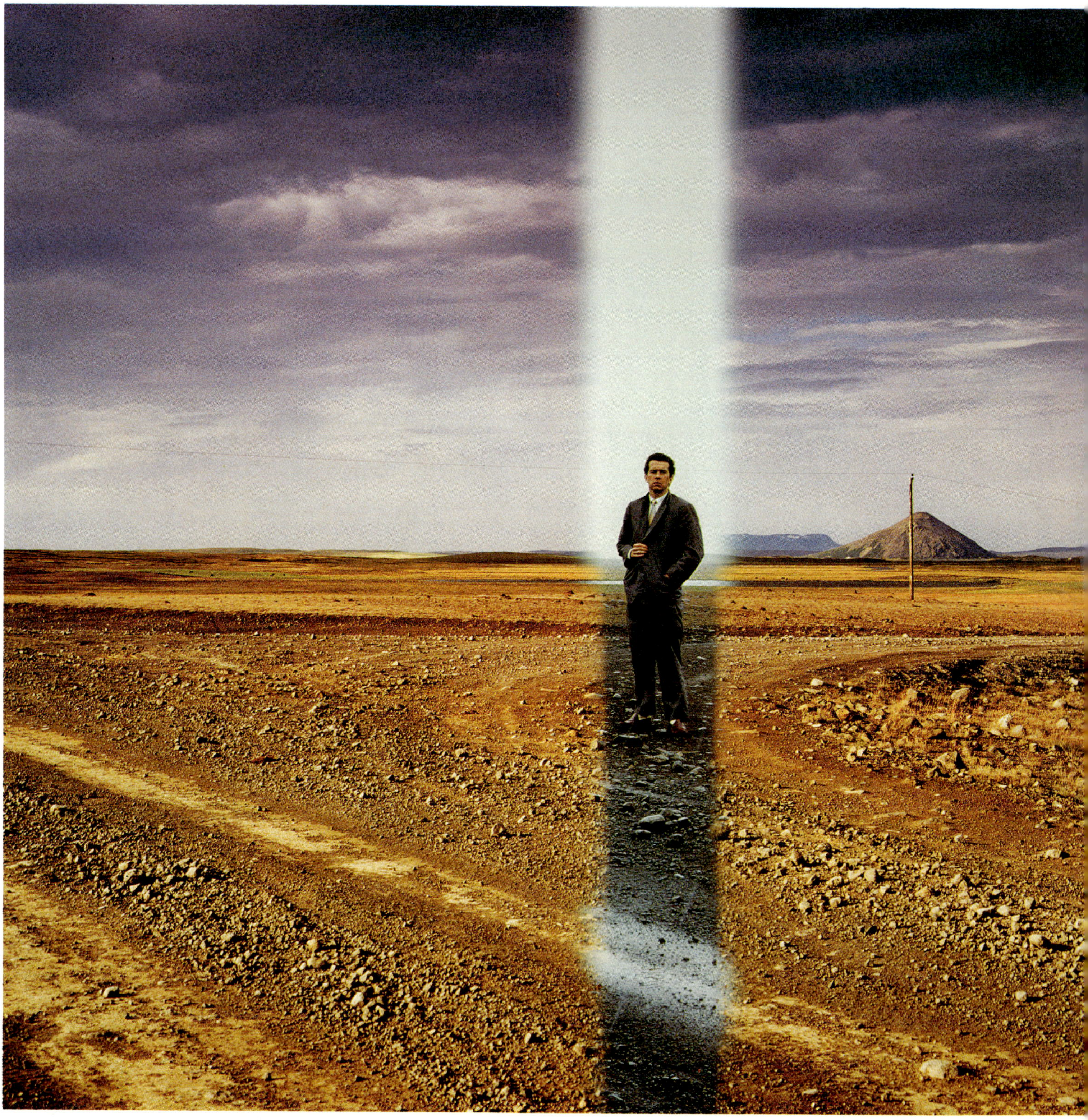

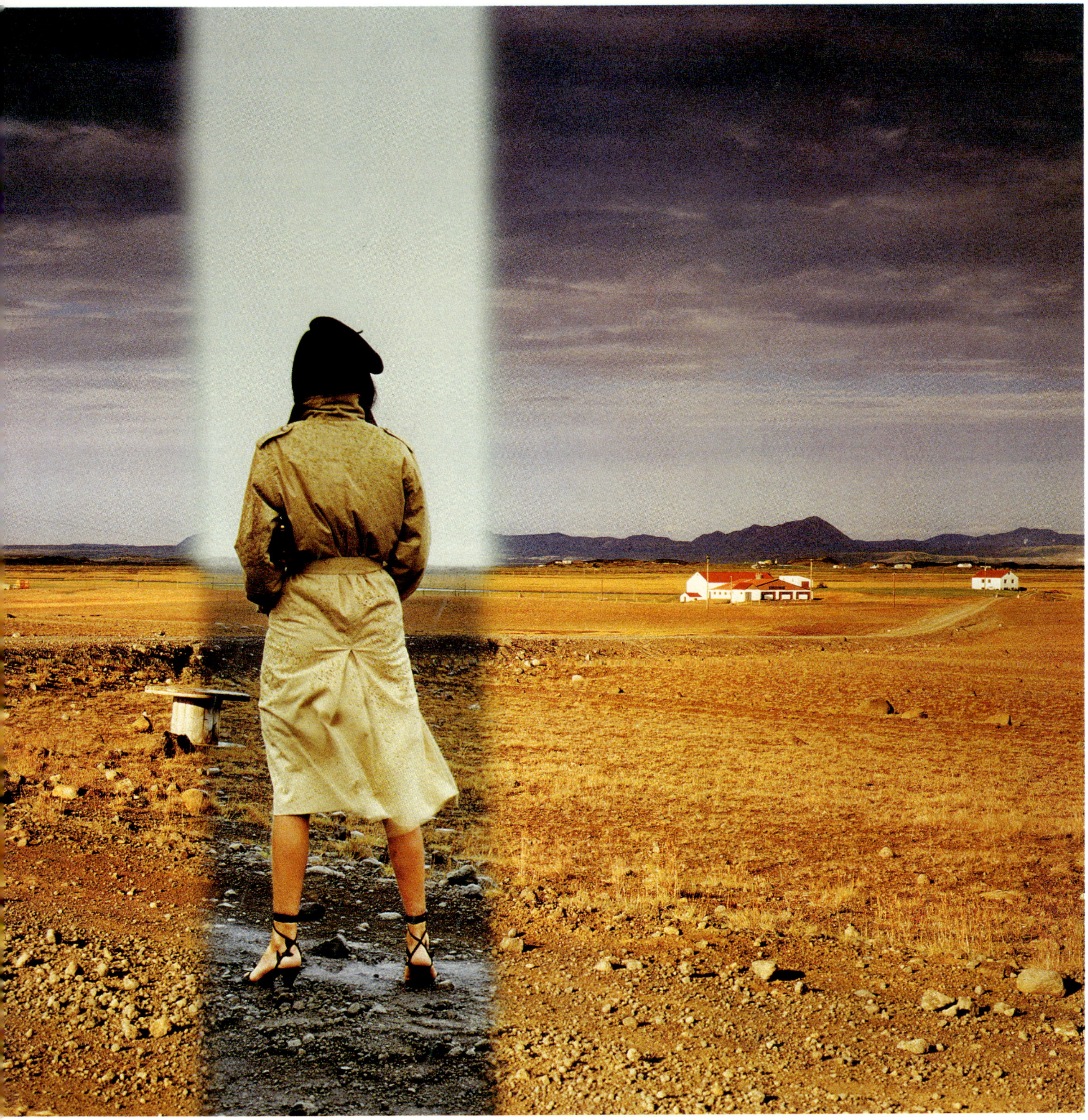

Yuming

X Frozen Hasselblad with normal lens, f22 at 1/30th, daylight Ektachrome, 62 ASA.

The models are friends. (It's not that we are total cheapskates, but we use friends when the budget is restricted and the outcome won't be affected.) The location is Iceland.

The panorama is achieved by panning the Hasselblad right to left for two shots that overlap slightly in the middle. Two halves can be joined by butting the two prints and losing the join on the spine of a record sleeve, or in the gutter of this book.

The mixture of weather is real. The camera position was marked, and background shots were taken on the Icelandic apology for a sunny day and the figures were photographed the next day when it was drizzling. The beam effect is achieved by contrast between the sun casting its oblique rays with a heavy cloud cover on the first day and the rain, a lot of mist and some low cloud on the second. We had no choice: Iceland is very expensive (£6 for a breakfast of fried eggs and bacon, for example) and we couldn't hang around for long. Funnily enough, Iceland was specifically chosen for its changeable weather, as well as for its desolate countryside.

⌖ The actual A/W is made up of R-type colour prints from selected transparencies. Two transparencies are needed for each half of

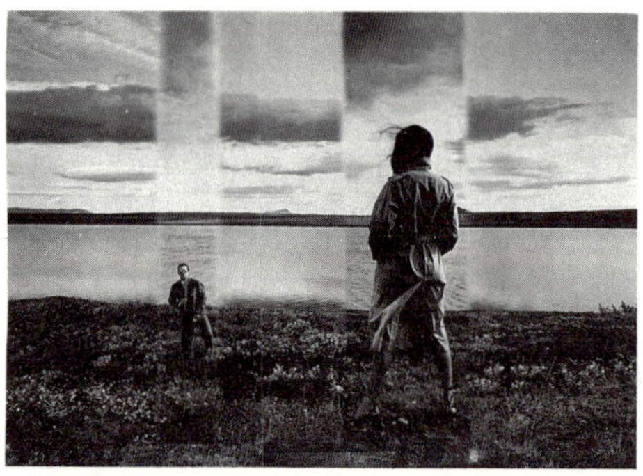

the picture. We used male and female masking films which allow the two transparencies to print onto the same piece of photographic paper. The films are pin registered in relation to the actual print and the transparencies registered in the enlarger carrier (cf. Nick Mason, page 23). The real trick is to make the masking films with vignetted edges. In fact, when you hold them together, they don't fit precisely because, as the vignette tails off, you have to allow some overlap to give a subtle superimposition where the two photos fade into each other. To make these masking films, Peter used that modern and highly scientific procedure known as trial and error.

⌑ This was used for an album cover for one of Japan's leading female singer/songwriters called Yuming. Her album was called something like 'Meet You Last Evening'. It seemed a little unclear to us, but we were assured that it was an entirely comprehensible Japanese phrase which alluded to the temporal paradox of existence as we know it. Or as they know it. The feeling was romantic, forlorn and a little sombre. It was appropriate to have a woman in it, one who might look like Yuming herself.

O This picture stemmed from some ideas we were exploring about people's individual realities. We envisaged a couple meeting, each wrapped in their own thoughts and feelings. For them things are not as they are for the rest of us. At first we tried to imagine a sort of egg shape, an amniotic sac enveloping a character in a secluded area all his own. But this looked very unattractive to the eye, so we made it into a beam, a slice of the picture, as it were, and not necessarily of reality itself. It's the lighting change on the wire drum that I like most, and the rain-soaked pebbles that merge with the dry ones.

In a more flippant vein, I think Scotty is about to beam them aboard the Starship Enterprise, or Enterplise.

'I think that this is a subtle and interesting image dealing with opposites. A man and woman trapped in separate beams of wet weather, meeting in but being separated by a dry hostile landscape. They seemed exposed and out of place, as if transmitted there (Star Trek style).' (Geoff Halpin – Designer)

'The basic theme of the album itself was to express the significance of a certain occasion by making it "time slip" into another state of time. I feel that this has turned out to be an excellent interpretation of the concept, with very strong visual impact.' (Yuming, translated from the Japanese?)

Voyager Poster

X Suicide picture taken with Hasselblad and 50-mm W/A lens, Tri-X film, flashlit from top right. Boys' picture: Hasselblad with normal lens, Tri-X, shot by available light. Photography by Paul Maxon and Peter.

Boys' location is situated just behind our studio, and the suicide is in our assistant's bathroom. Both in London. The blood is made by Peter from his own recipe. He assures me that it's all vegetable.

⌖ Two straightforward B/W prints from the negatives. The lettering is provided as a separate artwork and dropped in by the printer.

⌑ This was a poster for a rock band called Voyager in 1980. The brief was based on the album cover which also comprised two images. In both cases the images were to reflect the title – 'Act of Love'.

O One frequent element in our work, and, I suspect, in the work of other designers, is the use of more than one image at a time. Here I'm not talking about collage, montage, superimposition, multiples, mixed media, etc., but about the problems of arranging together two or more apparently quite separate images. A single image, framed, isolated or bordered, is problem enough. But two pictures can affect each other dramatically and unpredictably. They may enhance or undermine each other. They may reveal or conceal, mystify or illuminate.

Our idea in this case was to examine the effect of these two images on the interpretation of the words 'Act of Love'. The separate actions seem to be opposed. One is affirmative: the spilling of blood as a celebration of brotherhood and harmony. The other is a statement of depression and loneliness.

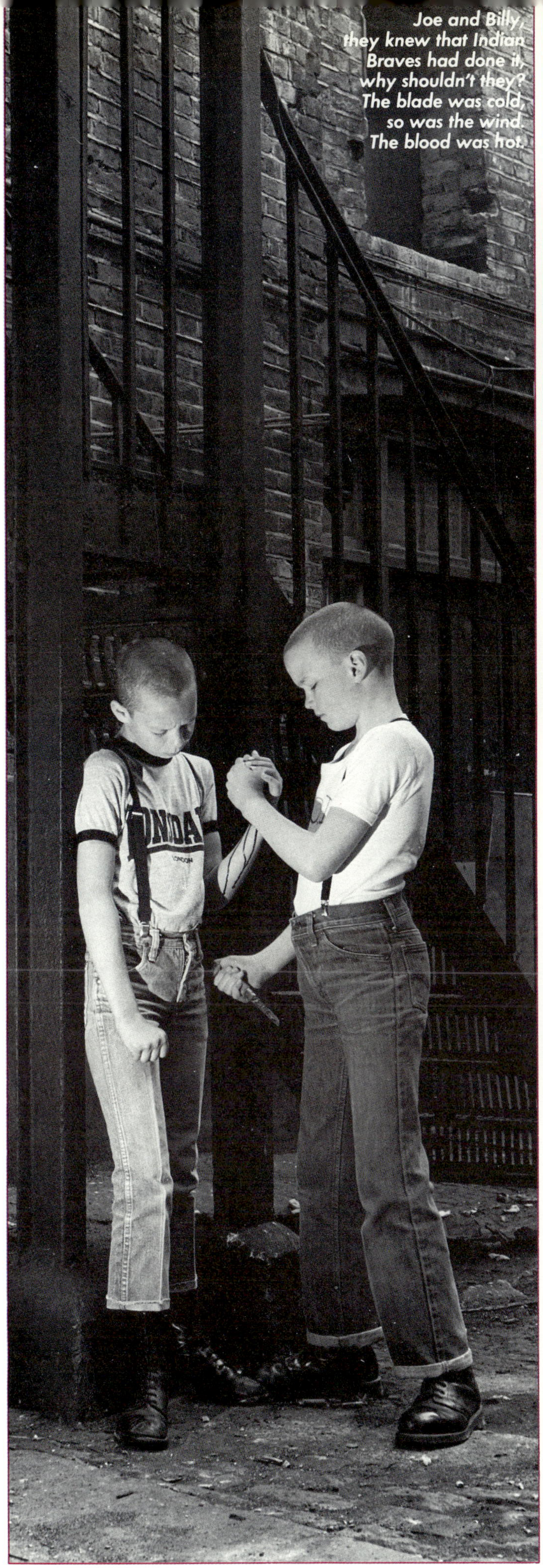

Joe and Billy,
they knew that Indian
Braves had done it,
why shouldn't they?
The blade was cold,
so was the wind.
The blood was hot.

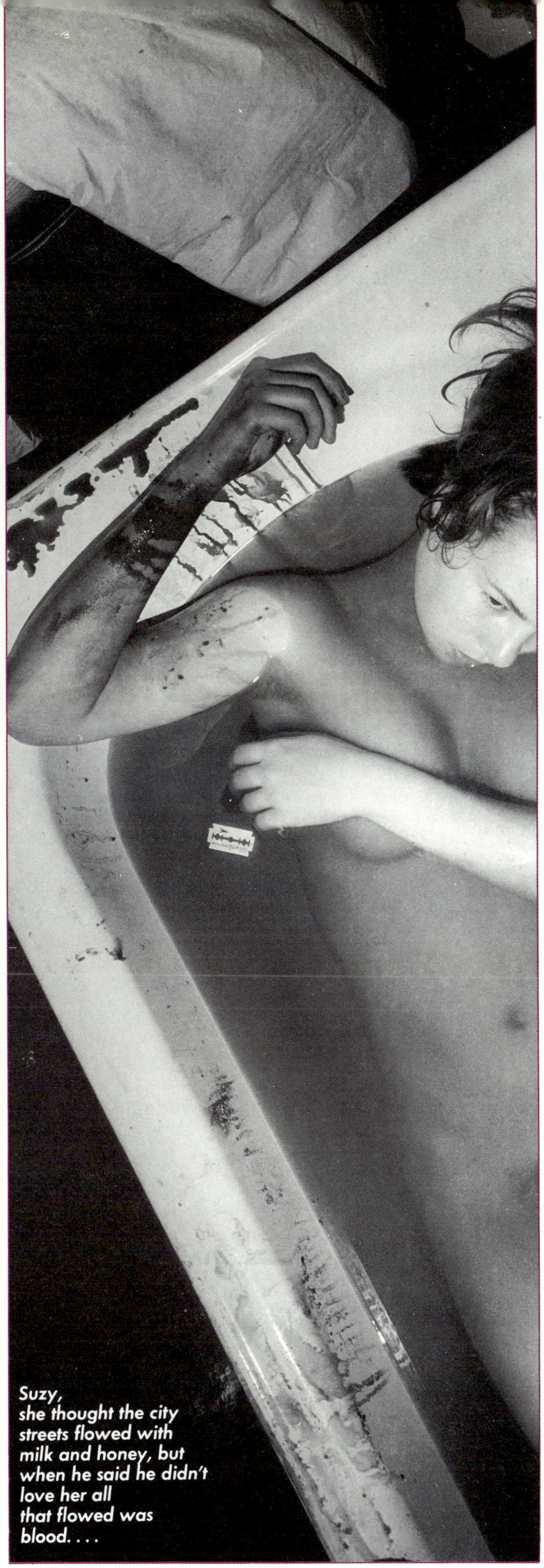

Suzy,
she thought the city
streets flowed with
milk and honey, but
when he said he didn't
love her all
that flowed was
blood. . . .

Mike Rutherford

Hasselblad with 50-mm W/A lens, Tri-X, shot by available light.

The character wearing simple overalls is from a model agency. The location is a pumping station in East Ham, London. These Victorian stations were built for the capital's water and sewerage system. They have wonderful pumps with brasswork and rivets, nameplates and wheels maintained in excellent condition. And great clocks and gauges with fantastic numerals, and a high-domed ceiling. This one had two or three subterranean levels reached by iron steps and floors made of wrought-iron lattices. It was like the inside of a large ocean liner from the 20s. Really splendid. The superintendent said that if the station went out of action or actually stopped pumping, central London would be submerged in one foot of shit over an area of ten square miles in approximately six hours.

The photographic image has appeared only where developer has been allowed to affect the bromide paper. The original negative is exposed onto a print. If this were developed in the normal way, the picture would appear continuous across the print, as in most photos. This is because the print would have been immersed in a tray of developer which would reach all parts of the exposed area. But if the developer is held back from some areas, only those areas which have admitted it will appear as an image. Areas that do not receive developer will stay white and can be fixed and protected.

As sometimes happens, we discovered this particular technique by accident. Our old assistant Richard Draper splashed developer all over the darkroom in a fit of hysteria, or was it depression? Some of the splashes went over a recently exposed print and revealed the photo where the fluid had landed. Richard experimented further. When we did this actual picture we made about forty different attempts, flicking developer on the print by paint brush, by hand, by spoon, and so on. Then we selected a couple of the best results, sepia-toned them and had them hand-coloured by Richard Manning.

Mike Rutherford (Genesis) used this for the front cover of his solo album 'Smallcreep's Day'. The title is from a book whose story inspired the music. Smallcreep is a guy in a large factory, making a part of some big machine. He hardly sees his fellow workers and has no idea what he is helping to make. He decides one day to go and find out, and that's all I'm going to tell you, otherwise I'll spoil the book and the record for you.

This is based on the brief. Little man in a factory, looking around, wondering where all of it leads to and what for. Our technique of splashing liquid across the page for image, rather than for colour, had no particular relevance to Mike Rutherford's record. It seemed like a good idea to us at the time, and gentle enough to suit his temperament. In fact, he was very unsure of it at first and paid us to do an alternative illustrated cover. Although it is his right, in our society, to spend his money how he likes, it struck us at the time as a trifle indulgent. It leads me to speculate on the spending habits of rock stars in general. Not all of them, of course, but a good few don't seem to know what to do with their money: they just throw it away. They should throw some of it your way, right?

'I think this sleeve reflects the music inside.' (Phil Stoker – Manager, Virgin Megastore, London)

'Clever (technique, that is. Picture dull).' (Malcolm Garrett – Designer)

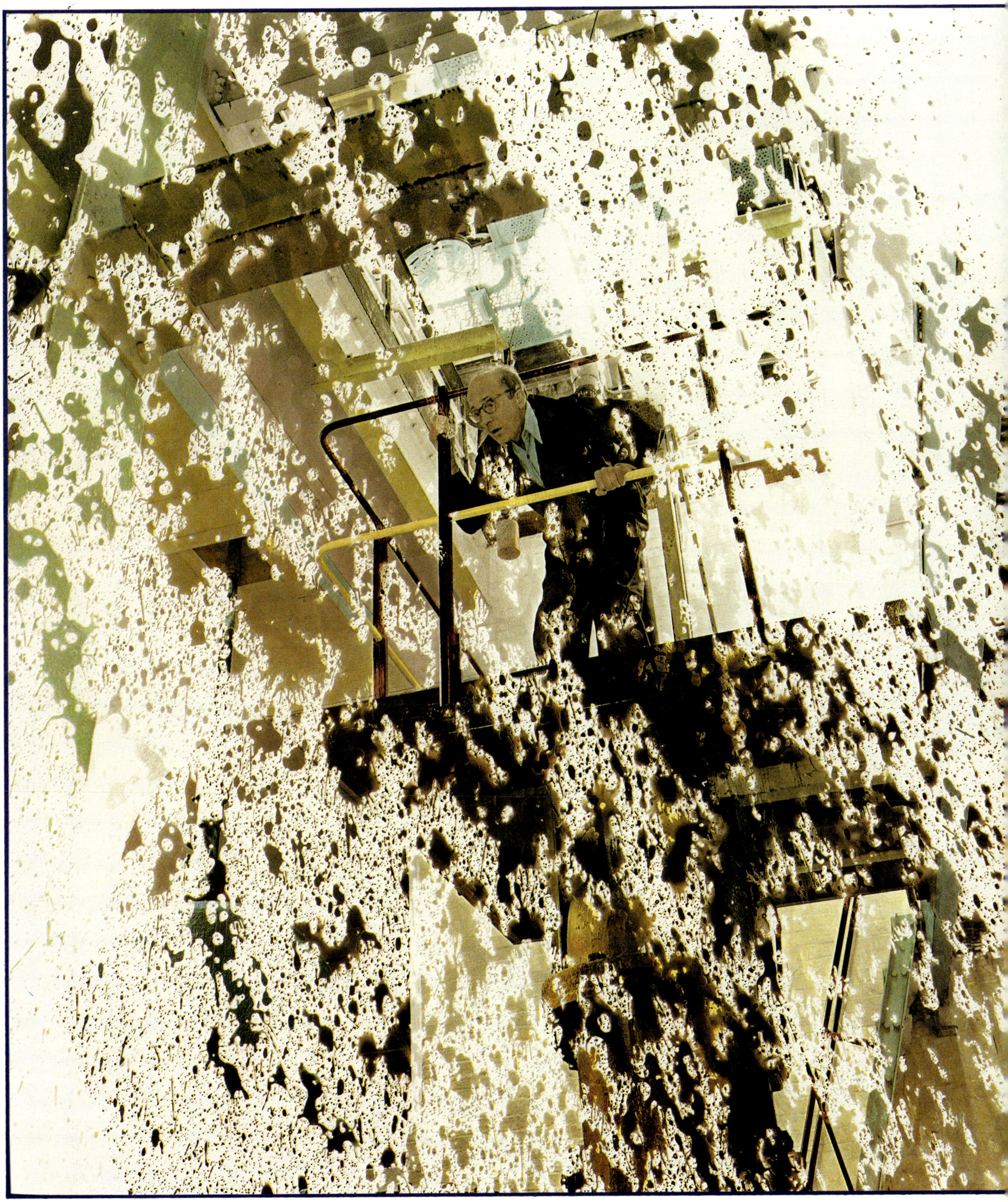

Ashra

We used a Hasselblad with a normal lens and a Proxar close-up attachment. The picture was lit by flash to freeze the water, using three heads (6000 joules), one for the background, one backlighting the water and the girl (as can be seen on the edge of her nose), and the third lighting the face from below and from the side. There was a problem in balancing harsh light (more suitable for the water) and softer light (more suitable for the face).

This was shot in our studio. The girl is an oriental model from an agency in London. The water was pumped through a Heath Robinson contraption and required a fair degree of pressure to ensure that it shot upwards towards the mouth and stayed there. The out-of-focus background comprised three bands of torn cyclorama paper in an attempt to reflect a variety of colours in the water spout. It looks very easy to shoot, but in fact turned out to be a minor nightmare, and a minor flood. It took seven sodding or sodden hours to shoot. I needed a drink after that.

There was a gentleman from Berlin with long blond hair called Manuel Göttsching. He was a guitarist, fond of long cascading notes with plenty of echo. To my simple mind his music seemed very like tumbling water: fresh, liquid, clean and a little on the cold side. This description hardly does it justice, but sometimes it is necessary to apply the reductionist principle – reduce the breadth of musical experience to manageable shorthand. Manuel and two friends made up Ashra. However, the album was never released here in the UK. Was it the cover?

We work in many different ways, but the most common procedure is to listen to the music, read the brief and lyrics and then, through a mixture of intuition and deductive reasoning, arrive at a suitable design. Thus, more often than not, the design is an idea which embodies the main feeling in the music. We then take the idea, discuss different ways of photographing it, and eventually arrive at a consensus. Since the three of us in Hipgnosis are very different people, this process is often very painful, and more prone to disagreement than agreement. At such times we either go home feeling bad, or else the main architect of the design gets to have the final say as to its realization. Swapping views, exchanging interpretations and listening to high-class criticism such as 'that's a load of shit' are vital procedures for group work. Our design meetings can provide stimulation and produce positive results. Quite often though they degenerate into drinking bouts and gossip sessions. Anything to avoid work.

Sometimes ideas, like this one on the opposite page, emerge from observation of everyday life: the act of seeing a commonplace event (in this case drinking from a water fountain) and then abstracting it to make a formal design. In the process we try to make it as appropriate as possible for the client and his brief.

The choice of an oriental model was partly a whim, and partly a desire to keep things cool and formal; I think the Japanese tend to use make-up in a very stylized way. And this helps to make the obvious phallic connotations a little bit out of the ordinary. It is overtly sexual but not sexy. Its idea is hot and sensuous, its manner is cold and detached. Sex in the head, not in the body. I knew I'd got problems.

'A real classical composition and content: on a par with "Drastic Plastic", Be Bop De Luxe. Something that can only happen after x hundred record sleeves is considering the square and what can happen in it, almost before the content (or even the client) arrives. Don't like the pancake.' (George Hardie – Designer)

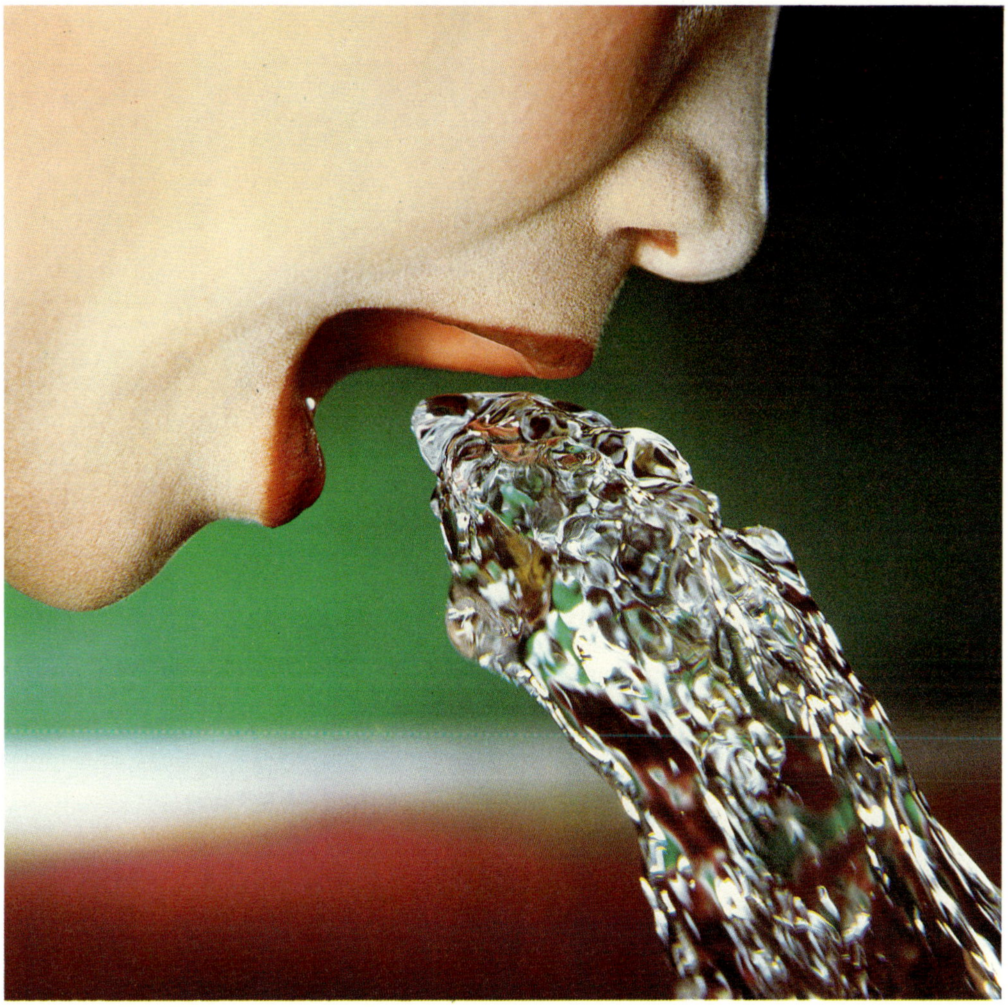

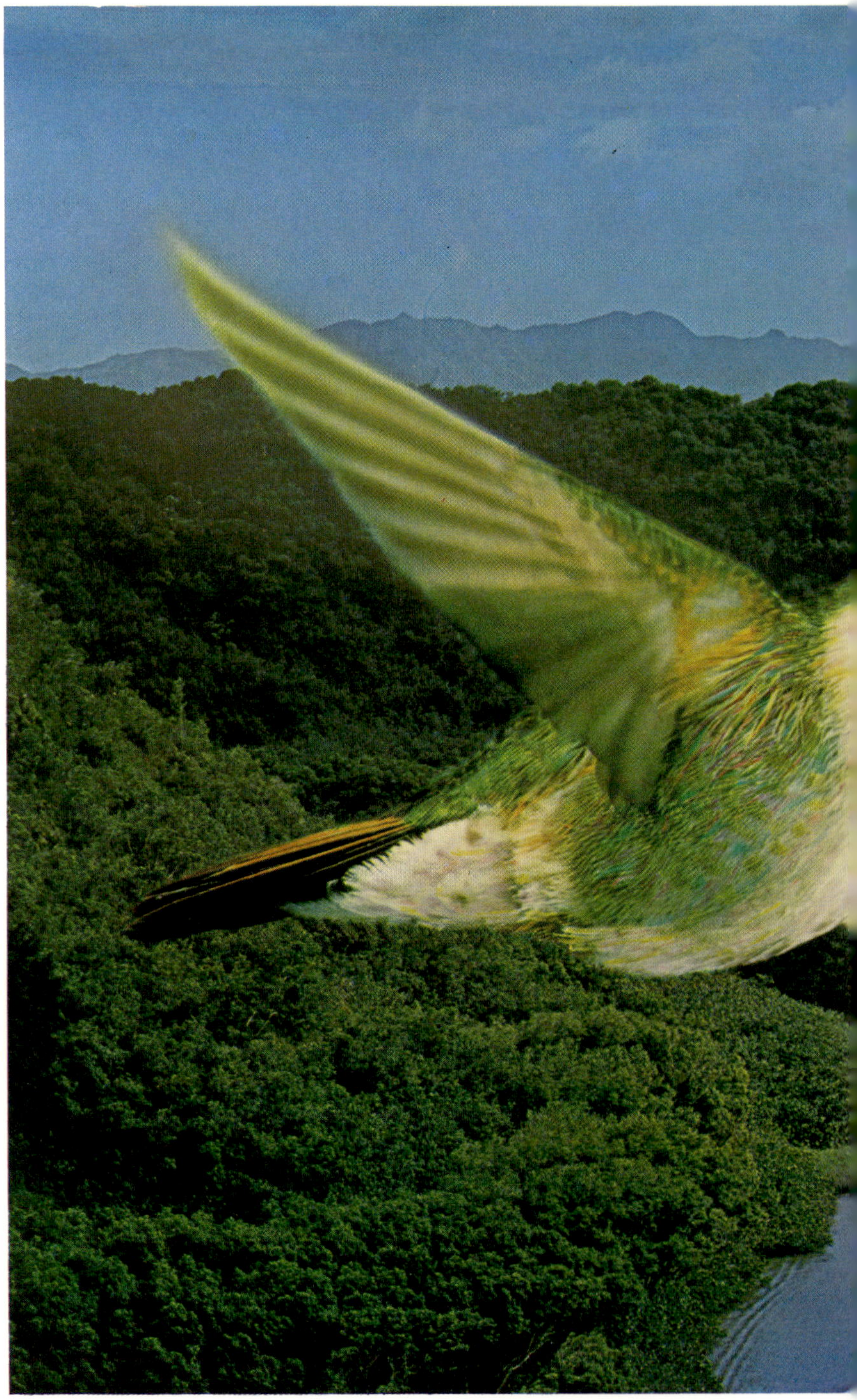

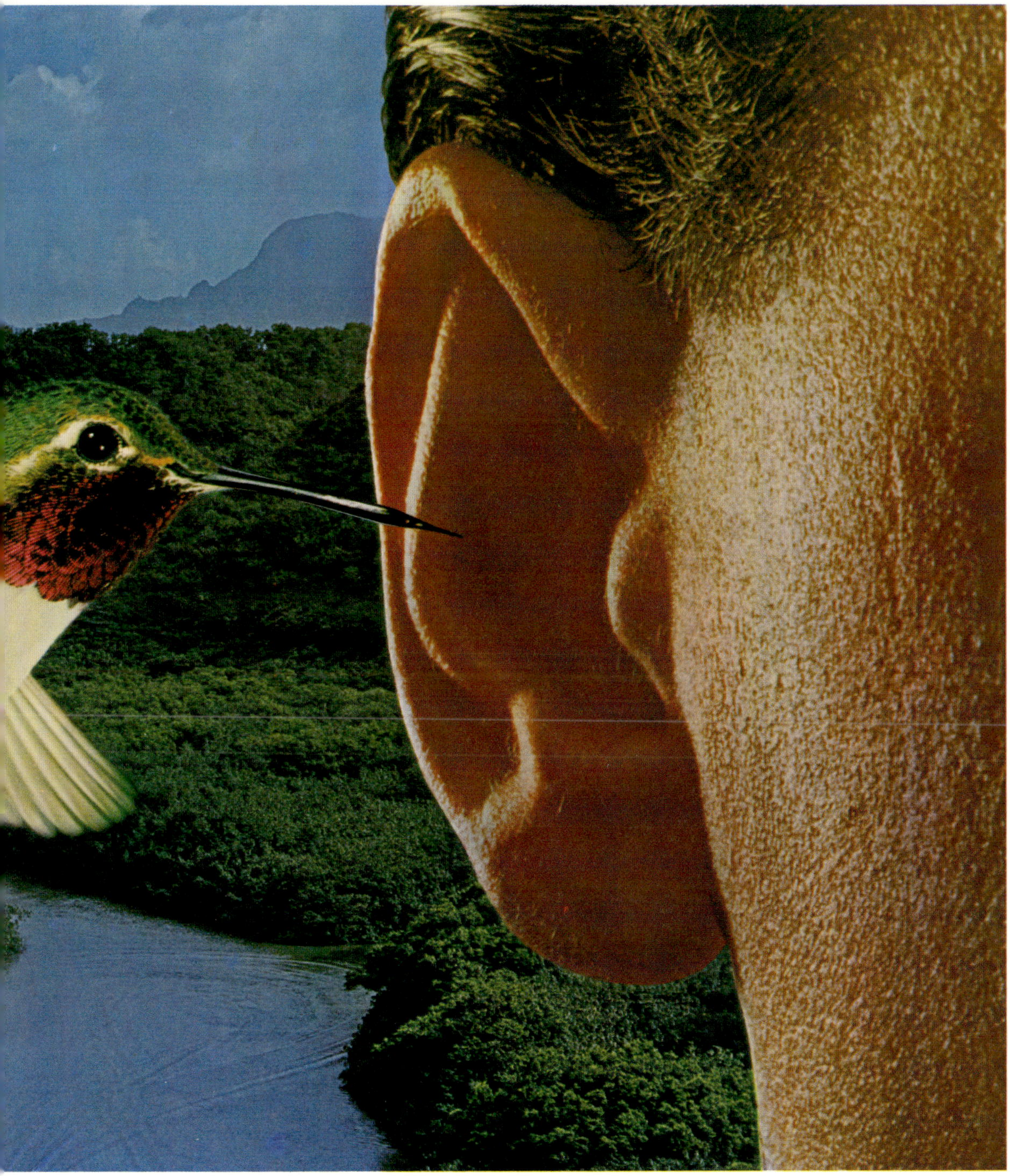

GGK Brazil

× The ear and face by Hasselblad and 50-mm W/A lens, flashlit, one head (2000 joules), daylight Ektachrome. Bird and countryside are separate shots bought from libraries.

⌖ This is known as a three-part dye transfer strip-in. That means there are three separate ingredients: bird, ear and background. These are different transparencies. Test prints are made to estimate sizes and colour matches and, most particularly, to solve compositional problems. These prints are done cheaply and are mutilated, cut up and stuck down, etc., until a satisfactory version is arrived at. And all this is performed in miniature to save money, spelt MONEY.

The exact composition is enlarged to about 18 × 12 on a Grant projector. The consequent tracing and the transparencies are sent to our dye transfer house. Here the pictures are turned into separation negatives and then transferred to one set of matts. The matt films pick up the dyes and deposit them onto a print by a rolling method. Three matts, three dyes, the recombination of which gives you all the colours of the original. Hence dye transfer.

Our three elements are now on one photographic print without any actual joins or edges. The dye is retouched to remove the signs of the joins as far as possible and to lend the wings of the bird the feeling of blurred motion.

⌧ This picture was commissioned as part of a set of fifteen pictures to comprise Polygram's 'World Atlas of Music' (see pages 18–20). This image referred to the music of Brazil which was seen as eclectic, with the samba and bosanova predominant, but with many other influences at work. Furthermore, there is a very fruitful cross-pollination between indigenous music and imported music. Polygram saw themselves as nurturing this fusion.

○ This piece is from the brief. The scenery is Amazonian. Hummingbirds are found in Brazil. They pollinate flowers by sucking the nectar. Here the bird is 'pollinating' the ear of a 'Brazilian' person. And the ear is an obvious way of indicating sound and music. There is also a sense of caring (nurturing) in this picture. As if the bird is telling the man something. Sweet nothings. Or a secret truth.

No Smoke Without Fire

× The background photo was shot in our studio; 2000 joules of flashlighting at the rear and reflector fill-ins from the front. Plus-X, f11 at 1/60th. The models are Peter and our assistant Richard. The only prop is the pen, pal.

⌖ The record company executives damn near had a collective coronary when we delivered this A/W. It *was* very complicated (*and* they didn't like it much). The base A/W was a straightforward B/W print by Peter, no retouching. The three diagonal bars were from an identical print which had been exposed for less time, and the circles from a print that had been exposed longer. Colin Elgie drew most of the illustrations in air brush, one in pen and ink (top left), and executed the graph patterns and 'oscilloscope' wave as mechanicals. There is also one small piece of a full-colour photo above Peter's eye.

All these items were separately drawn and mounted. There was a Kodatrace overlay across the base B/W print indicating where the illustrations were to appear, and their size. However, it was the printer's job to amalgamate all eleven or twelve items, including the type. We thought separation would be improved by being able to camera all the pieces individually. They could also be drawn larger, thus preserving quality. This was probably true, but the separator hated us for all the extra work, known in the trade as aggravation.

An A/W like this was a bit nerve-racking really. We couldn't tell what the finished result was actually going to look like until it was proofed. By then it was too late to change anything. And too late to cool the clients' wrath!

○ The title 'No Smoke Without Fire' suggested rumour, hence the image of one person whispering into the ear of another. But on its own this didn't seem interesting enough, so we introduced the cutaways. Remember the 'Eagle' comic? Somewhere in the middle they used to have a huge drawing of an aircraft carrier or something like that. There were cutaways showing sections of the hull, seamen's quarters or engine room. I used to love them. Apart from the circular rings in our design, representing sound waves, the majority of it is therefore embroidery, or rather medical versions of cutaways.

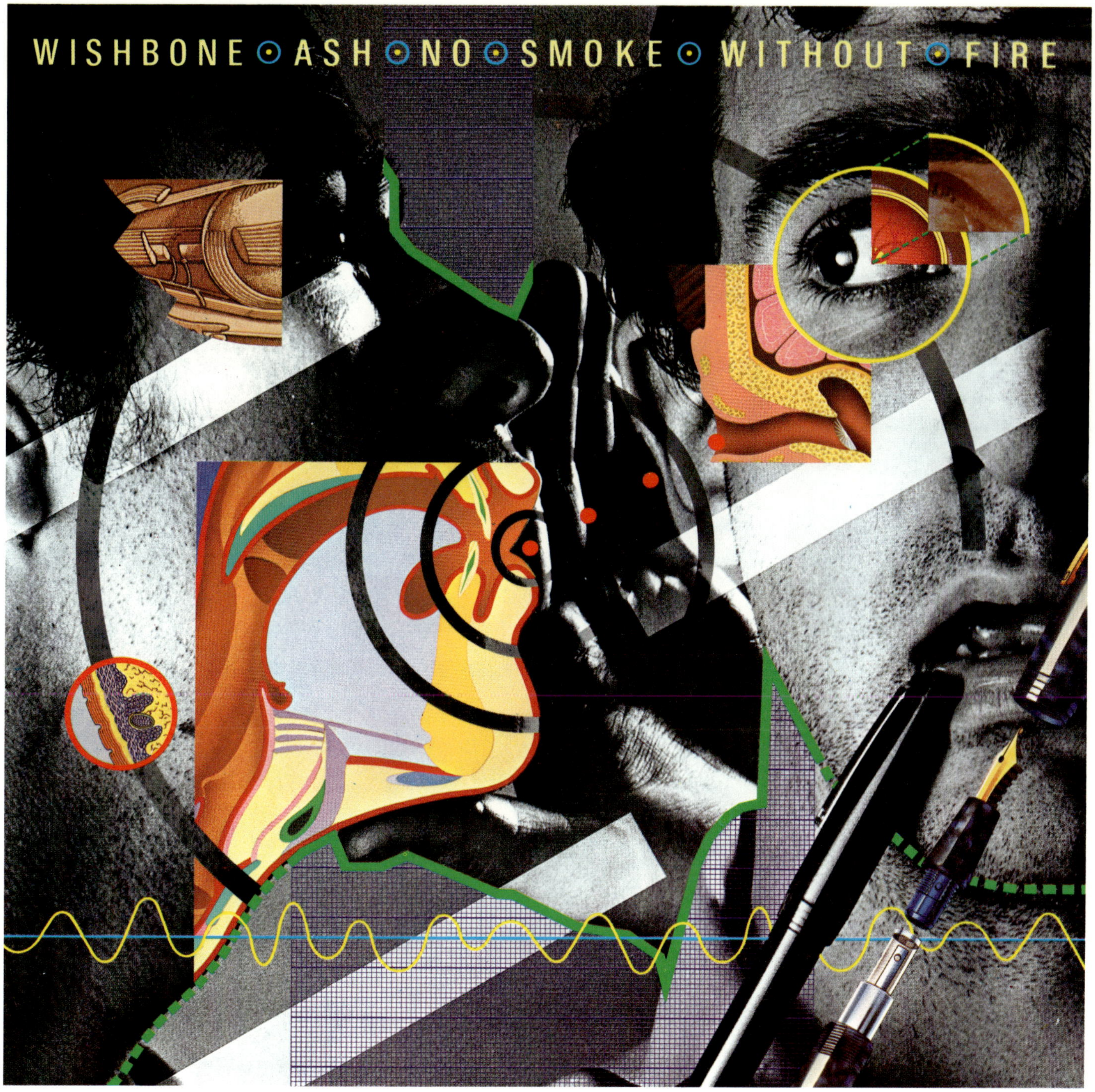
WISHBONE ASH NO SMOKE WITHOUT FIRE

It is also part of our long history of throwing illustrations, graphics and photos together and mixing colour with B/W. This is nearly an obsession and it is very difficult to relinquish it completely. It keeps getting revisited like Brideshead – or Maidenhead?

Although they accepted the design, Wishbone Ash didn't speak to us for two years. They detested it with a unanimous vengeance. The manager hated it. The record company hated it. The bitterness and, I suppose, the disappointment (it didn't sell well) far outweighed any rational consideration of the piece. Since I like it, I could never genuinely sympathize. A parting of the ways. Funny life, business. Funny business, life.

Scorpions Lovedrive

Hasselblad 500C (again) plus 50-mm W/A lens. Daylight Ektachrome rated normally, f8 at 1/60th. Flashlit with Bowens Quad system, 8000 joules, with two heads for couple, two for lights outside. Heavy use of tracing paper on car windows to soften light.

This picture is taken in the back of a Mercedes saloon in an underground car park in London. The couple are models; hair, make-up and clothes by themselves (er ... limited budget). We thought a location would be cheaper than a set. True, but hazardous. The car park was pervaded by the pungent petrol fumes from a zillion automobiles. Would the entire place explode when the flash went off? You may think us silly for worrying, but since the place was underground, it was almost entirely sealed off. We turned religious.

And that pink stuff actually is bubble gum. The boys in the studio chewed twenty packs and regurgitated. God's truth.

This is a dye transfer print taken straight from the chosen 2¼-inch transparency. A little retouching was needed to smooth attachment to the breast, and clean up the faces, etc.

The Scorpions, a German rock band, used it for the front of their album 'Lovedrive' in 1978. The singer and drummer came over from the fatherland to see me. They sat in my little sitting room, introduced themselves, and then asked me if I liked sex. Although their English was excellent, I thought it was some kind of trick question. Was it an invitation? I mean, I hardly knew them. They said they wanted something curious and sexy. Something with an attractive lady. And sex. As long as there was sex.

This piece was designed for the album title. I was interested in glue (visually, not nasally), particularly when items glued together were being disengaged. I imagined two classy people returning from the opera in their limo. It's nighttime in the city. She is indulging a harmless fetish of his involving bubble gum. Instead of blowing it out, rolling it around, extending it, stuffing it back in his mouth or stashing it on the underside of a chair, he likes to stick it on her flesh. And then stretch it. She doesn't care either way.

I knew the image was potentially very annoying to women. I also knew it would elicit heavy criticism. Yet, to me, its very absurdity makes it something other than purely sexist or chauvinistic. Reactions were predictably violent. America didn't use it at all. The English record company received a barrage of angry complaints. Every woman I know hates it. I see it as poking fun at the whole feminist/chauvinist debate. I don't think it is violent, merely odd. Anyway, whenever I told anybody that I was consciously trying to point out possible ironies in the whole issue of the portrayal of women as objects, I was shouted down: it was, I was told, just rationalizing to cover my guilt at doing a sexist picture. It still makes me smile. After all, it's only bubble gum.

There are some who consciously plunder source material and unashamedly rework it. We prefer to invent images. But this one for the Scorpions, I now realize, came in part from something particular, although I was unaware of it at the time: Les Krims's 'Fictcryptokrimsographs'. I'm sorry about this, Mr Krims, but inspiration comes from all sorts of places. Imitation, they do say, is the sincerest form of flattery.

'Perhaps it is the sardonic expression on the face of the man and the frozen look in the eye of the woman – whatever – this sleeve repulses me. At least, it has overtones of sexism, at worst, rape. Amusing? I seem to have lost my sense of humour.' (Jill Furmanovsky – Photographer)

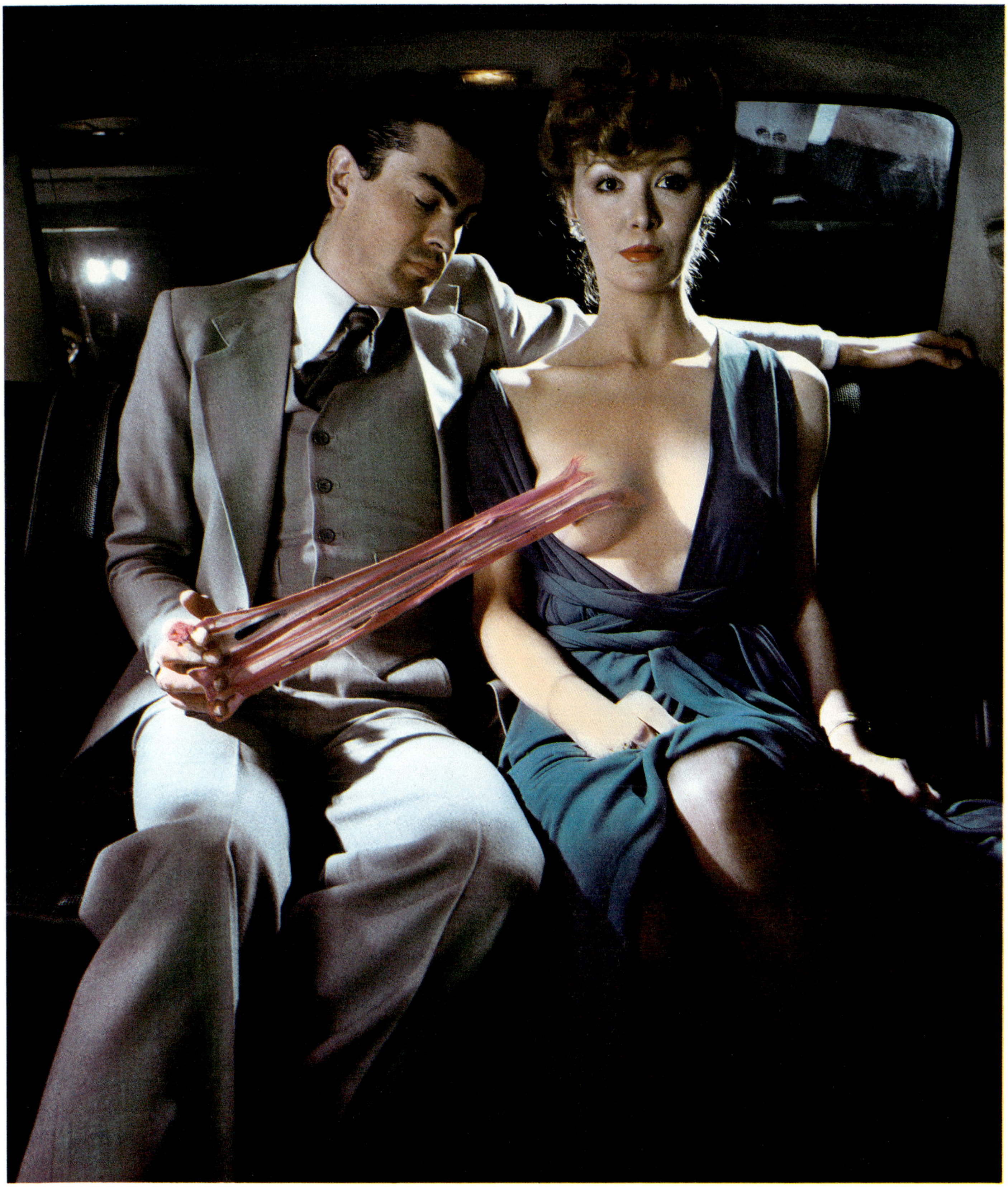

Peter Gabriel 2

(a) The photo of Peter is taken with Hasselblad and normal lens, using Plus-X and shooting by available light and outdoor reflector.
(b) The lyric insert is mixed media of B/W and colour photography with a variety of line drawings, blueprint and mechanical drop-ins. Designed with Colin Elgie.

The model is Peter Gabriel, well-known gent and sometime bizarre rock 'n' roll performer. The choice of clothes is his. The location was going to be New York but it didn't end up that way. It's just round the corner from our studio. The lyric insert, however, is New York in the winter: thick ice and snow, and very cold. There are some shots from a recording studio, the Record Plant, also in New York.

(a) Picture of Peter is simple B/W photo print. The tears are made with strips of white paper stuck on top. They were ripped strips in order to simulate the action of the hand and fingernails.
(b) The blueprint is one piece. The B/W photos are another piece with an overlay indicating their position. There is a further overlay for the mechanicals, line drawings and copy. There is one last overlay which tries to explain all the previous overlays.

Peter Gabriel used these pieces for his album released in 1980. This was his second solo album after leaving Genesis. It had no title. It had no brief. The only thing I can remember him saying was that he wanted it monochromatic and also that he wanted it to be a picture of him. But the picture could be obscure, hidden, unflattering, weird or whatever. He didn't have to look attractive or upfront.

To my horror, I saw exactly the same idea two years later executed by an Italian photographer. His version was different in feeling, but conceptually the same (it was in a French book, 'Photographes Fantastiques', along with our Pink Floyd's burning man). Wheels within wheels, shared consciousness. It just goes to show that *all* ideas inhabit a world of their own, one to which every conscious mind has occasional access.

The idea for the cover is just another of our sporadic forays into the world of illusion. The world of the visual conundrum. The only way in which Peter Gabriel can scratch his own photograph is if he is three-dimensional and can stretch out and back onto the surface of the print. And the scratch leaves a trail of white: the paper beneath the photo image. This scratch is therefore 2-D, in which case Peter is 2-D. On the other hand, we've just explained that he has to be 3-D in order to make the scratches, and so on and so forth. Further screams against the limitations of two dimensions. I shall become a sculptor. Tomorrow.

The lyric insert is related to the tearing of paper but not to the trompe l'oeil of the cover. It is like a scientific textbook or technical manual, which is trying to illustrate how something works. In this case we are examining Peter in a certain pose, at a certain time, in a certain downtown New York street. We explore the internal structure of his body, the place he inhabits. We have a blueprint of the area. Various isolations and enlargements are made to clarify particular details: odd symbols and bits of scientific jargon are interpolated amongst the data. Parallels are drawn and themes proposed. It's hocus pocus, that's what it is.

'Totally relevant to Peter and his music. People who buy Gabriel albums are usually more intelligent than the average punter. They know what they're looking for so it doesn't matter that there's no title, etc.' (Keith Johnson – Manager, HMV Record Store, London)

'When the time came for our regular sleeve discussion, I asked for a moody little piece to explore alienation, surveillance, frustration and other wonderfully modern maladies. I was shown the usual portfolios of partly-mades with various images of animal cruelty, multiple metallic eyeballs, accident victims and laser-loaded lighthouses – the initiation ceremony for most Hipgnosis clients, or so I presumed. I passed through that and Storm showed me a prototype he had designed for Lumiere & Son. It looked both strong and right. I was sold.' (Peter Gabriel)

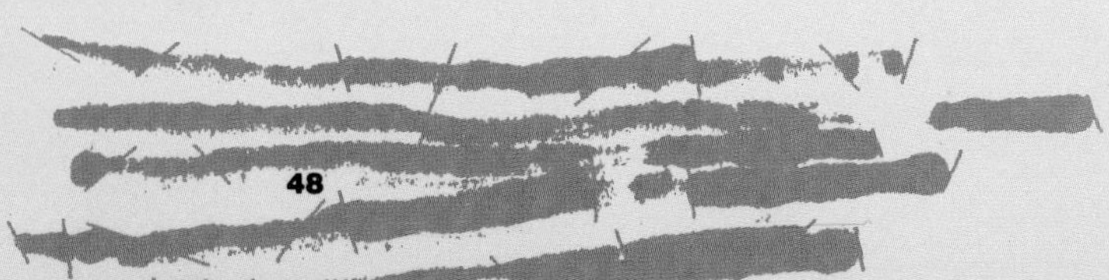

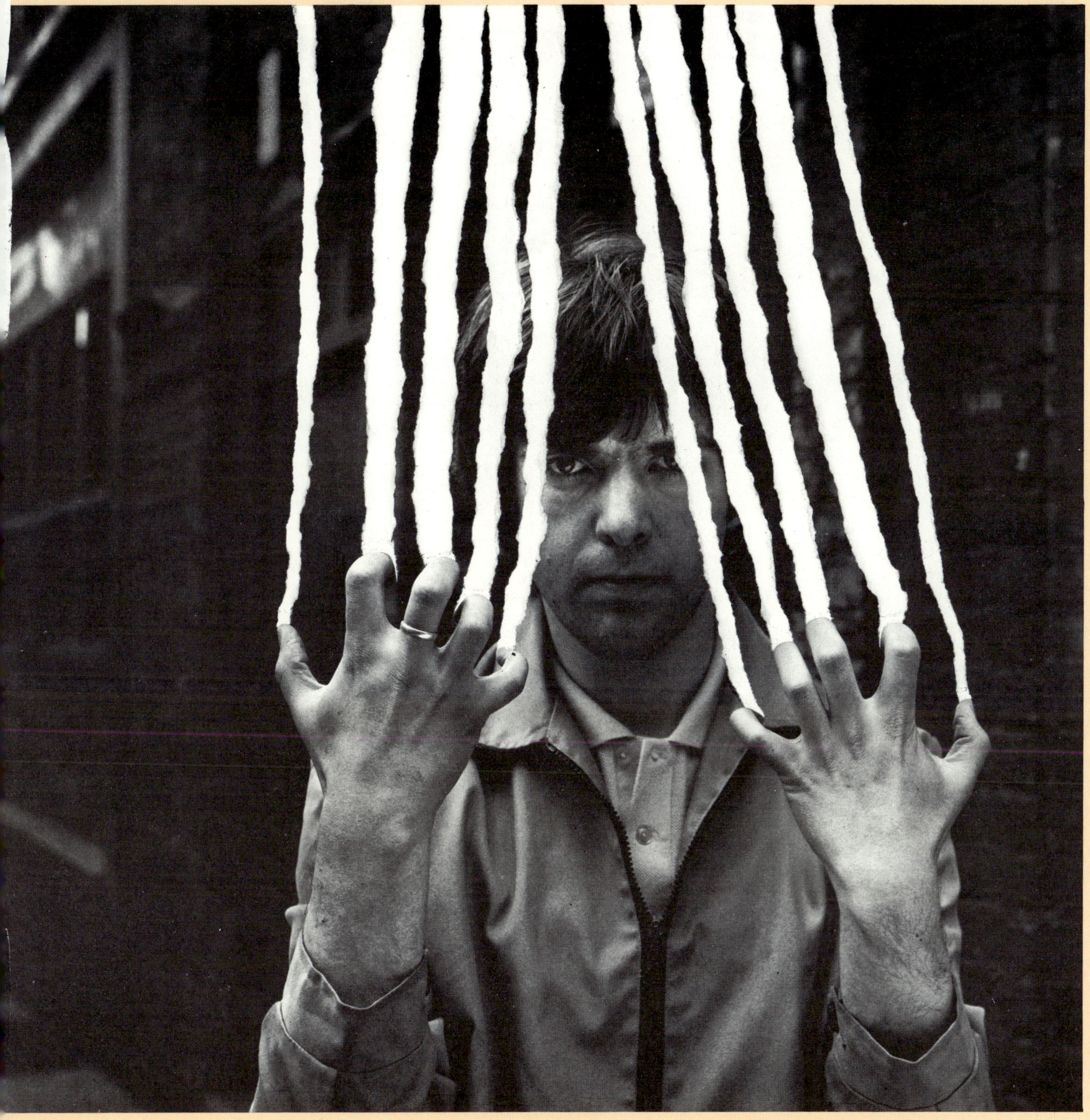

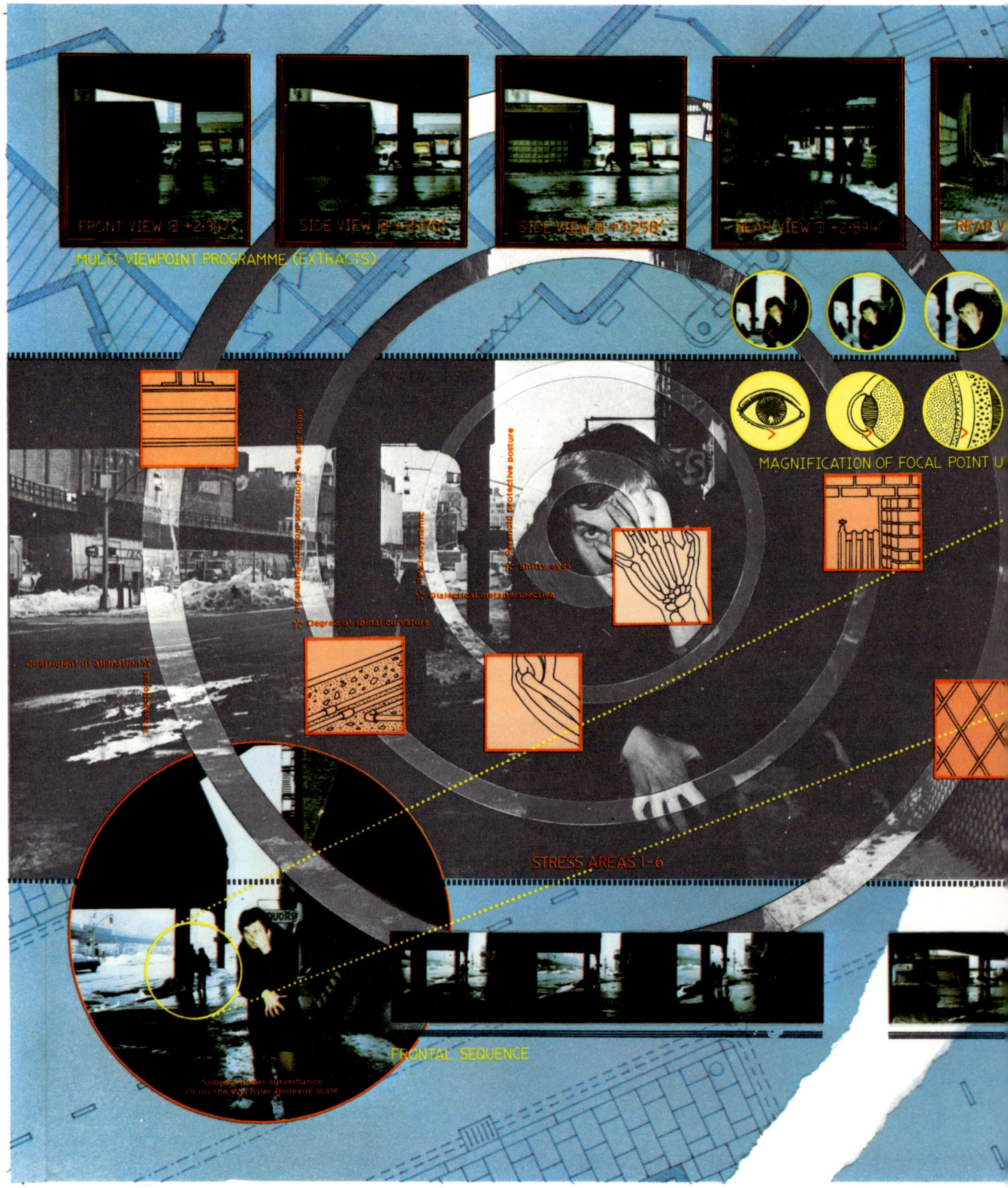

FRONT VIEW @ +2·347′
SIDE VIEW @ +2·170′
SIDE VIEW @ +3·258′
REAR VIEW @ +2·894′
MULTI-VIEWPOINT PROGRAMME (EXTRACTS)
MAGNIFICATION OF FOCAL POINT U
Increasing adrenal secretion 24% and rising
Paranoid protective posture
Psychodynamic
Shifty eyes
Dialectical metaperspective
Degree of spinal curvature
Coefficient of alienation
Transactional
STRESS AREAS 1-6
FRONTAL SEQUENCE

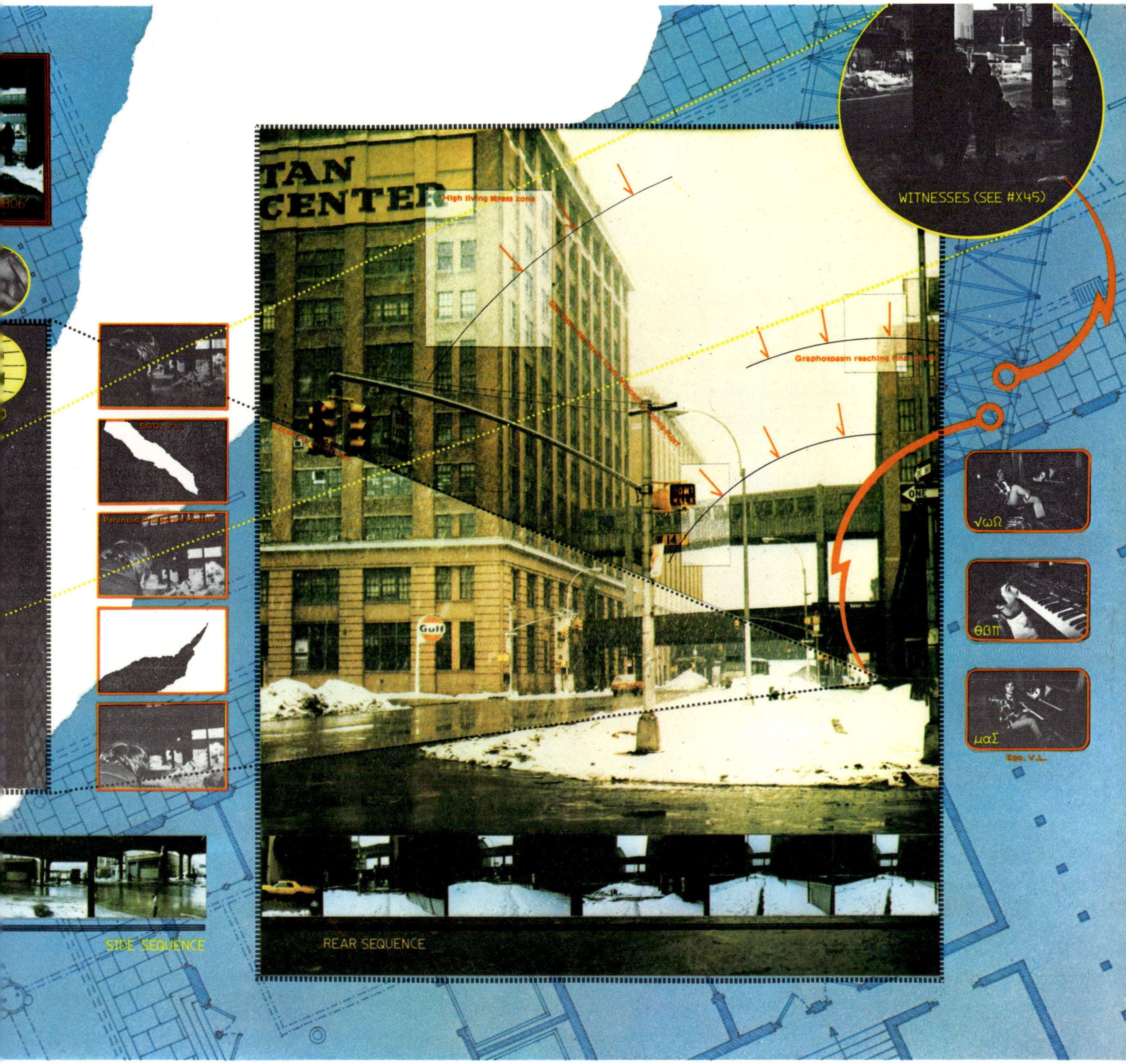
TAN
CENTER
High living stress zone
Eccentric projection
Graphospasm reaching final phase
DON'T WALK
W 14
ONE
Gulf
WITNESSES (SEE #X45)
√ωΩ
θβπ
μαΣ
Ego, V.L.
SIDE SEQUENCE
REAR SEQUENCE

2

A commercial break, but nobody really gets up to go. I mean, a break is *never* commercial. Images are. And commercial images are the *best* there are. They have to be. They are the documentaries of the endless war between things to gain ascendancy over one another.

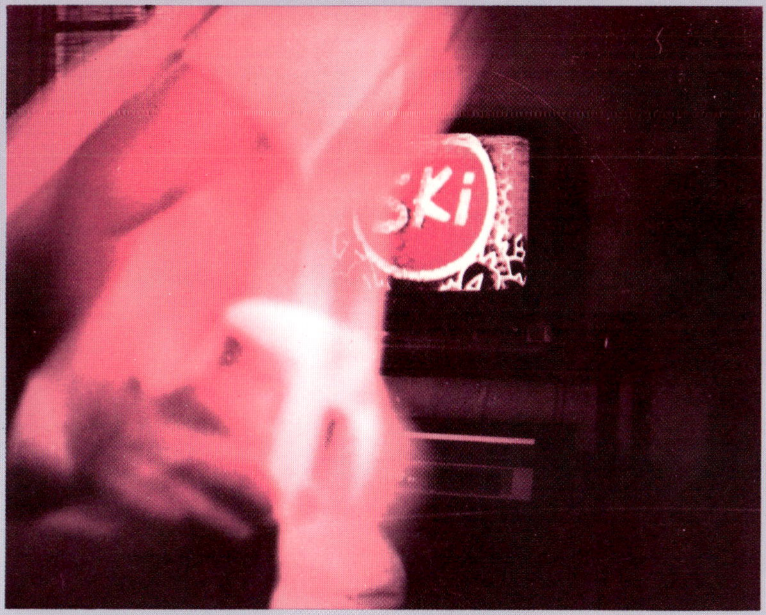

Bloody Tourists

✕ Hasselblad plus 50-mm W/A lens. Daylight Ektachrome with Chromafilter, f11 at 1/250th. Illumination by Caribbean sunlight.

This is real: Barbados in the spring. Po and his friend Gabi are the models. The map is made up to look as if it had been blown onto Po during heavy turbulence. He is wearing it like a mask. The clothes are his. He wears a Hawaiian shirt, Bermuda shorts, straw hat, wicker moccasins, etc. Very dashing.

⌖ The focus would not carry between foreground and background, not if we wanted the main character to be that close. So there are two shots: the figure plus the map, and the sweeping line of palm trees with sea, sky, etc. Both shots are exposed similarly and taken at the same place so that there are no undue lighting changes. As a result the combined picture has a chance to look like one shot.

R-type prints were made and collaged together. That's it. A minimum of retouching was required. B/W negative prints were done first to ascertain the most favourable ratio of sizes and the best composition. The really difficult part came in actually lining up two sets of overlapping background shots – the Hasselblad has a square format and we wanted the whole thing to stretch over a gatefold. The camera was panned at the time of shooting to provide two pictures that fit together.

◻ 10cc used this for the front cover of their album 'Bloody Tourists'. They wanted something positive and colourful. They added that they had been doing a great deal of travelling before they had made this album, touring all over the world visiting far-flung places, but never having the time to see anywhere. They had crossed continents in one box after another. An apparently endless cycle of plane, limo, hotel, dressing room, limo, hotel, plane, etc., passing through exotic locations which they were unable to experience.

○ This idea directly ties in with notions of travelling without being there; looking without seeing. The 'tourist' syndrome of never really appreciating any place that is visited; of never attempting to soak up the atmosphere or understand the rhythms. Just passing through. More time spent in photographing the place than absorbing it: places enjoyed only in retrospect.

So the picture shows an avid tourist, his ghastly shirt proclaiming his identity, camera slung round his neck. He has been examining a map to see where he's going. The wind gets up suddenly and blows it into his face. At this moment he can't 'see' where he's going. The very thing that would point him in the right direction obscures his vision. His fear of experience is symbolized by the map being under his nose and in his eyes. Why doesn't he worry less about tabulating his environment, and spend more time responding to it? His tourist mentality is what makes him miss the experience in the first place. A tourist through life. And there are a lot of them about.

Aside from all this, it is also a surrealistic oddity. You can't see the guy's head. It's supposed to look humorous and a little strange. We have, of course, cheated in so much as the map should be facing inwards, as if he had been looking at it. But this is artistic licence, renewable at great expense.

‹ 'I don't see the point of this.' (Phil Stoker – Manager, Virgin Megastore)

'When I first saw this it looked like another one in the eye for old surrealism: *another* ambiguous Hipgnosis cover. Although I suspected that if I took the time to wade in, all would be revealed – I couldn't be bothered. Some time later I arrived at the idea and, having missed the point, felt like the bloody tourist in the picture – blinded by the thing that's trying to direct him.' (Bush Hollyhead – Illustrator/designer)

'Said in one picture what I felt like on tour.' (Graham Gouldman – 10CC)

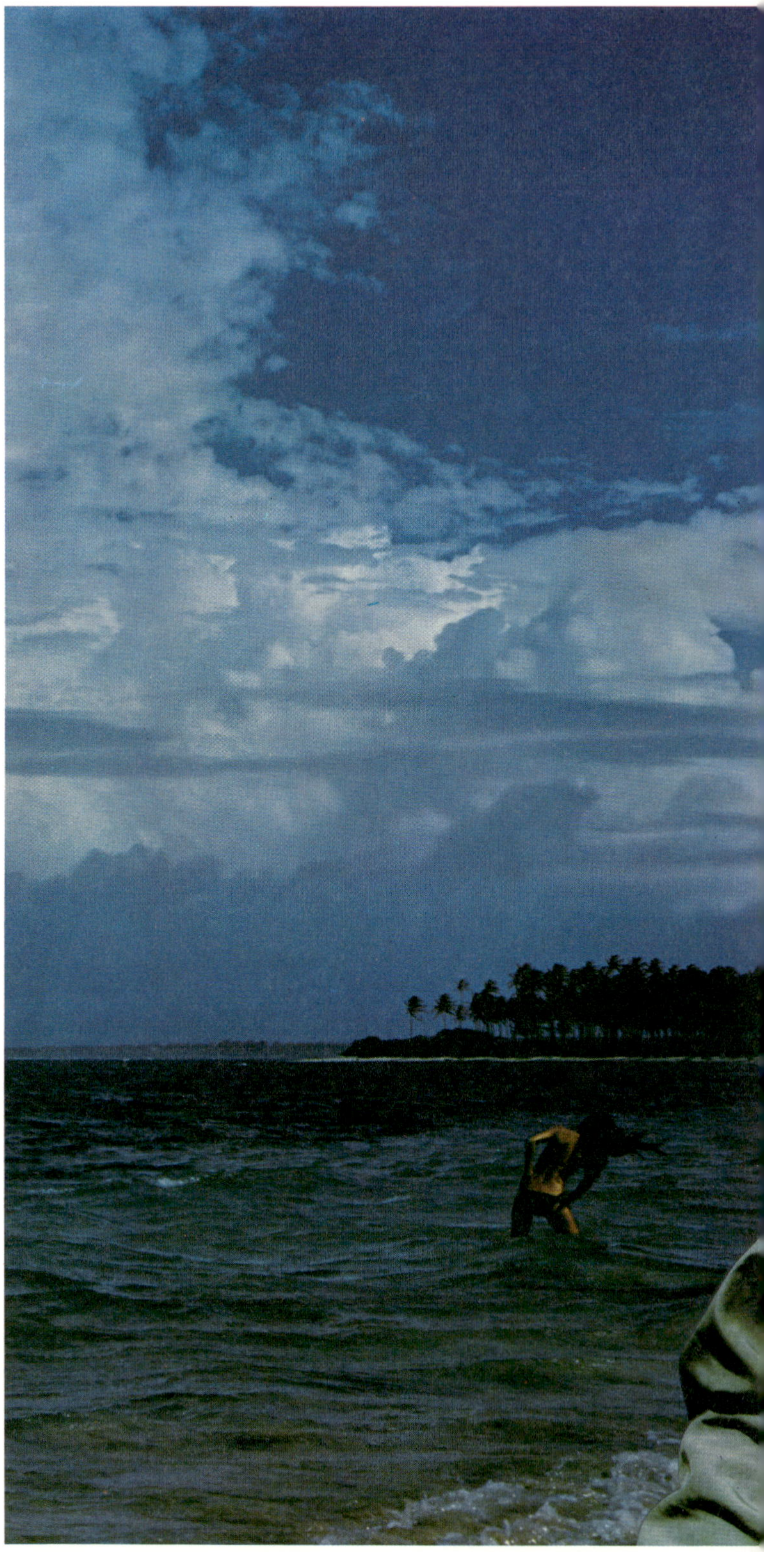

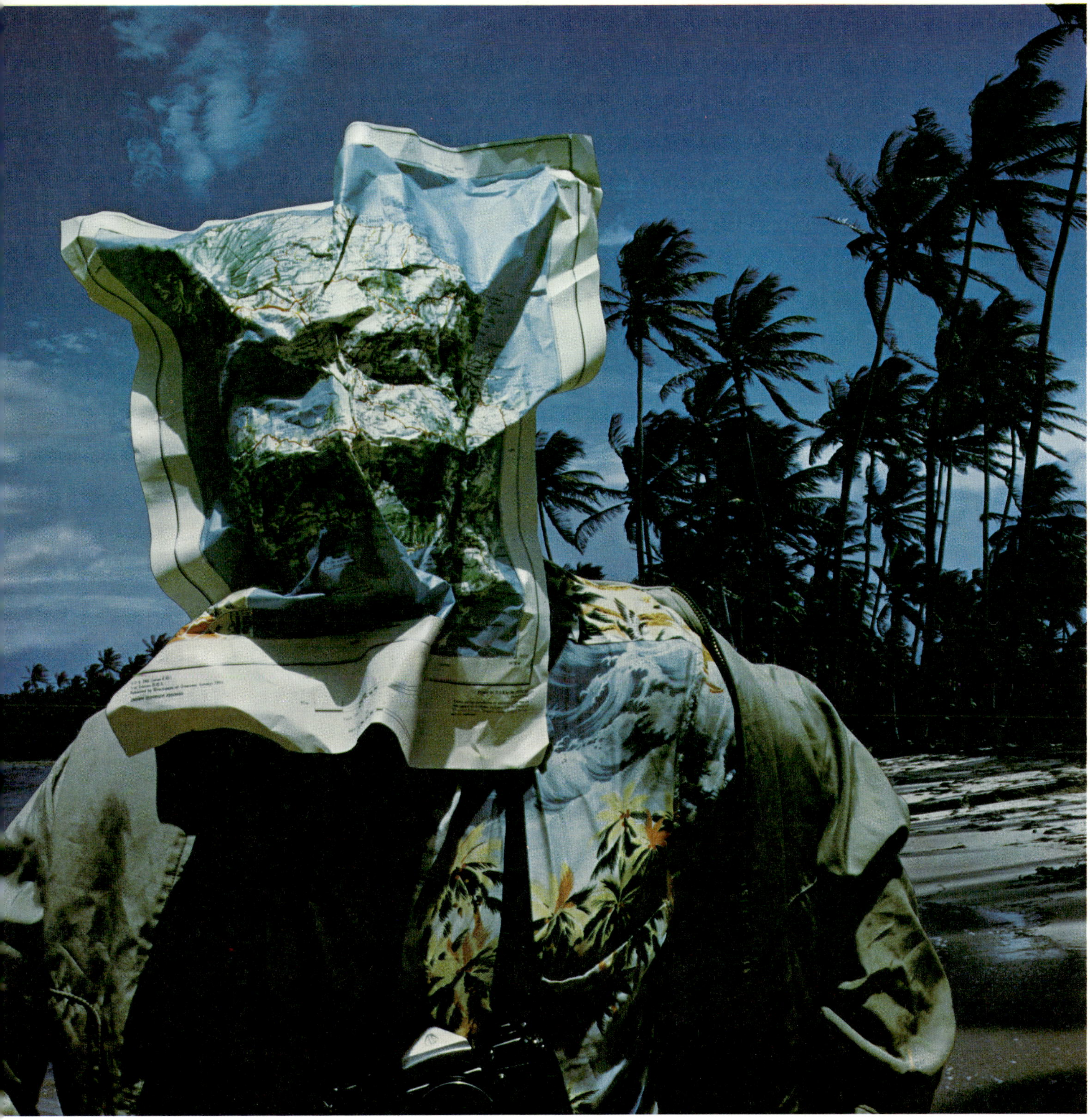

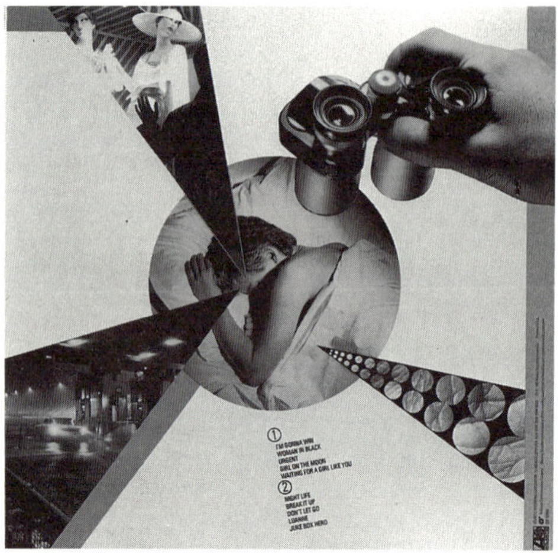

Foreigner

Two photographs, both Hasselblad plus normal lens. Flashlit in the studio with one head and snoot for the figure (2000 joules), side top lighting and two heads (4000 joules) for the binoculars, top lit and reflectors below. (It took five minutes to shoot the figure and five days to shoot the binoculars.) The rest of the photographs were also taken in B/W using Hasselblad, 35-mm Nikon 28-mm lens, 6/7 Pentax, and a variety of tungsten, daylight and flashlight.

Most of the dramatis personae were friends, except for the poster when we were, quite reasonably, obliged to use the band. The locations included a Holiday Inn hotel room, a tollgate near Bristol, Peter's house and a shopfront in the West End. The band was photographed in New York. The background buildings were shot at night in Manhattan by available light and long exposures, courtesy of Mr Peter Moon. Po shot the band. Peter and our assistant, Paul Maxon, photographed the rest.

Simple B/W prints from negatives, collaged together. The binoculars are cut out and stuck on the black background. No copyprint necessary. The only retouching was spotting and the occasional sharpening. The main difficulty here was the quality of the prints. We needed to keep clarity for the bins yet hold enough tone for the person asleep to achieve a grey and slightly dated quality. Peter spent weeks in the darkroom struggling to obtain just the right feeling in the photograph. That's what *he* claimed he was doing in there, anyway.

The rock band Foreigner commissioned this piece as a cover for their album 'Silent Partners' in 1981. It was later retitled 'Foreigner 4'. They asked us to do a 'typical Hipgnosis piece', and to remember that the music was striking and very powerful. And, finally, to pay attention to the lyrics.

It's very difficult to respond to lyrics except in the context of a song. Unsung and without music, they tend to lose rather a lot of their sparkle. We read through Foreigner's songs several times and endeavoured to make some visual sense of their themes. Trying to elicit a single image (or feeling) from lyrics or music is a daunting task since separate pieces usually express separate ideas. We tend to extract what are, to us, the most salient amongst them and forget the rest. On this occasion we ended up with nighttime, a sense of breaking frontiers/boundaries, a sense of intrusion, of watching things, and an image of shopfronts at night. All these elements are to be found in various parts of these designs. But they all stem from the front cover, and this design emerged from a dream.

I've only ever dreamed two designs: this one, and one for Peter Gabriel. I once dreamed of exploring a record shop of the future and seeing many of our covers, but as yet undesigned in reality. The problem was that I couldn't recall any of the specific covers when I woke up! However, in this particular dream, a person was asleep with a syringe suspended above him. The binoculars seemed a more pertinent symbol for intrusion and in the final design replaced the syringe. They hover close above the sleeping figure even though they are an instrument designed specifically to see things from afar. This closer-than-necessary scrutiny feels threatening to me, doubly so since the person, the victim, is asleep – at his or her most vulnerable time.

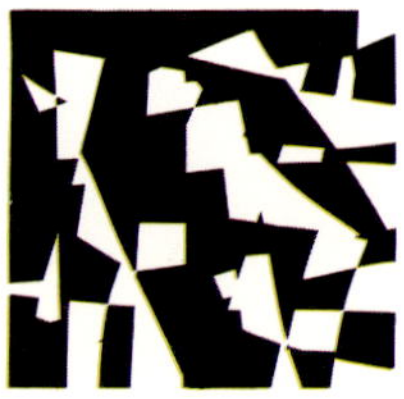

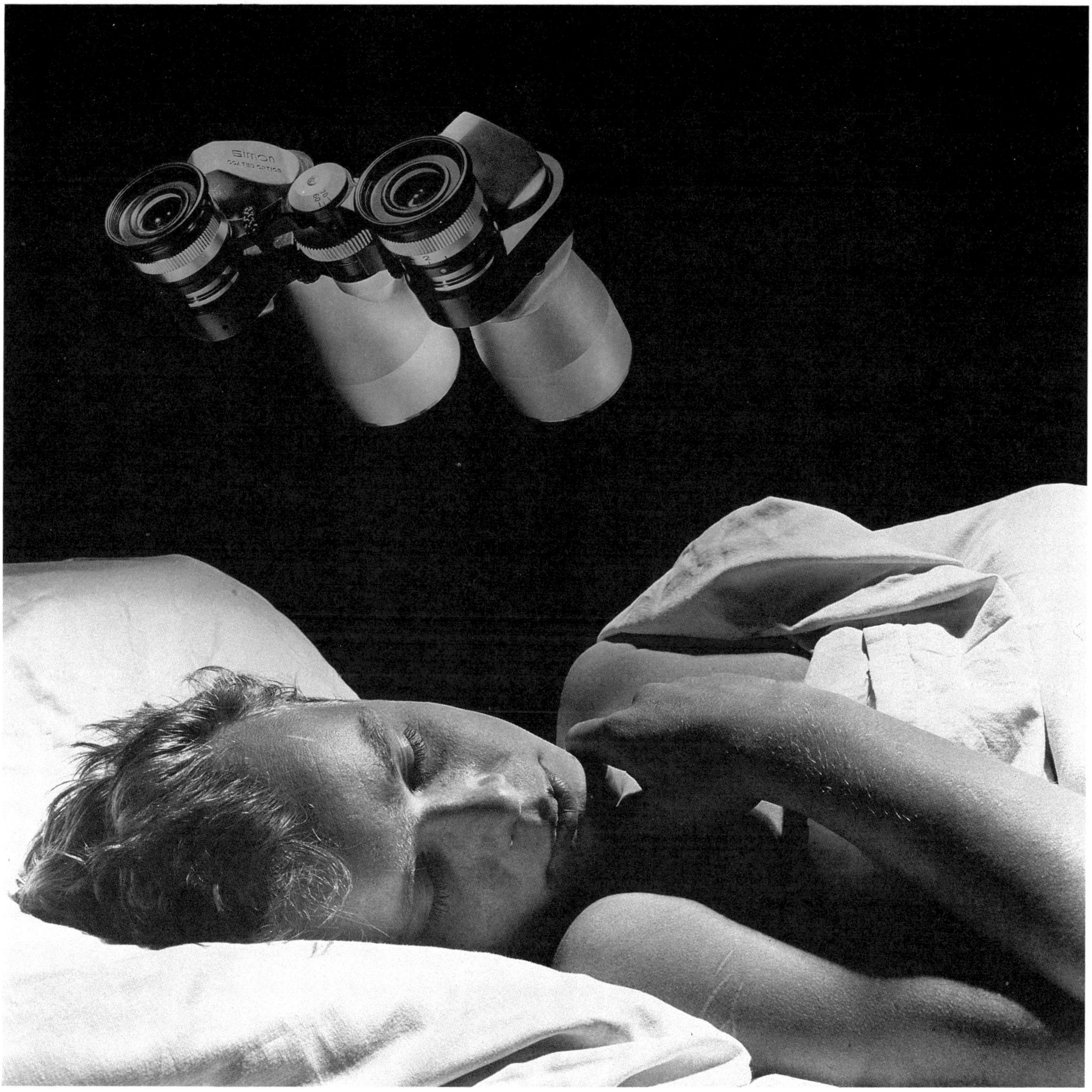
simon

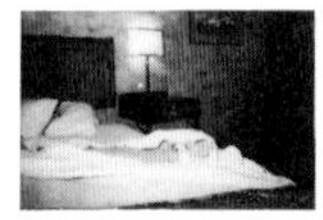

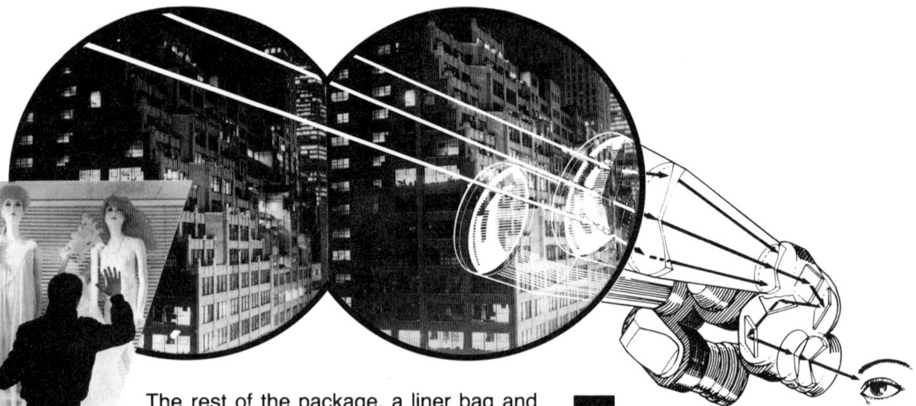

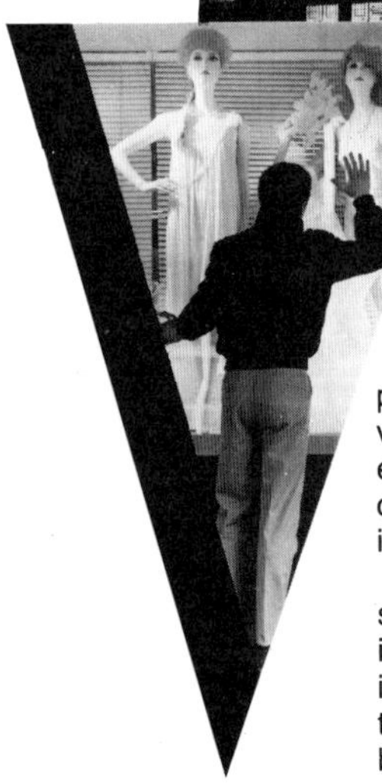

The rest of the package, a liner bag and poster, explores themes of intrusion and surveillance. Perhaps the binoculars can penetrate into the mind itself, passing through our defence systems as we lie in sleepy ignorance.

Foreigner wrangled over this design for six months. Finally they accepted it and had it proofed. The band then decided it was inappropriate and junked the lot. It only saw the light of day as a single bag in Germany, by mistake I believe.

'I found this a compelling range of images, as the complicated odd arrangement and mass of different imagery suggest, without actually showing, heavy, dangerous, sordid or criminal activity being observed by an unknown intruder: like a detective story which gets more complicated as you move from one picture to another, but is never explained. The drama of the situation is further emphasized by the use of optical effects and devices, i.e. enlargement of small areas of type and pictures and the continuous use of the binocular shape.' (Geoff Halpin – Designer)

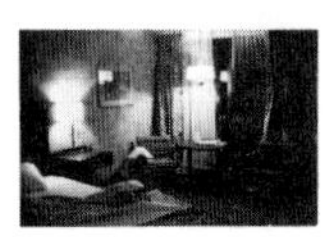

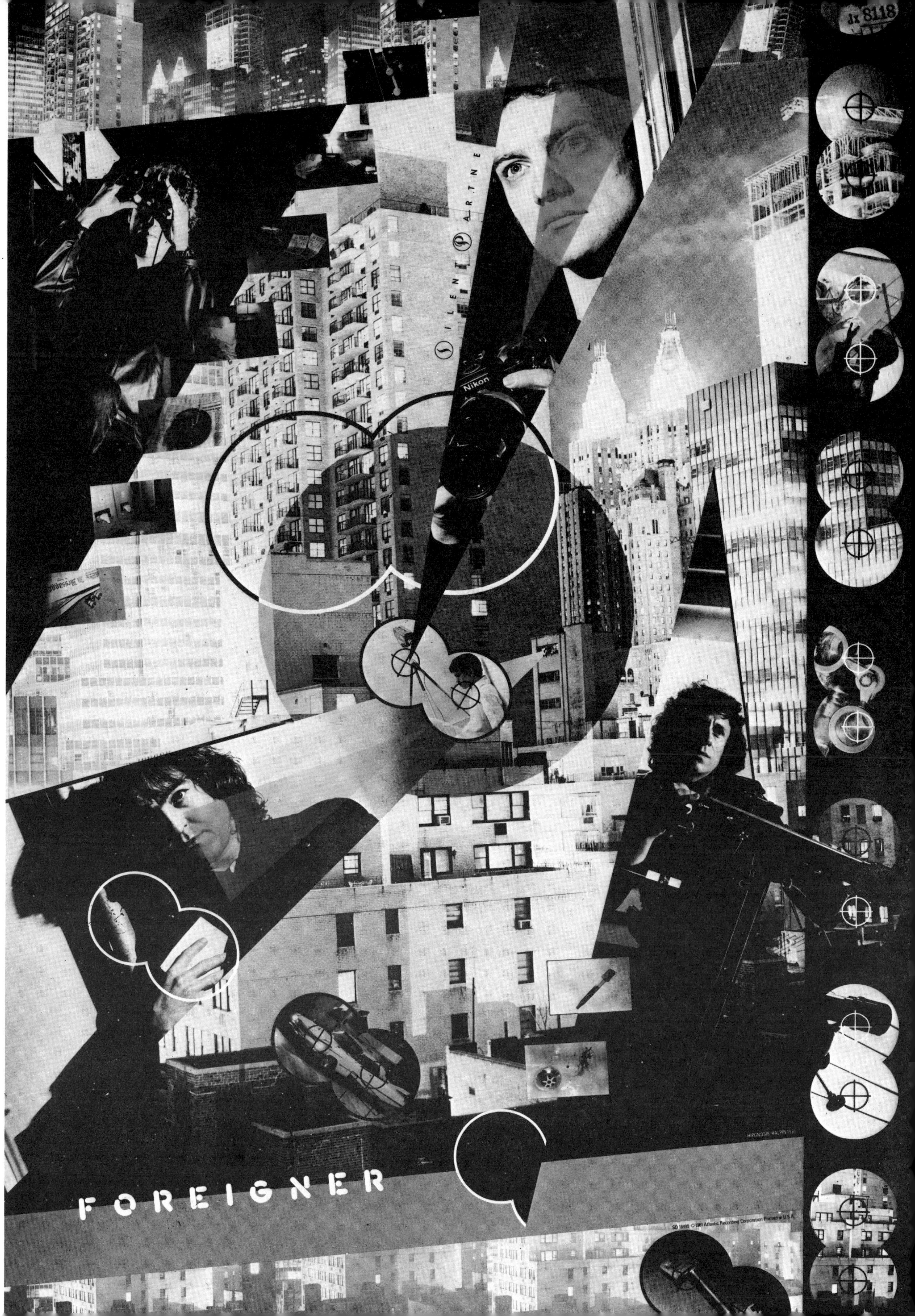
Jx 8118
SILENT PARTNER
Nikon
HIPGNOSIS HALPIN 1981
FOREIGNER
SD 16999 © 1981 Atlantic Recording Corporation Printed in U.S.A.

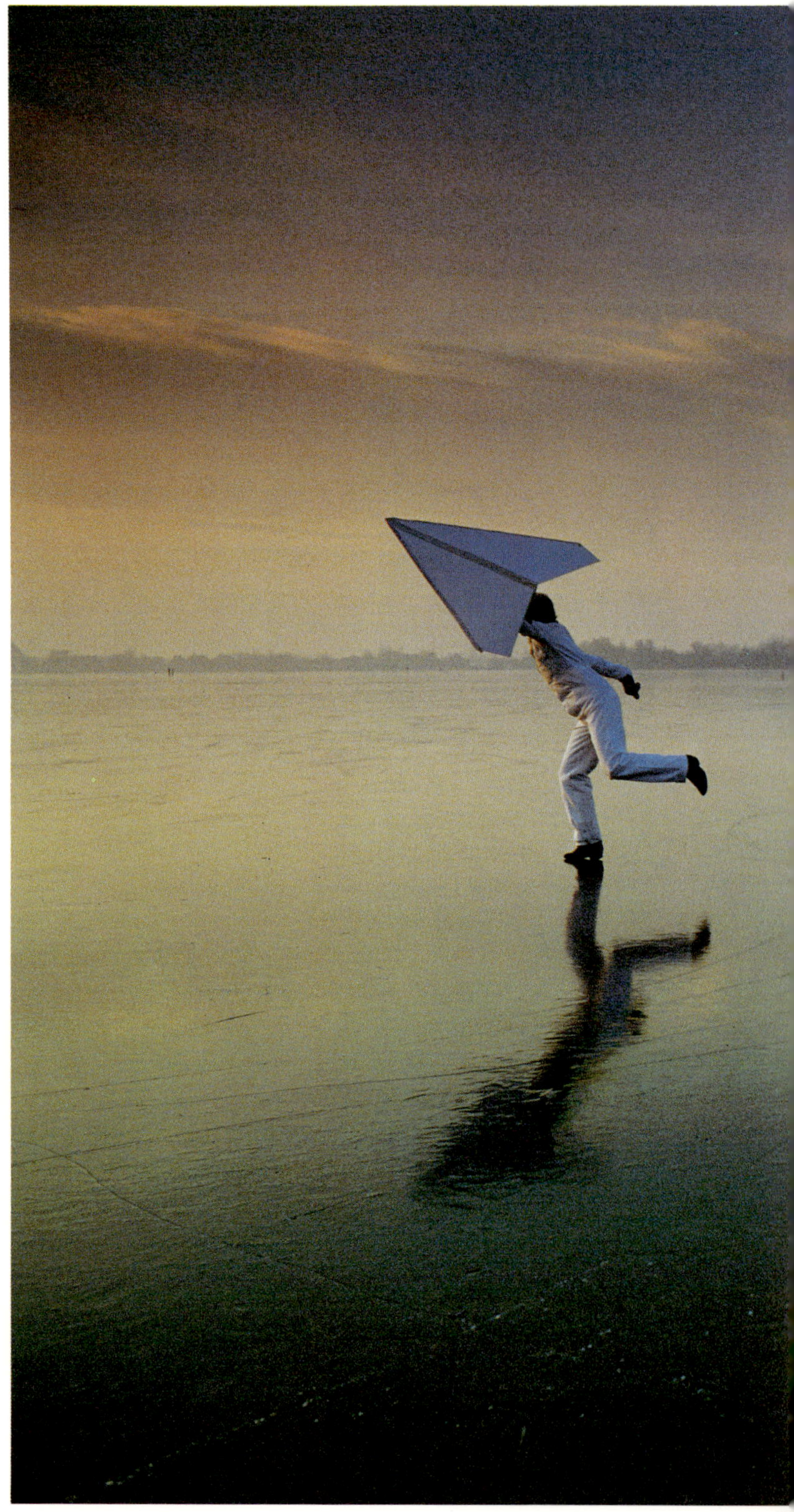

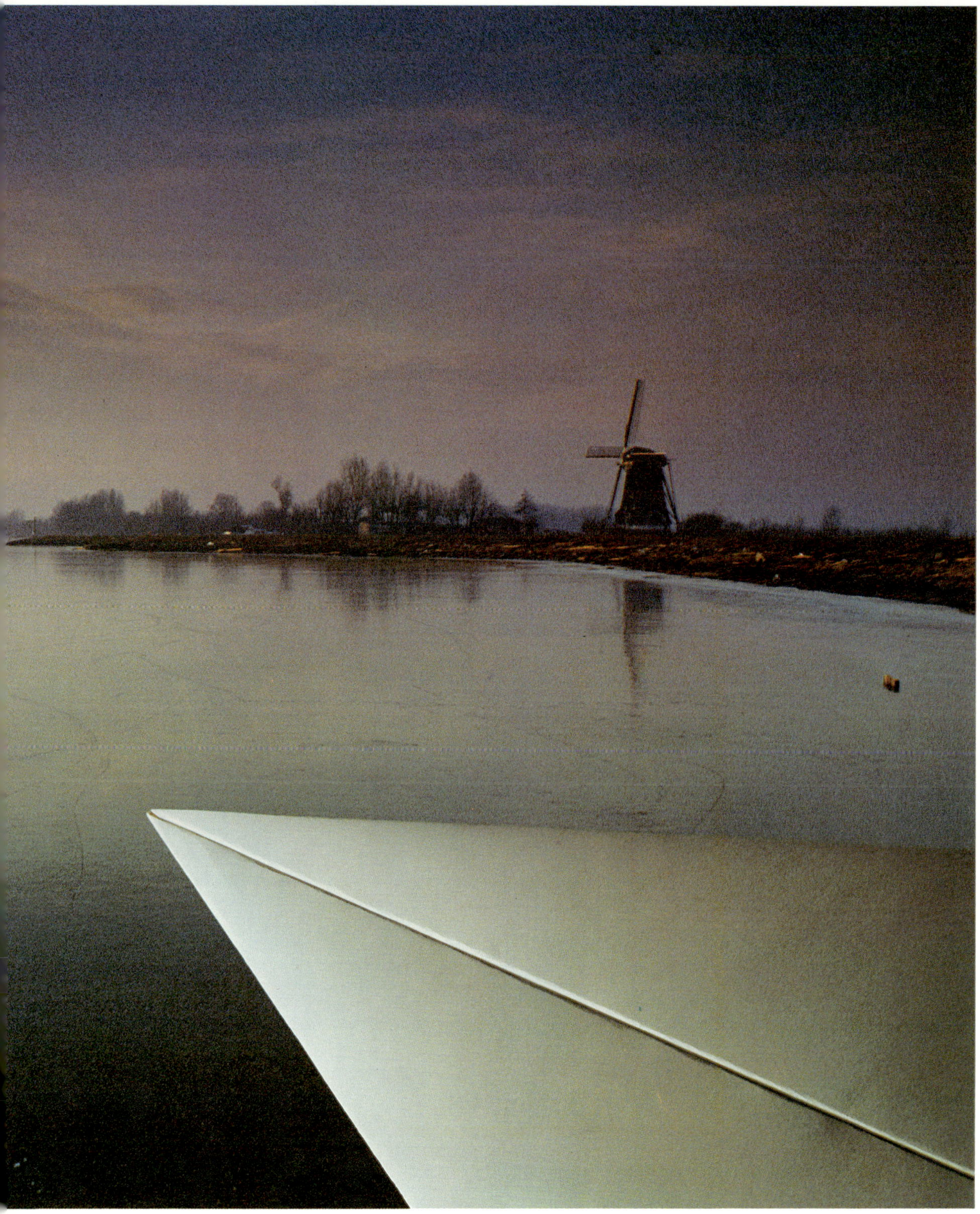

Best of Rainbow/GGK Holland

Photographed with Pentax 6/7 with W/A lens, using Ektachrome. Shot by daylight with Chromafilter. Foreground dart photographed in the studio with flashlight, single head (2000 joules), from front top left.

Late afternoon light on a frozen lake in Holland, not far from Amsterdam. The dart which the model holds was made from stiff white card. A smaller version of the same was used for the close-up. The Chromafilter helps to bring out the colour in the sky. The frozen lake reflects this delicate colouring and provides the lakeside reflections.

The A/W is a masked R-type double print, easy to do since the edges of the large dart are straight. A minimum of retouching was required to clean up the print and scuff the edges of the inserted foreground dart. The masking process is a simplified version of the process used for Nick Mason's cover 'Fictitious Sports'.

This was originally one of a series of pictures (see GGK Brazil, pages 42–3) for an advertising campaign illustrating the music of different countries. This was for Holland. We were told that Dutch music was primarily experimental. New ideas and approaches were readily tried and the culture seemed more receptive to innovation. When this campaign finally died a death, we were sufficiently enthusiastic about this picture to re-present it to Polydor (ironically enough) for the 'Best of Rainbow' album cover. This album was seen as a collection of classic rock songs. We suggested this image for its classical qualities, its simplicity and purity of line. We made other suggestions but this one was accepted by Polydor, which both surprised and pleased us. We think it is an elegant piece, but possibly a bit rarefied for the likes of Rainbow. We heard that Ritchie Blackmore admired it, but thought it unsuitable.

When you think of Holland, don't you think of tulips, dykes and windmills? In tune with the brief, we therefore thought of flower experiments (whatever they could be), water experiments, and wind experiments, but the last seemed the most promising. We considered a number of things that make use of wind currents, such as kites and gliders, and decided that darts would be the most interesting visually. Peter recalled that in the design meeting we had for this job, our inability to think of anything was so marked that Po, in frustration, fashioned the brief into a paper dart and hurled it across the room. Design by exasperation.

On reflection, if you'll excuse the pun, this picture works for me because of its photographic quality. The concept and the lines are satisfying enough, but it's the location and the light which make the difference. And these Peter found by chance. Since there was neither time nor money for a proper recce he just took off into the unknown Dutch countryside trusting that he'd eventually find a suitable dyke. The reward for which was a long hard weekend in naughty Amsterdam. There are some things a young man cannot resist.

'I like this picture a lot because I think it illustrates in an interesting way the contrast, yet strange harmony, between nature and technology. This is done by using the colour and atmosphere of classical painting in the landscape, but doing it as a photograph. There are also other references to the contrast, i.e. the running figure looks still compared to the flying dart, and the smooth machine-like dart contrasts with the texture and tranquillity of the landscape, creating a very quiet, yet powerful and disturbing image.' (Geoff Halpin – Designer)

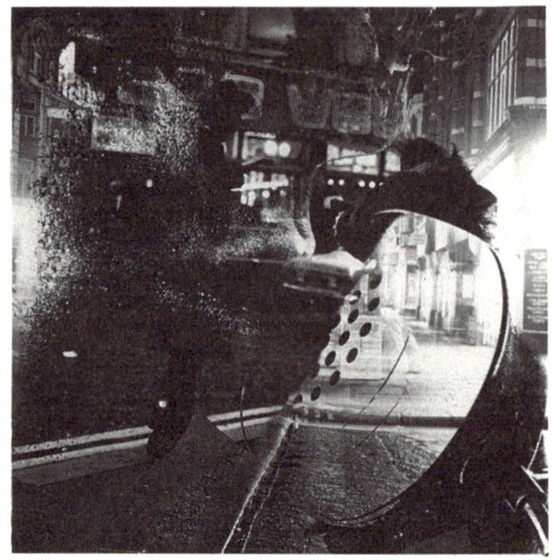

Matting

This process combines two different transparencies on one print. Two masks are made on acetate. Certain proscribed areas are made black on the clear film on one mask, and the other way round on the second. Thus if an exposure is made through the first, then a different exposure through the second, every part of the paper gets exposed just once. We've tried this process many times with different pictures, and quite recently we tried using a line image on the masks, rather than plain abstract blobs. The results, although interesting, were very variable.

The blue picture of the windmill was taken during another job in East Anglia. The street shot is in the New York docks area, and also taken whilst we were doing something else.

We originally did something like this for Steve Hillage, but regrettably we didn't like it as much as others we had done. Since then we've been trying to sell the telephone version (of which the picture above is a rough), but without success. No wonder, I hear you say. How dare you?

The origin of this is the film travelling matte process, without which Superman would be an ordinary chap. Peter was mucking about in the darkroom one day and stumbled on it (in the dark, you understand) and we've been fiddling with it ever since.

'The idea was to use the matting technique to explode contrasting images of city and country. Unfortunately at first glance it resembles puke. Maybe the strain of blending urban and rural life drives a man to drink. Ars longa, vita brevis.' (Steve Hillage)

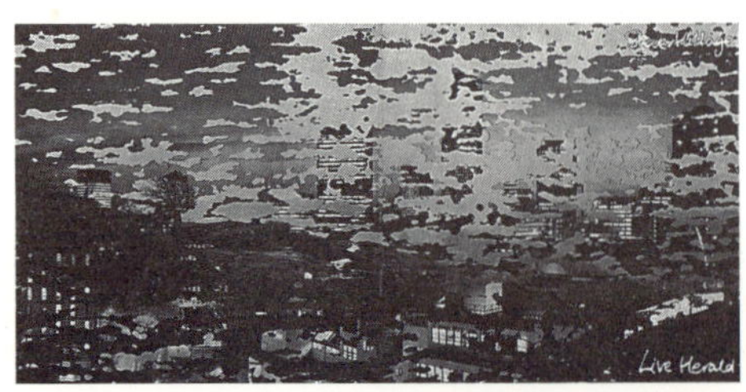

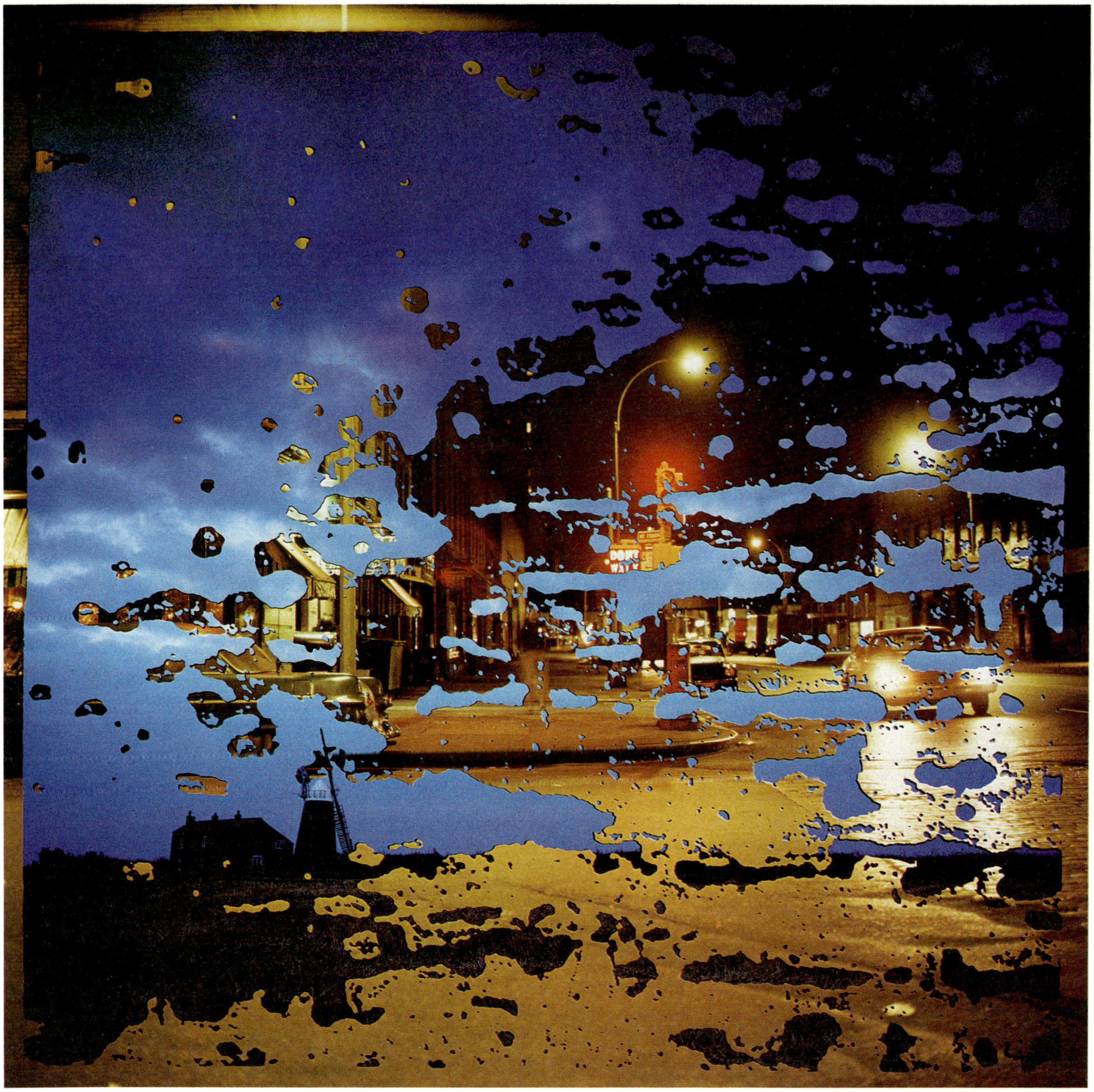

Freeze Frame

Hasselblad camera plus 50-mm normal lens. Ektachrome 64 ASA transparency rated normally. Shot with Bowens Quad flash (4000 joules), using three heads bounced off polystyrene sheets. Exposure f16 at 1/60th.

This is a set-build: simple bathroom, blue tiles, white bath. Designed by ourselves or, rather, undesigned – 'studied simplicity'. The blue was chosen to go nicely with the tanned flesh. The set was built in our studio by John Whitely.

First of all we were going to paint the models but memories of Shirley Eaton in 'Goldfinger' and death by pore asphyxiation dissuaded us. Then we thought we would paint the photograph itself. This seemed too clumsy. Then we thought we'd over- and under-expose when shooting and use the shapes from the underexposed print to create the piebald effect, but this would involve copying and a possible generation loss. In the end we used a single transparency and played with it in the printing. The piebald shapes were carefully painted in black on a clear acetate mask which was laid over the paper during the exposure of the final R-type print (obviously in a registered position so that they fitted). As a result these areas received less light and ended up darker than the rest, since R-types, unlike ordinary negative prints, are black when unexposed. In this way the dappled areas not only retain skin quality, but also follow contours, and display any lighting fluctuations, for it is just the one transparency.

This was used as an LP cover by Kevin Godley and Lol Creme for an album called 'Freeze Frame', released in 1980. It wasn't designed for them, it was just an idea that we were interested in. When their job came up, we designed lots of things to their brief but, at their request, also worked on other things we liked, even if not strictly relevant. They chose this one in spite of it being designed for someone else two years previously. I remember XTC went through a similar process (for 'Go 2', see page 85) when they took a design which had been previously but unsuccessfully submitted to 10cc when Lol and Kev were still part of that band. Small world, ain't it?

Many of our efforts emerge from group discussion, but others arise because one of us is interested in a particular theme. Peter dreamed up this image when he was exploring what he called 'piebald people' – mutants, odd people, outcasts, people with marks of mysterious meaning or of incurable disease. Society views such phenomena with distrust and fear, and occasionally with secret admiration. People don't quite know how to react. Are the people in Peter's vision lepers or privileged? Are they hiding away or just quietly and disinterestedly going about their business? This ambiguity is enhanced by the ordinariness of the setting and the cleanliness of their camouflage. It is unsettling. It seems as if their markings distinguish them from others. But why?

The faces are not clearly seen because we don't want them identified as particular individuals or even specific types. They're just a couple of 'piebald people'.

'It's not a bad cover but it doesn't reflect the music. Godley and Creme weren't particularly well known when this album came out and the sleeve certainly didn't help to give them an image or sell the album.' (Nick Turnbull – HMV, London)

'In order to save money we decided to use a still from a movie for the album cover of "Freeze Frame". So we got Hipgnosis to shoot a full-length feature film about two people in a bathroom, in the hope that in at least one of the frames they would end up with spots on. Incredibly, they did.' (Lol Creme)

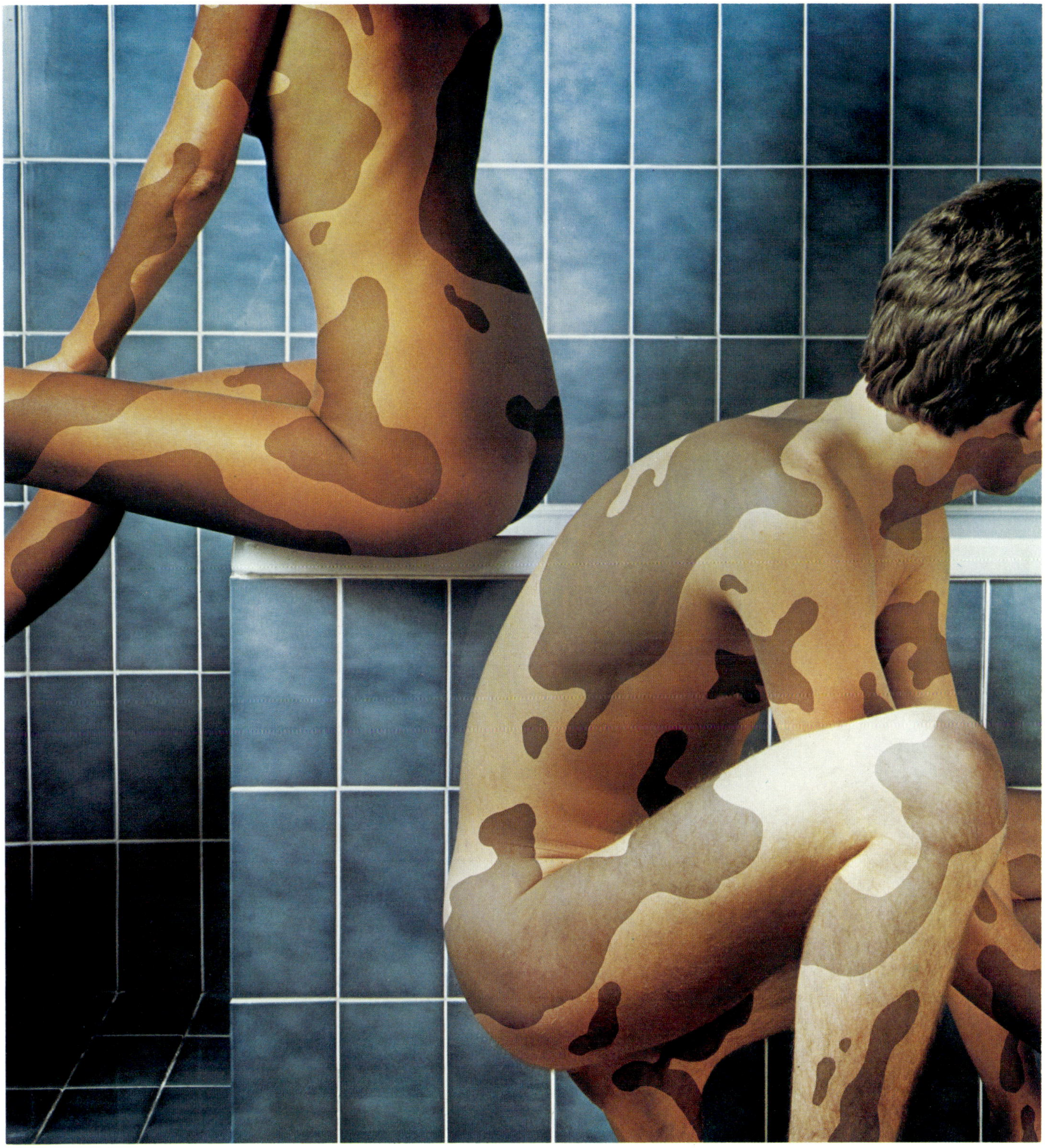

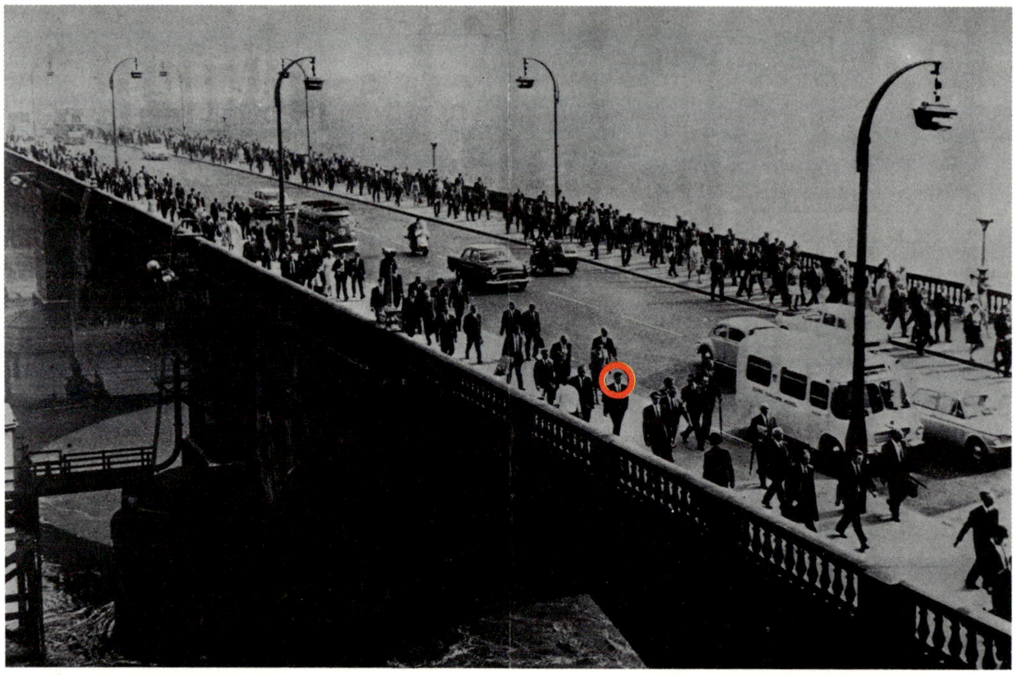

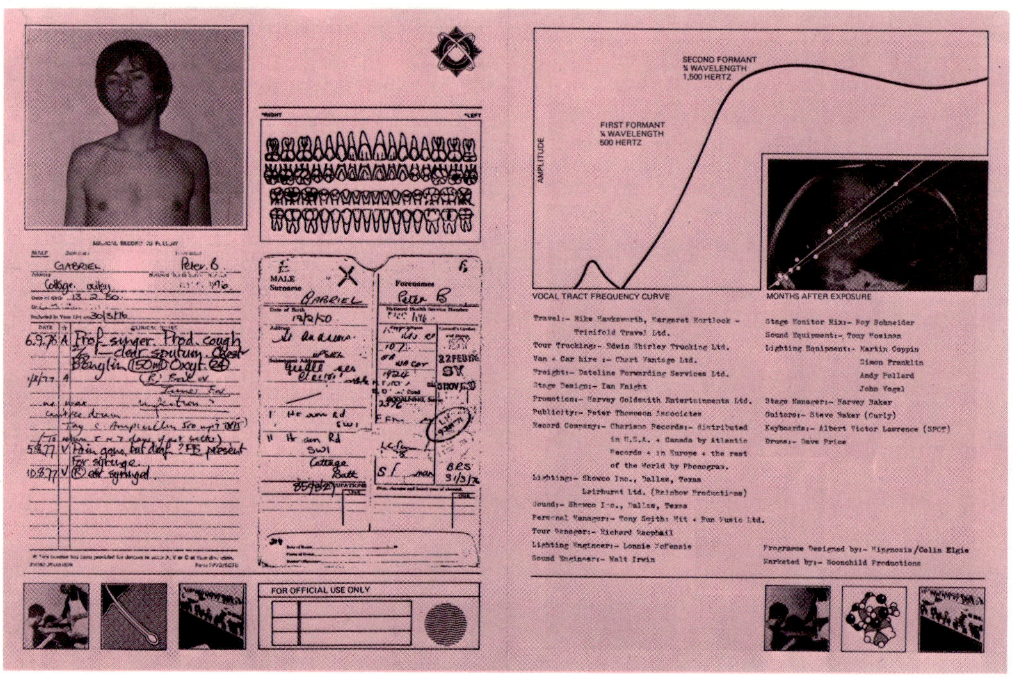
FOR OFFICIAL USE ONLY
SECOND FORMANT
⅕ WAVELENGTH
1,500 HERTZ
FIRST FORMANT
⅕ WAVELENGTH
500 HERTZ
AMPLITUDE
VOCAL TRACT FREQUENCY CURVE
MONTHS AFTER EXPOSURE
Travel:- Mike Hawksworth, Margaret Mortlock - Trinifold Travel Ltd.
Tour Trucking:- Edwin Shirley Trucking Ltd.
Van + Car hire :- Chart Vantage Ltd.
Freight:- Dateline Forwarding Services Ltd.
Stage Design:- Ian Knight
Promotion:- Harvey Goldsmith Entertainments Ltd.
Publicity:- Peter Thompson Associates
Record Company:- Charisma Records:- distributed in U.S.A. + Canada by Atlantic Records + in Europe + the rest of the World by Phonogram.
Lighting:- Showco Inc., Dallas, Texas
Lairhurst Ltd. (Rainbow Productions)
Sound:- Showco Inc., Dallas, Texas
Personal Manager:- Tony Smith: Hit + Run Music Ltd.
Tour Manager:- Richard Macphail
Lighting Engineer:- Lonnie McKenzie
Sound Engineer:- Walt Irwin
Stage Monitor Mix:- Roy Schneider
Sound Equipment:- Tony Mosimann
Lighting Equipment:- Martin Coppin
Simon Franklin
Andy Pollard
John Vogel
Stage Manager:- Harvey Baker
Guitars:- Steve Baker (Curly)
Keyboards:- Albert Victor Lawrence (SPCT)
Drums:- Dave Price
Programme Designed by:- Hipgnosis/Colin Elgie
Marketed by:- Moonchild Productions

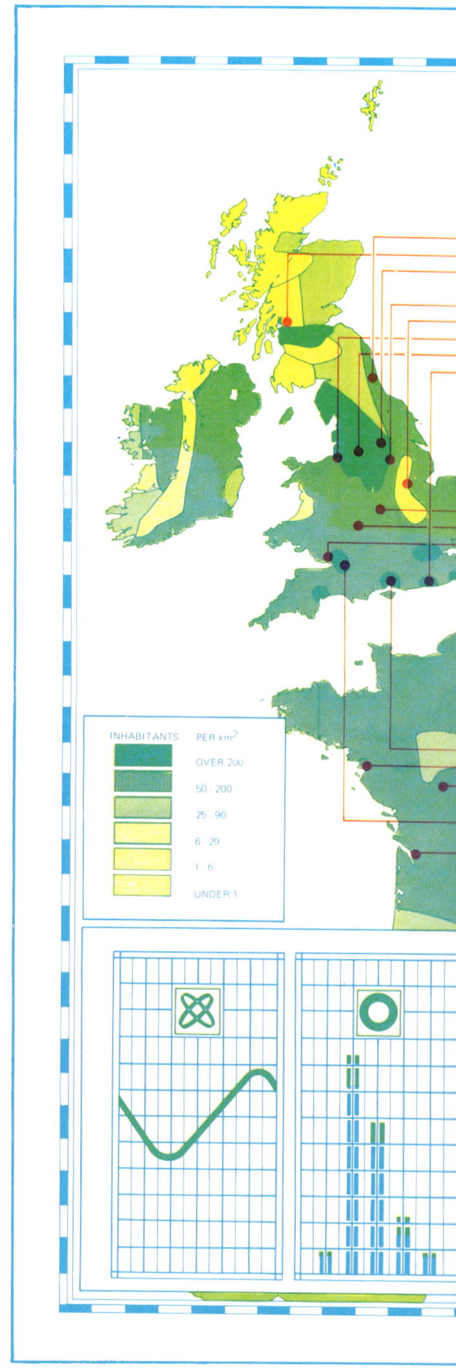
INHABITANTS PER km²
OVER 200
50 - 200
25 - 50
6 - 25
1 - 6
UNDER 1

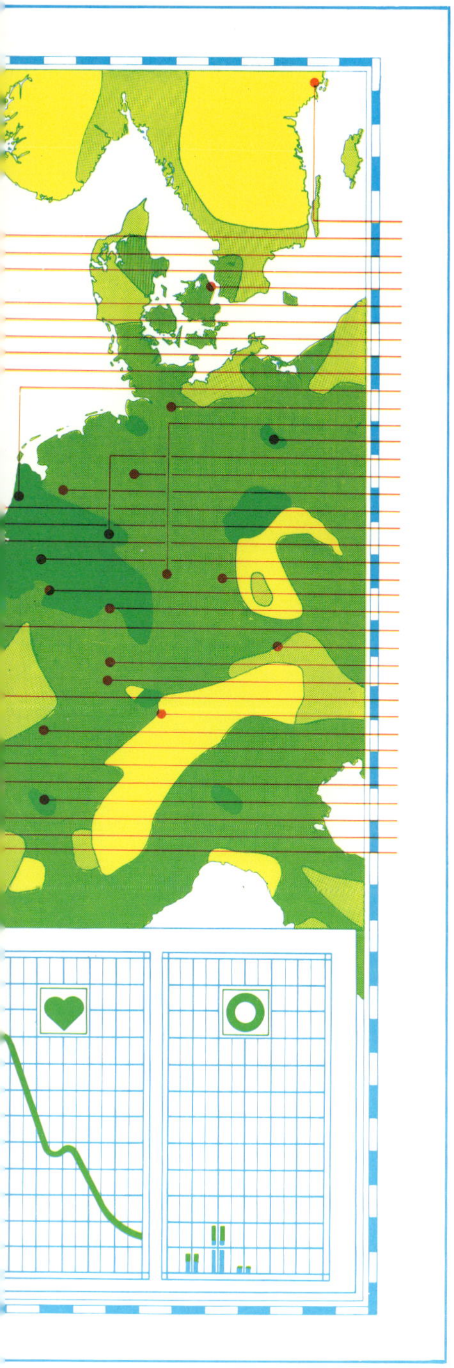

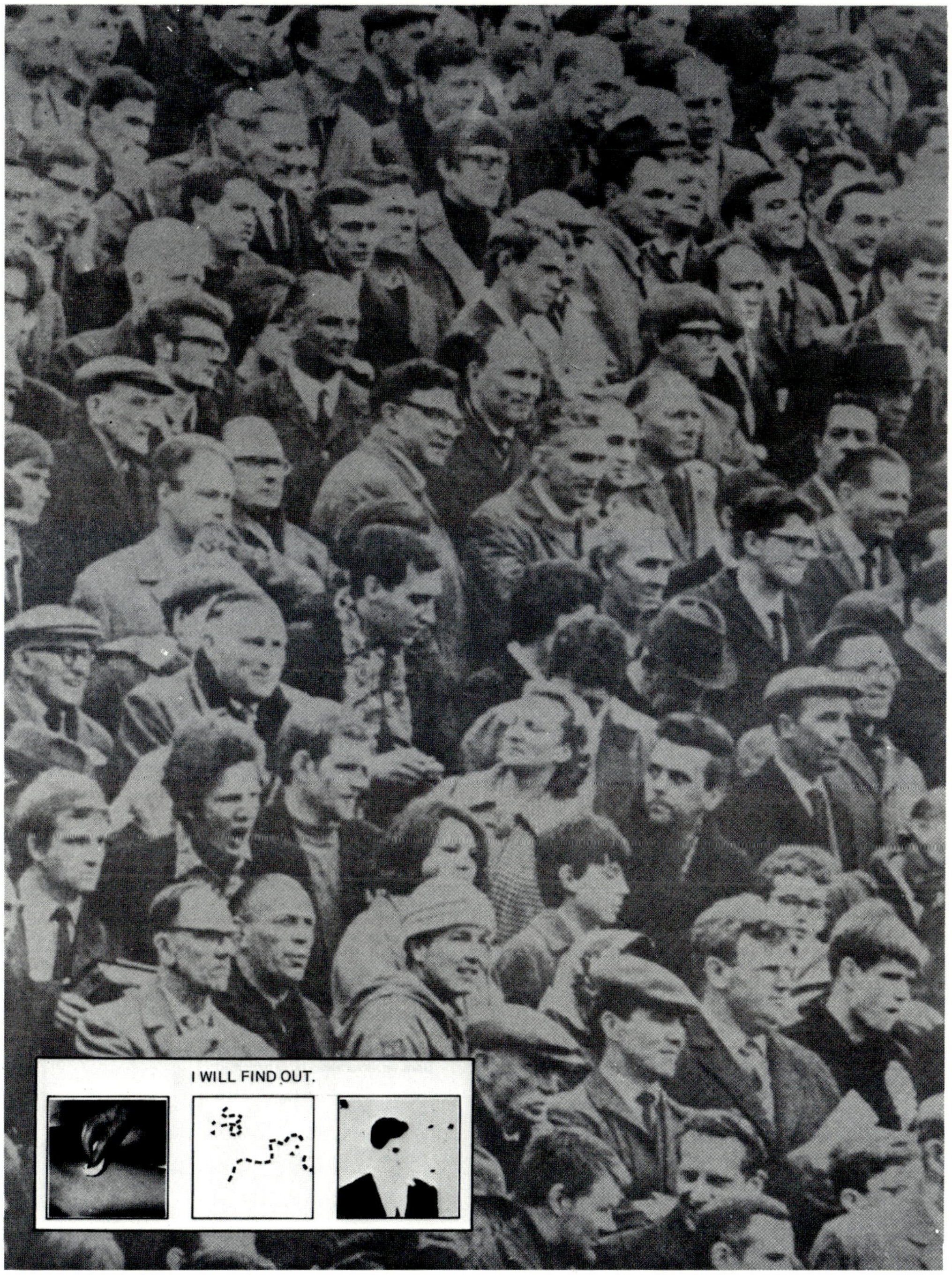
I WILL FIND OUT.

Peter Gabriel Tour Programme

A combination of photos by us (except the commuters on the bridge, which was from a library) and drawings/graphics suggested by us and drawn by Colin Elgie.

All this material was for a tour programme for Peter Gabriel with whom we have a good relationship. He encourages us to suggest whatever we like, no matter how outlandish.

This design concerns viruses and strange diseases, supposedly carried by Peter as he toured the cities of Europe. None of this is stated too clearly though, and the finished piece is the stronger for it, having built its sense of secret medical stigma by implication and association. All total nonsense, of course, but fun. That's what Peter thought. He's such a clean-living chap. Not a foreign body in sight.

'Another showy visual piece of packaging. We wanted to parody the lifelines of the 60s fanzines with real medical and dental information on the performing article. This was coupled with a desire to present "Gabriel in motion" as an anonymous medical corporation complete with medical garb, surgical gloves, etc., all with company logo. I like the front photo in particular and the questions suggested by the ring of red.' (Peter Gabriel)

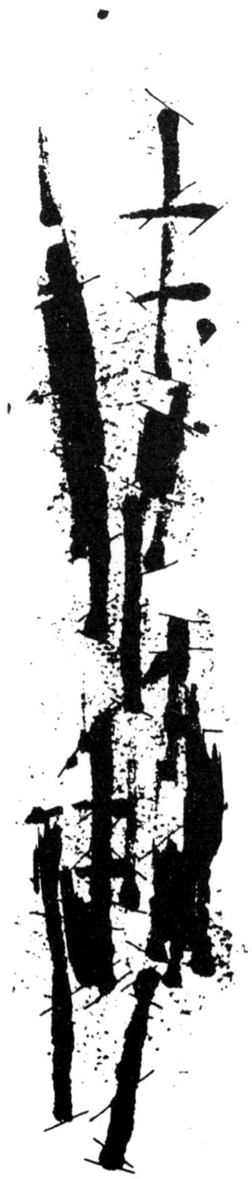

Bethnal Crash Landing

The couple were photographed with 2¼-inch Hasselblad plus normal lens, using Tri-X treated normally. They are flashlit with two heads (4000 joules), one back lighting from the right, the other bounced from the front. The background shot is taken on the same equipment using daylight. The plane is a library shot.

The woman is a model, the man is our assistant. The figures behind are the band Bethnal, escorted by a pair of real nurses we befriended at a local hospital. The lovers are photographed in our studio, the background is a large park in North London.

This is a three-part collage photographed according to a pencil drawing we had made to illustrate the idea for the band. The background clouds were given added exposure in order to accentuate both the stormy weather which forced the plane down, and the tempestuous nature of the love affair.

Bethnal was the name of a short-lived rock band in the late 70s. This was their first album. The manager requested a strange collage, not unlike 'Burning Man' or 'Deceptive Bends' in feeling, but a touch simpler. We were asked to take the title 'Crash Landing' as our main influence.

This is unashamedly in the style of a film poster. The hero and heroine are seen against a backdrop which indicates how they came to be together in the first place. It is either very romantic (no matter what the circumstances, love finds a way), or very sentimental ('Darling, I don't care what you look like, I will love you always'), or very cynical. In spite of death and injury all about, they will swear loving allegiance to each other. Their eyes meet midst bandages and drip feeds. That's it. The plane crash with all its attendant horror has brought them together. She looks so lovingly into his eyes (they're *all* she can see) that it almost convinces me. I know she will wait at his bedside for ever. Hurrah!

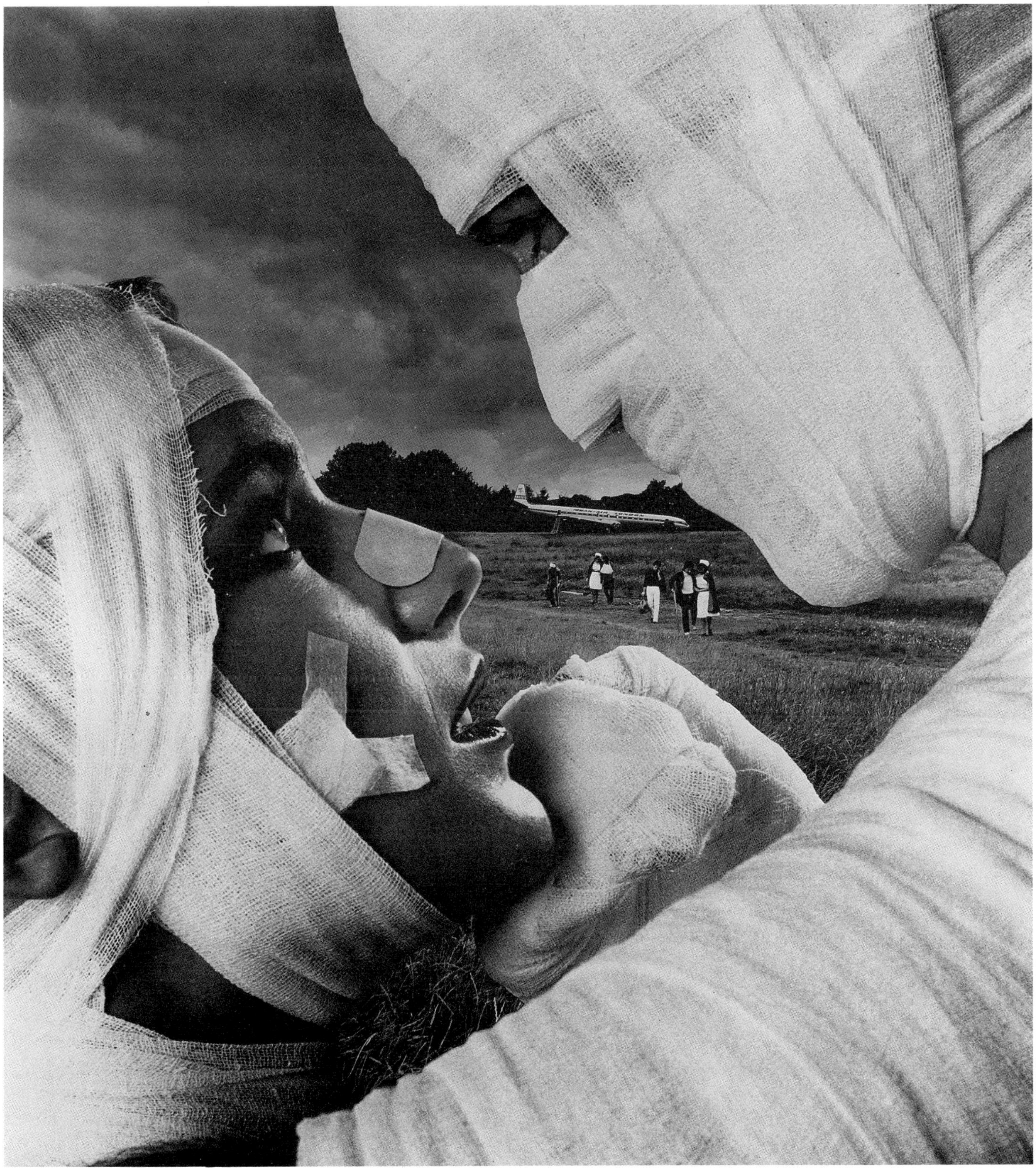

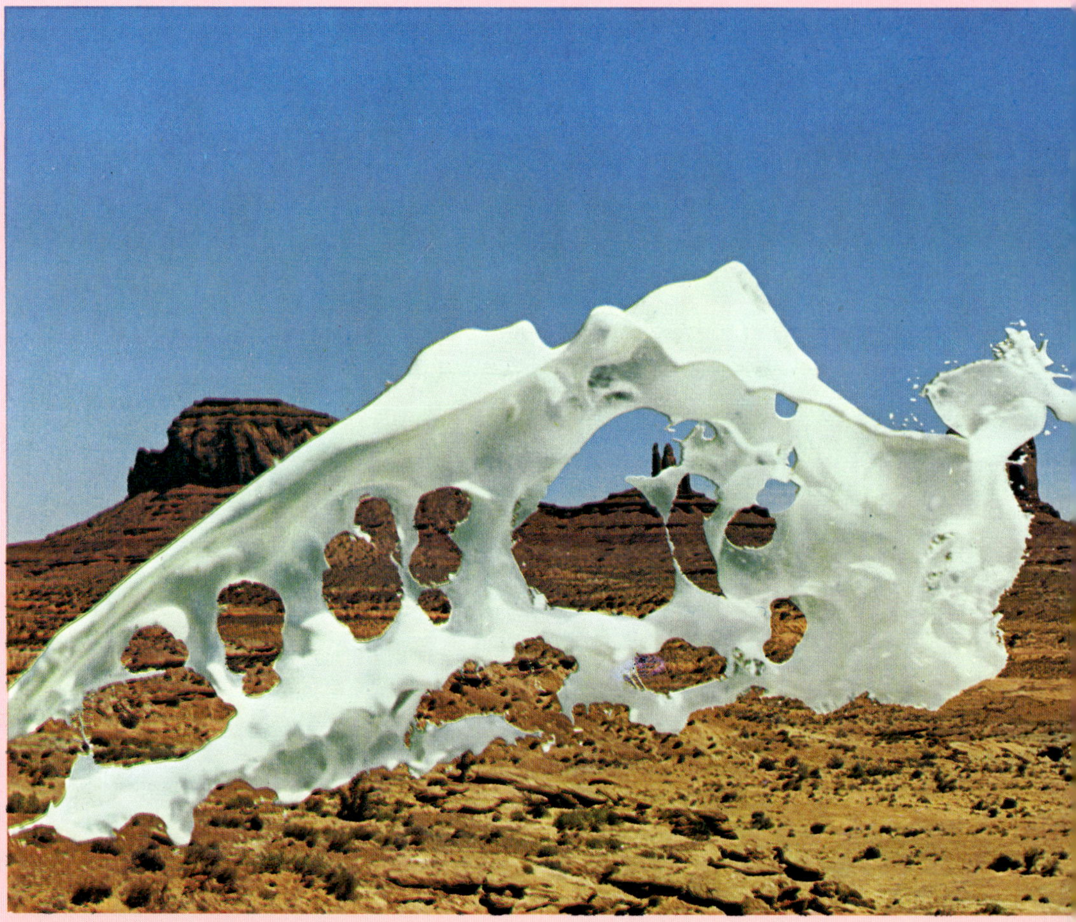

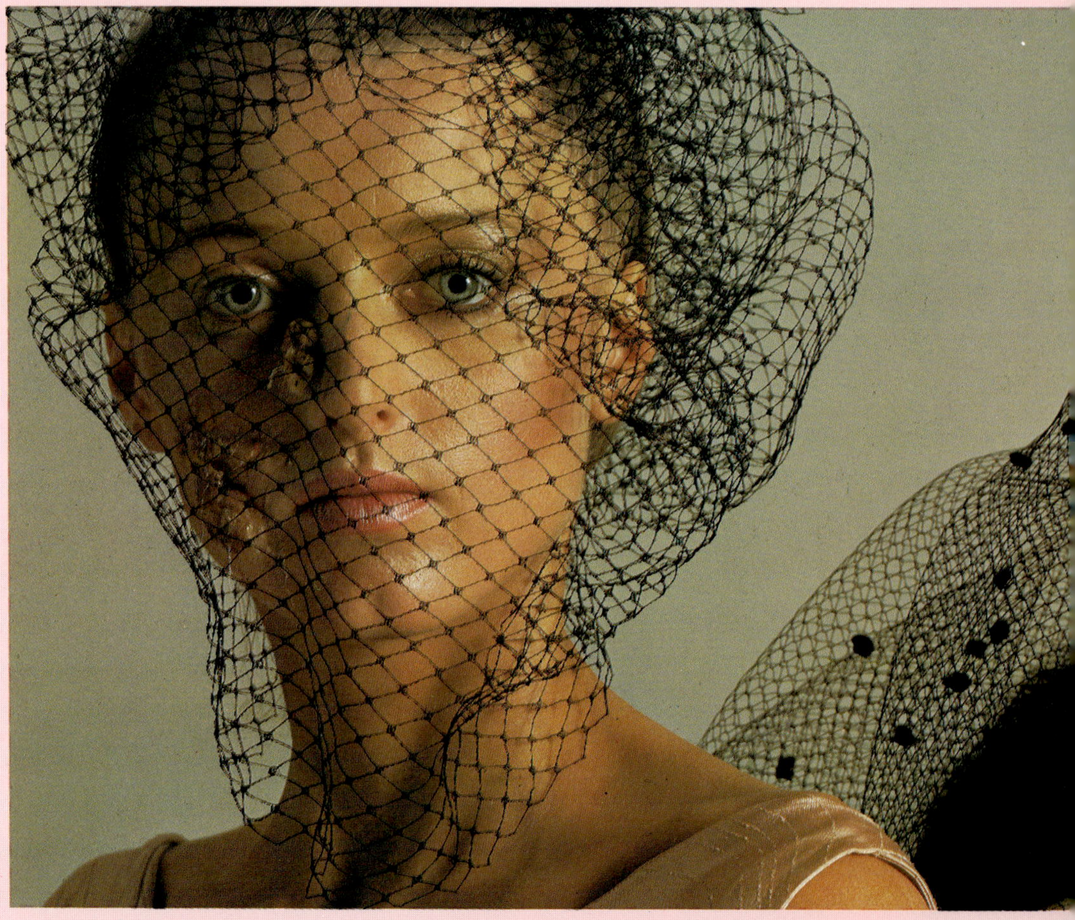

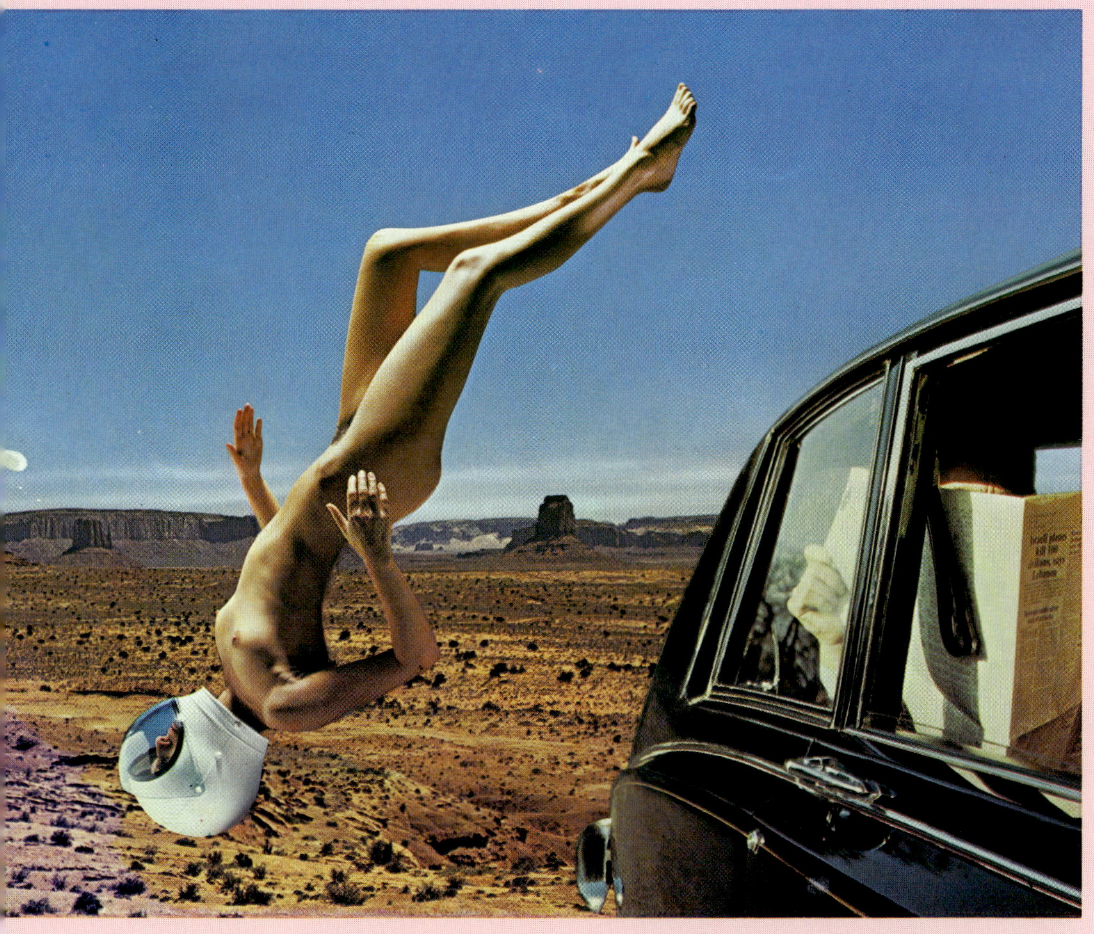

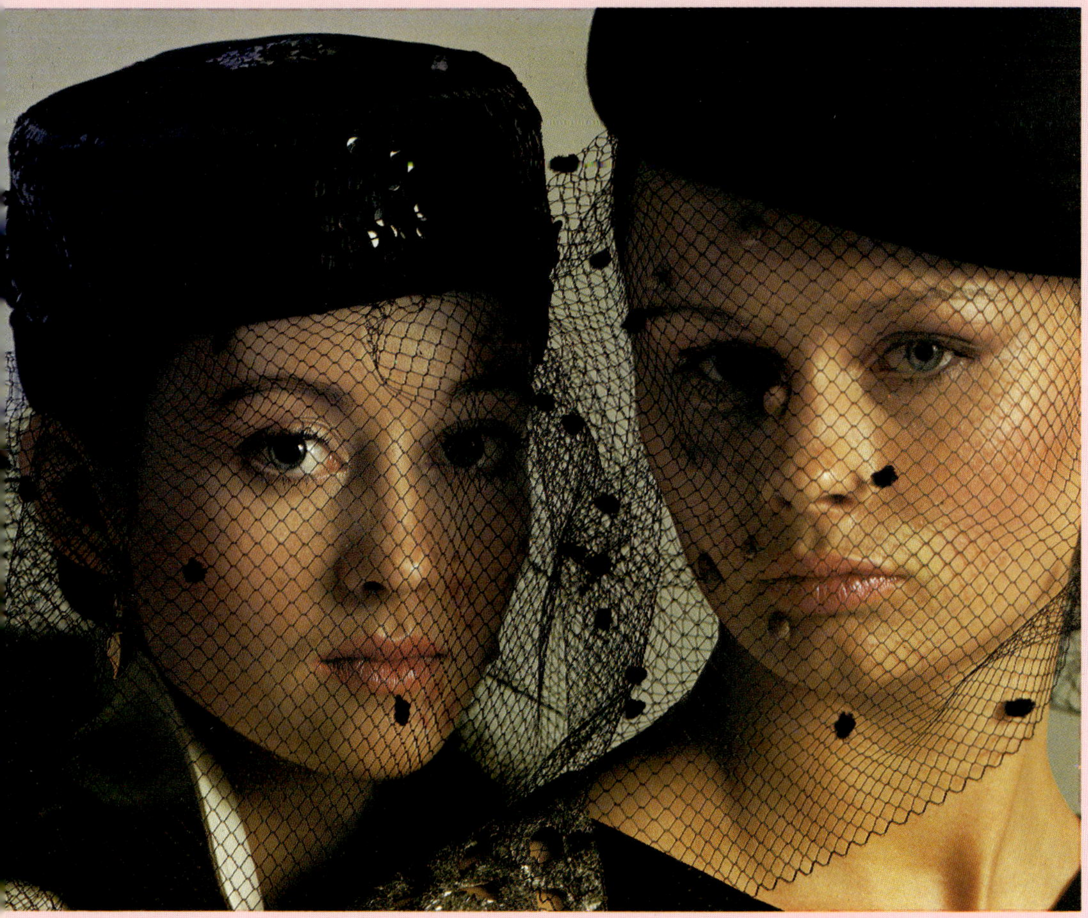

Eve and Space

The ladies with veils were shot on a 10/8 Sinar with portrait lens, using daylight Ektachrome sheet film and lit by flash – 8000 joules through a fish-fry top right front. The soft light was reflected all round by a white cyclorama. Exposure f22 at 1/60th (and even then the focus drops off dramatically).

'Eve' was shot in a studio in south London. The girls were models. Mary Vango was responsible for the hair, clothes and ordinary make-up. Tom Smith (see Sad Café) did the spots, sores, boils and disease. He is a gifted make-up artist, working mostly in the film industry.

The other picture comprises a background shot on 5/4, the remaining elements shot on Hasselblad with normal lens. The girl was flashlit in the studio, the flying white stuff was photographed with a fast shutter speed to freeze it, and the car was shot on location in London, using available light plus a W/A lens to increase the sense of being driven out of the frame.

The background landscape for this is a library shot of Monument Valley in America. The girl was positioned upside down so that we could see her shape better (for the composition of the overall design, you understand) and so that her toes could be pointed. The flying white stuff is milk, thrown from a plastic bucket, and photographed at a rubbish dump.

'Eve' is a colour print from a transparency. Space is a four-part montage: background, girl, milk and car. The first three of these are done with a dye transfer strip-in (see GGK Brazil, pages 42–3) and the car is added as an actual piece of collage because it has a straight edge and does not need retouching.

The Alan Parsons Project required a gatefold sleeve for their album 'Eve' in 1979. The darker side of woman was mentioned as a theme to consider. The other picture is for a gatefold sleeve for an album entitled 'Deliverance' by a French electronic disco outfit called Space. They wanted something very atmospheric. They saw their music as a way of getting people out of the confines of normal living; as a deliverance from the rigours and constraints of everyday life.

Both these pieces are derived directly from their briefs. In the first one we were trying to suggest that the sinister side of women can be represented in a directly physical way. Women can look gorgeous and behave grotesquely; alternatively, they can seem deformed and behave like angels. Appearances are deceptive. In our picture, the women are beautiful and glamorous, until you look a little closer and see the disease and ugliness. One side of each face is clean and elegant, the other side is deformed and horrible. The viewer is not supposed to notice this discrepancy immediately, any more than Adam did, rather to think of it as an ordinary glamour shot from a glossy magazine. The idea incorporates a comment on all superficial fashion that tends to concern itself only with the surface of things. Disease and scars are for real.

Space is a little old-fashioned. We feel that it's the end point in the collage, event-oriented phase of our work. The car represents the humdrum world, the girl represents the music tempting businessmen away from their interest in the arena of everyday events. The milk is there because: (a) there was an empty space in the picture, (b) because it is odd and atmospheric, and (c) because the movement seemed like a possible analogy for music. The girl is naked because her nakedness makes for a purer image. If she'd worn something, it would have been too prescriptive. Anyway, the client was French, as I said. She wears a helmet because that used to be the client's logo. I would normally reject on principle any inclusion such as this, but in fact when we tried it, it looked good. It adds to the atmosphere, suggests rarefied air, that she needs oxygen. I like it for its distinctive dreamlike quality, and because it is not an event. It's just a collection of images bound together in a scene.

'A visual sick joke. Eve, the original woman, flawless? Perfect, shot in the style of a beauty photograph from a woman's magazine; immaculate accessorizing, styling, hair and make-up. Now look at the shadow area.' (Alex Henderson – Photographer)

'As a result of the "Eve" sleeve which, according to Storm, was meant to depict the darker side of women, copies of this record were ritually burned by religious protesters in some American states. My own view is that their action was much too passive.' (Eric Woolfson – Manager)

I've Had Enough

We can dispense with categories here. It's a pretty silly picture taken with a pretty silly Hasselblad plus normal lens, Tri-X exposed at f16 at 1/60th, with one flash head bounced on right-hand side, in our pretty silly studio. Some pretty cold and pretty silly spaghetti bolognese was purchased from a café next door. The model is pretty silly too.

The artwork is a B/W collage of badly cut-out eyes (taken with a close-up lens attachment) and stuck down on the base print in a very hasty fashion. This was because it was only a rough version of an idea that we submitted to Paul McCartney for a single entitled 'I've Had Enough'.

Obviously he'd had enough too. He accepted the idea and insisted on using the rough. We protested, but perhaps he was right. There's not a lot of point doing something so ludicrous proficiently, or expensively. Part of its charm, if that's what it is, lies in its immediacy, and in its thrown-together quality. So thrown-together, in fact, that by the time Paul received it at his Scottish island retreat one or two of the original eyes had fallen off the A/W. Not the ones on the face, I hasten to add, for these were obscured with a dash of opaque white paint.

The idea comes from the title. I envisaged an occasion where one could say 'I've had enough', and mean it. Having rejected various matrimonial and work situations, I returned to something quite basic. Being full. Or, in this case, being horrified at the thought of trying to get through a plate of cold and indifferently cooked spaghetti. Instead of throwing up, the eyes have 'popped out', multiplied, and met some friends outside the window. It's silly. But love can be silly. And governments. And TV.

'We were looking for an idea for "I've Had Enough" and had a bit of difficulty thinking of one. We asked Hipgnosis, and Storm came up with this insane interpretation. We immediately decided it was an "eye catching" solution to the problem.' (Paul McCartney)

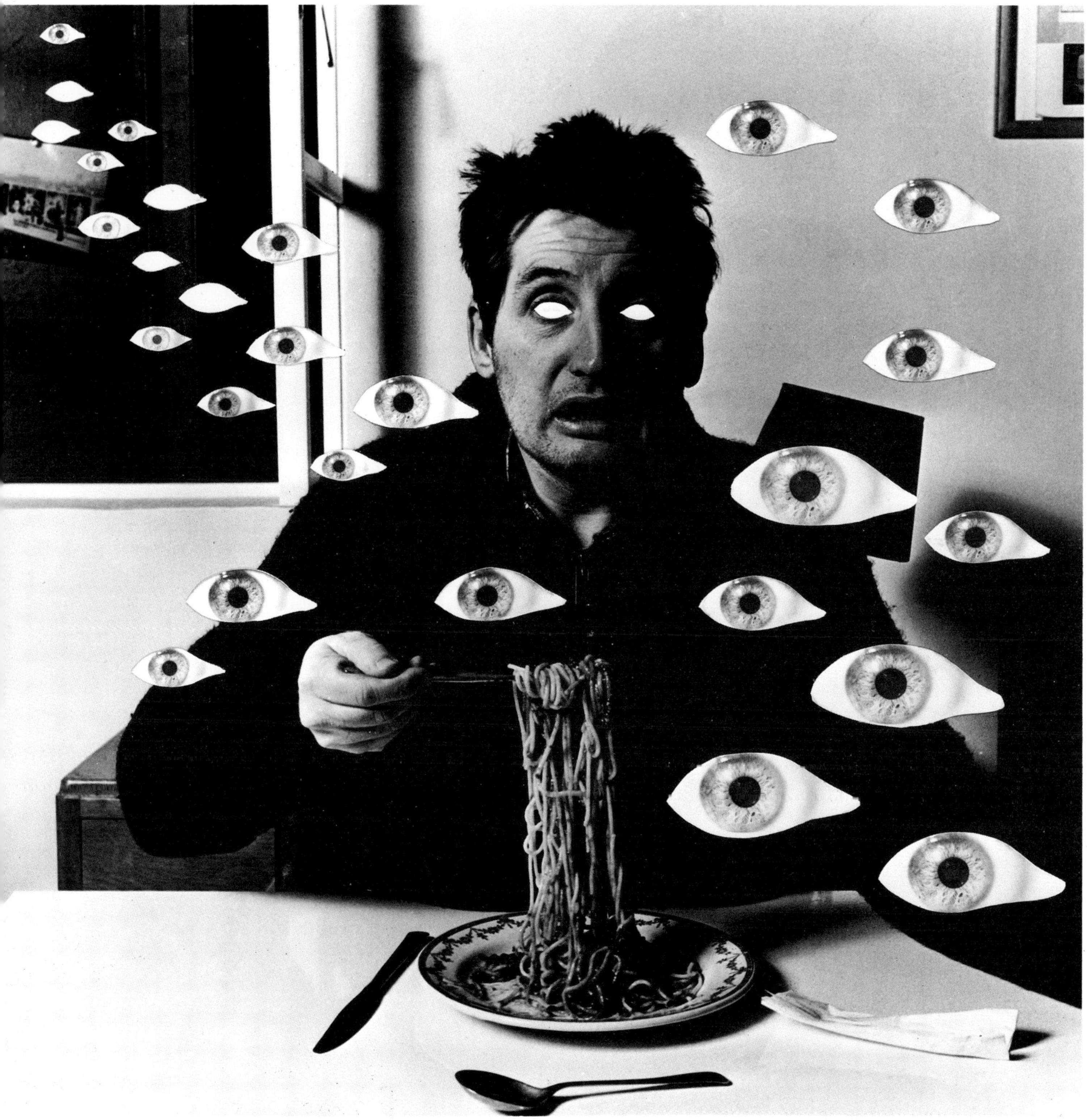

Herman Rarebell

× This was photographed with a Hasselblad plus normal lens. It would have been tempting to use a W/A lens to lengthen the legs but this would also have given us some other unwanted distortions. The film was 64 ASA daylight Ektachrome, exposed at f22 at 1/60th, and lit by flash – three heads (6000 joules): one front lighting bounced, another back lighting from the left-hand side, and the third top lighting with heavy trace, but placed close enough to make it lighter above the table than it is below.

The set was constructed in our studio and augmented by hired Italian chairs and tables. The set and the models were dressed by Po. The legs on the left were the most expensive legs in London at the time, and were insured against disfigurement for a cool £¼ million, or so we heard.

⌖ The A/W is a straightforward print, taken from the chosen transparency, with a little corrective retouching. The choice of the transparency, however, was not in the least straightforward. It was one of those situations where the idea was pretty thin and the success of the design rested heavily on the realization. In such cases, variations are called for, particularly in terms of lighting and composition. The picture on the opposite page just nosed ahead of another in which the lighting was more moody but the legs were less symmetrical.

⌧ Herman Rarebell is the drummer for the Scorpions (see pages 46–7) and in 1981 produced a solo album called 'Nip in the Bud'. He rejected designs involving exotic Japanese women emerging from flowers and accepted this one because . . . well, because . . . he likes women, and pictures of women, and pictures that make him feel sexy. He emphasized, however, that straight sexy pictures, or glorious nudes, were not enough on their own. Could have fooled me.

○ This design is derived from two main sources. One is a pop art book which was lying around our studio, containing a painting of legs in a sculptured pose, probably by Allen Jones. The other source is previous work of our own, involving designs which are separated into two by natural dividers. I remember one in particular: an escaping soldier is hiding under the water whilst his pursuers are seen above ground. The design is divided into two by the surface of the water, giving us two different worlds in one photograph.

I was interested in the legs primarily for their shape. I thought that an attractive way to see them would be under a table where they would be in a natural setting but would also be isolated, i.e. the viewer gets to see them privately and exclusively. Normally one gets interested in what happens above the table top, whereas in this case we have focused on what goes on below.

The symmetry of the legs adds a final edge of strangeness. Both pairs of legs look as if they are walking, fingers pretending to amble across the surface of a page, or the edge of an armchair. They remind me of a dance: disembodied legs quickstepping up and down a restaurant. The owners of the legs are too busy chatting to notice.

< 'Sexist.' (Keith Johnson – HMV, London)

'Romantic.' (Nick Turnbull – HMV, London)

'Unashamedly plagiarized from stocking advertisements both in lighting and style. Is this Hipgnosis's revenge on art directors who, over the years, have "borrowed" their designs for advertising campaigns? I like the legs on the left.' (Alex Henderson – Photographer)

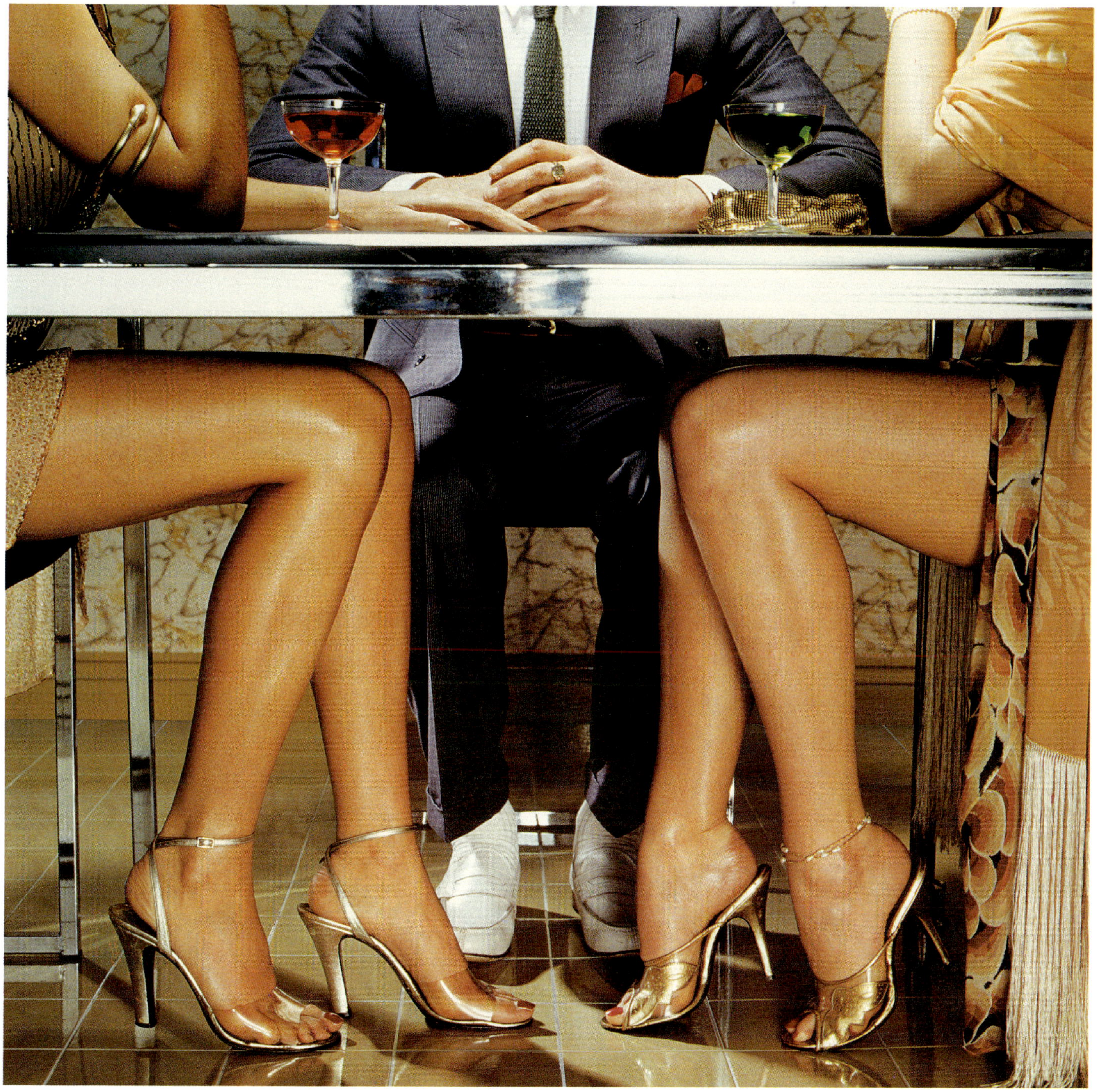

3

Once when I was separated from someone, at the panic-stricken end of something, but long before its real end, I had occasion to make an urgent call to Oakland, California, from a tiny village on the Adriatic coast of Greece. The kind of place where goats roam unfettered through the streets. There was one phone booth outside the post office, a tin box blistering in the fierce heat of the August afternoon. From here the Oakland number ran into fifteen digits and I'd get as far as the first two or three in the series and then be cut off. So I'd start again, but the same thing would happen almost immediately. I dialled for hours, roasting in that metal drum, my fingers swelling and bleeding. Eventually, miraculously it now seemed, the creaking Greek machinery slipped into place and linked into the fast and brilliant American communications grid, and I was through! Screeched greetings, and a barrage of questions for the next twelve seconds. Then nothing. The line went dead. And I couldn't go through all that again. The point was, the lines *were* dead. Had been for months. And I'd known it in that weak way we sometimes know a thing, persuading ourselves we don't.

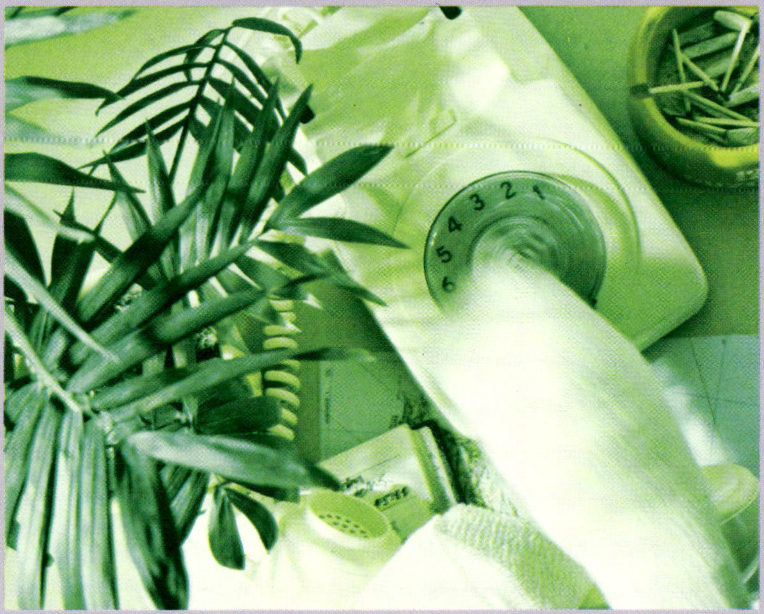

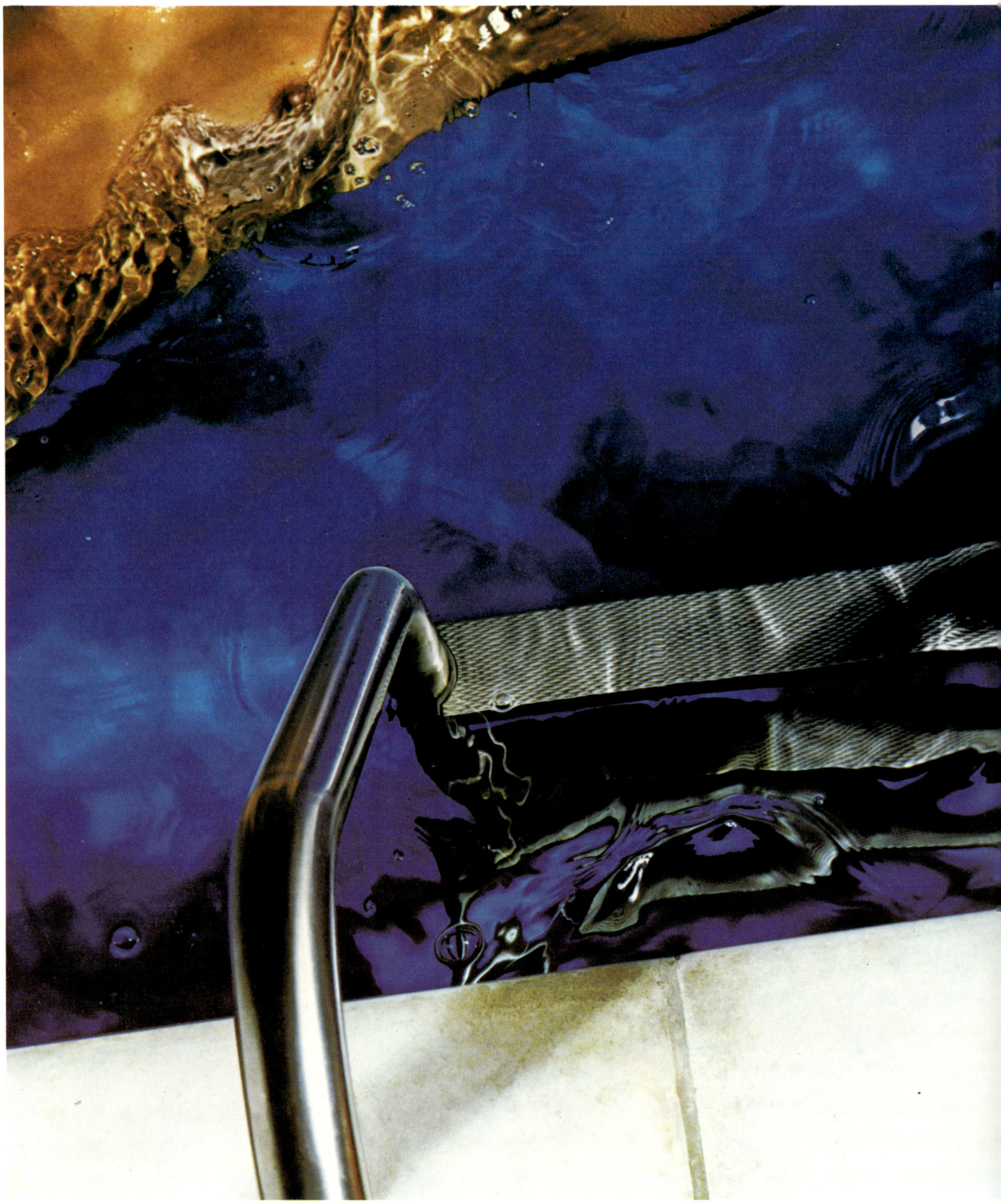

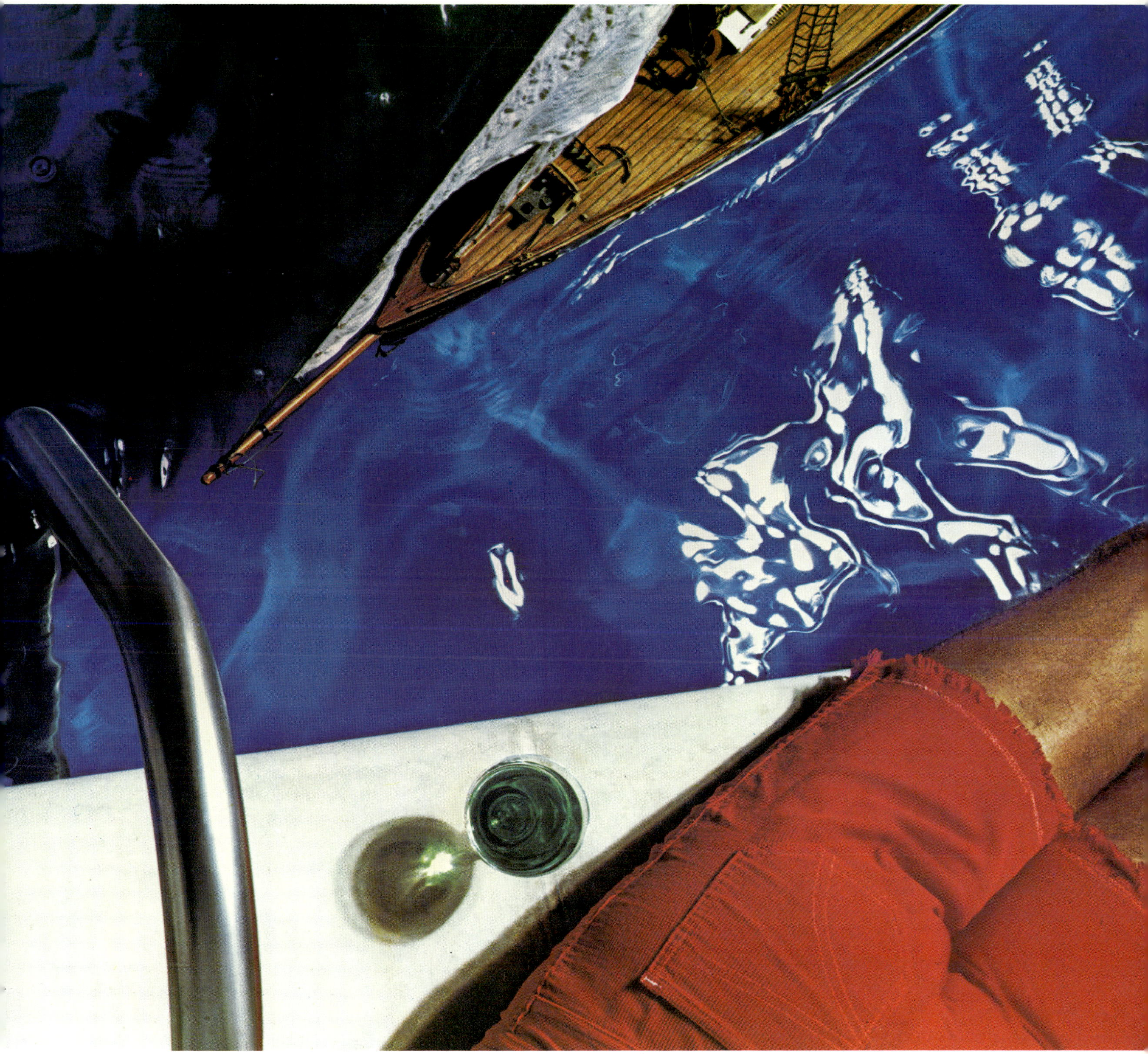

Wet Dream

× **This picture is another sortie of ours into the world of 10/8. We used a Sinar with W/A lens and daylight slides. It is lit from the top right with a fish-fry, and left-side reflector fills.**

The pool belonged to a friend of Po's. We added the rest, including the steps! The man is a model and the girl is Po's friend, Gabi, who often helps us out (see Yuming, pages 34–5) and deserves a great deal of gratitude for her patience. The boat is an extremely expensive model: about £350-worth. The beautiful depth of blue in the water was achieved by laying a false blue bottom, rather like an aquatic cyclorama, which extended only as far as the camera view required.

⌖ **A dye transfer print was obtained in order to be able to remove the cotton which tethered the boat: other types of colour print are much more difficult to retouch, especially when you want to get rid of something. R-types, for example, do not bleach in any controllable way, and you can end up with bizarre and unwanted discolorations.**

◲ **Rick Wright of Pink Floyd made a solo album, released in 1980. This is the gatefold front cover. He said he preferred bright, colourful things with clean lines. He didn't want anything very meaningful, lest it border on the esoteric or pretentious. Nor did he want anything bizarre, unusual or even overtly funny. Nothing, in effect, like a Pink Floyd sleeve. We also knew, through our relationship, that he was fond of women, sailing and boozing, not necessarily in that order.**

○ **This design is representative of what we frivolously call the advertising end of our spectrum. We are, and always have been, greatly enamoured of the swimming pool (cf. Tilt, page 114), as well as being aware that it is an overworked image. Yet the pool and the water were appropriate to the client's brief, so we discussed how to vary an old theme, and decided that if it was an aerial shot, and if it was an unusual colour, and if it contained something unexpected (the model boat), but not surreal or impossible, it might then stand a chance of working. The choice of colours was crucial, hence the red shorts, the green drink and the blue water. The woman is, I now admit, a problem. She could easily have been in the pool at the time (thus she is not a *forced* inclusion), but why is she naked when the man isn't? It now seems like a mild piece of chauvinism. A case of following the advertising approach too slavishly? I find it more disturbing than, say, the Scorpions' sleeve (page 47). But do women, I wonder?**

< **'Strong bright colours, dramatic composition and clever use of scale give this image impact. The ingredients complete the picture – a naked girl, a yacht, lying by a pool with a drink – a nice wet dream.' (Alex Henderson – Photographer)**

The Shape of Things to Come

× Photo–B/W collage. Hasselblad, normal lens, Tri-X, flashlit. Illustrative print is made up of photo, line drawing, air brush retouching, Xerox, heat photos, bits of cotton, Japanese text, Letraset, colour bars, plastic and old bogeys. You name it, it's in there somewhere.

The models are friends, photographed in our studio. The location is near Cambridge, on the edge of the Fens. It was autumn, hence the long shadows. We also took a photograph of a common earthworm (that's for you to find) and did some retouching to affix the man to the woman, and to paint head suckers on him for the picture on the right.

⌖ Mixed media collage – the left-hand side is a collage, retouched, then photocopied. The right-hand side is a 3-D piece. The two halves are joined and then rephotographed to make it 2-D.

◲ A Mr Jim Slattery was editor of 'The Creative Handbook Diary'. The theme for 1982 was 'Predictions'. He said that the monthly divider he wanted me to consider was September, and the specific predictions for this month involved sex and gender. And I was to make it as futuristic as I could.

Jim Slattery left the diary before I gave in the A/W. His successors didn't think too much of it and rejected it. Were we surprised? The word they used was 'disgusting'. I suspect they were looking for something stylish and modernistic, not so biological. Nor something set quite as far into the future.

○ It strikes me that the origins for this manifest some of my deepest fears and hopes. Terror of the mother figure on one side, and visions of large male genitalia on the other. Is it the fear of women and of the feminine principle that define men, in male fantasy anyway, as redundant organisms except for reproductive purposes? Women can do everything without men, except reproduce. If the basic purpose of life was only the motive to make more life (the salmon dies, the turtle lumbers far inland), then man has a limited usage – limited, I mean, to sperm banks for reproduction.

The male *is* needed, but only in a reduced form. His reproductive organs develop, the rest atrophies. His size and mobility decrease, his feet and hands become vestigial. He is best carried round permanently attached (for safety) to the woman. His head develops suckers, like the remora, so that he can hold on. The parallel can be seen in the angler fish where the female is one hundred times larger than the male, which is permanently fixed to the female's underside. Reproduction is achieved by the female ingesting the male, but this was obviously too weird and painful even for my twisted vision.

The picture is a page from a future textbook on the human species. Perhaps it's for alien viewing. It shows the human in its natural habitat (the photo) and a biological drawing to illustrate the internal viscera and the bodily functions. Humans control the heating of their planet, so they don't need much clothing. It is set far into the future. The farther the better. I'm a man, and I don't want to be taken for a ride.

< 'Quite an interesting little sketch on the right here. Would have liked to have seen more integration with the photo on the left, although I like the depth created by the repetition of figures and the hints of gender confusion. I'm not at all sure about the purpose of that chap sticking out of the poor girl's ribcage. And why fields and trees, Storm?' (Malcolm Garrett – Designer)

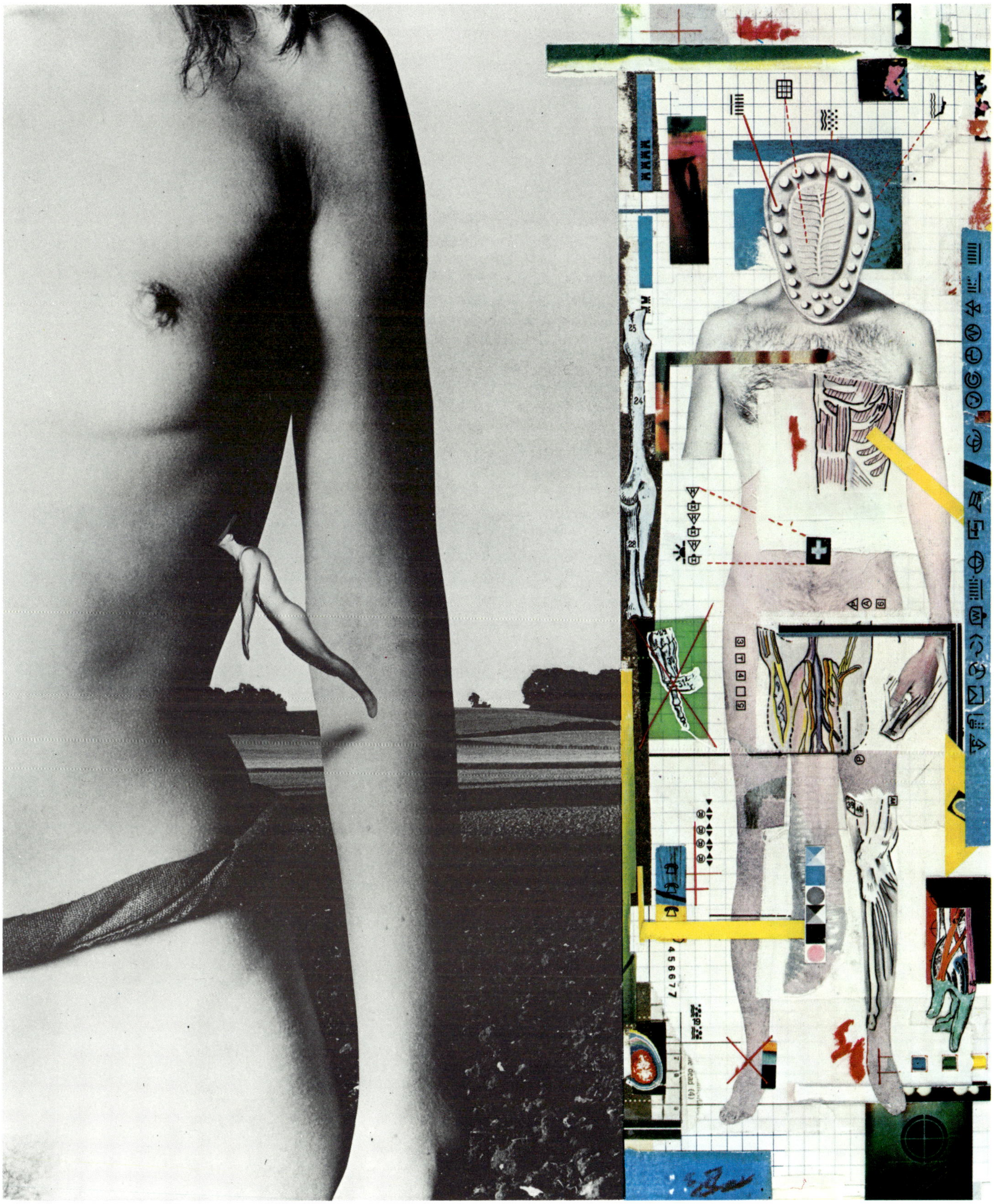

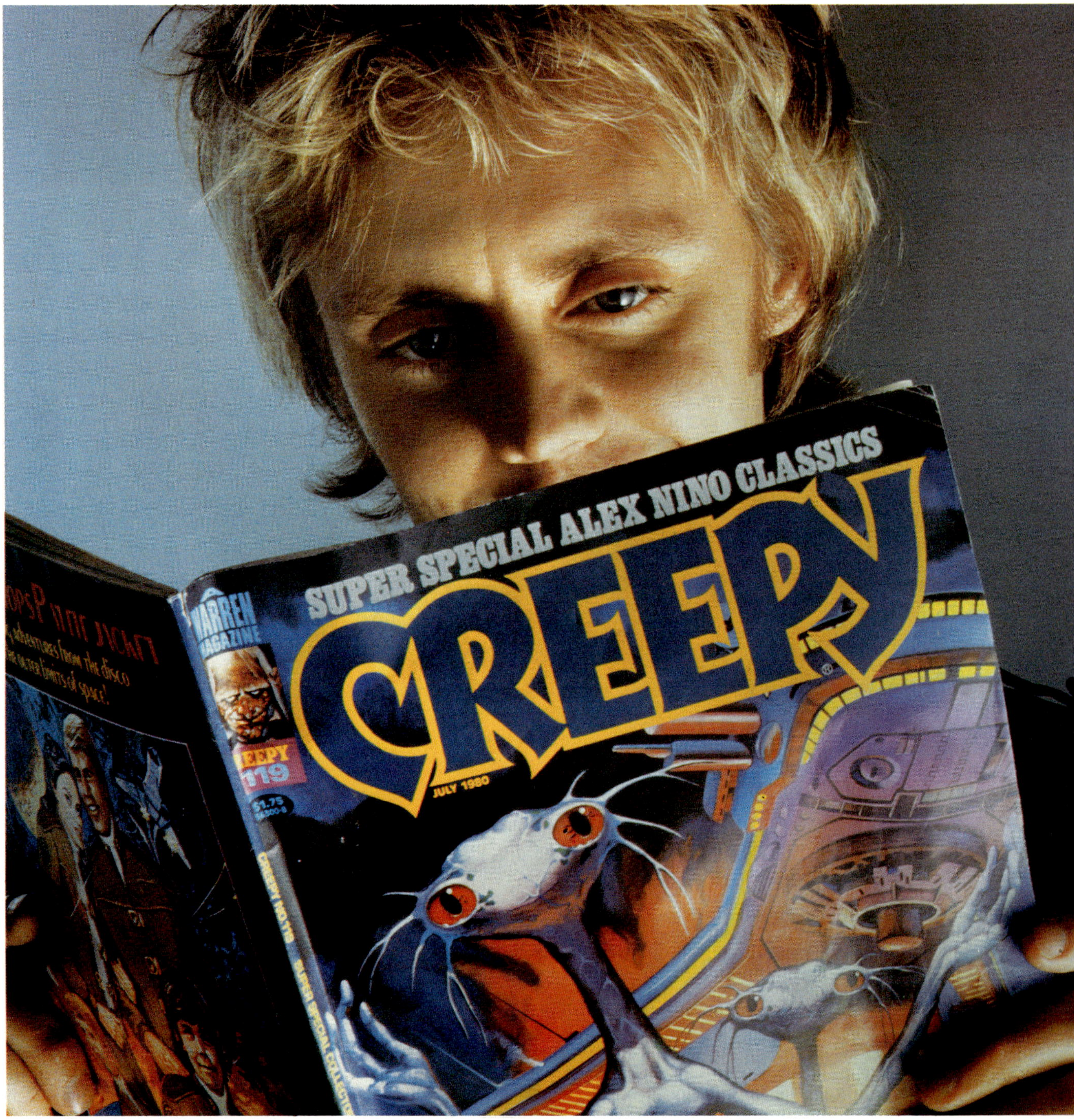

Roger Taylor Fun in Space

Hasselblad 500C with normal lens and daylight Ektachrome transparency, lit by flash, two heads (are better than one) (4000 joules), top right and back left, with reflectors all round the front. White paper on the inside of magazine to light underside of chin. The monster's eyes are also lit from within. Balanced exposure therefore necessary, f16 at ¼th. In left-hand photo Roger is underlit and back side-lit.

Shot in our studio. Roger Taylor is the human. Creepy is the alien. When I had the idea, I researched a nearby sci-fi shop called Forbidden Planet. I found this 'Creepy' comic and fell in love with the monster. He seemed so friendly. We could have designed our own monster but this one seemed perfect. Roger Taylor agreed, so I flew to New York to meet Mr Warren, owner of 'Creepy' magazine, and asked him if I could use it. He agreed, if properly credited, so thanks again to you, Mr Warren and the illustrator Jim Laurier. Alistair Bowtell, model-maker extraordinaire, then made a model of Creepy out of latex and polystyrene. It stands about 18 inches high and unfortunately has no body, just a neck, head and hand. Poor Creepy. There are light bulbs in the head to give the eyes extra life. They are positioned to look as if he's actually reading the magazine. I think he now lives with Roger.

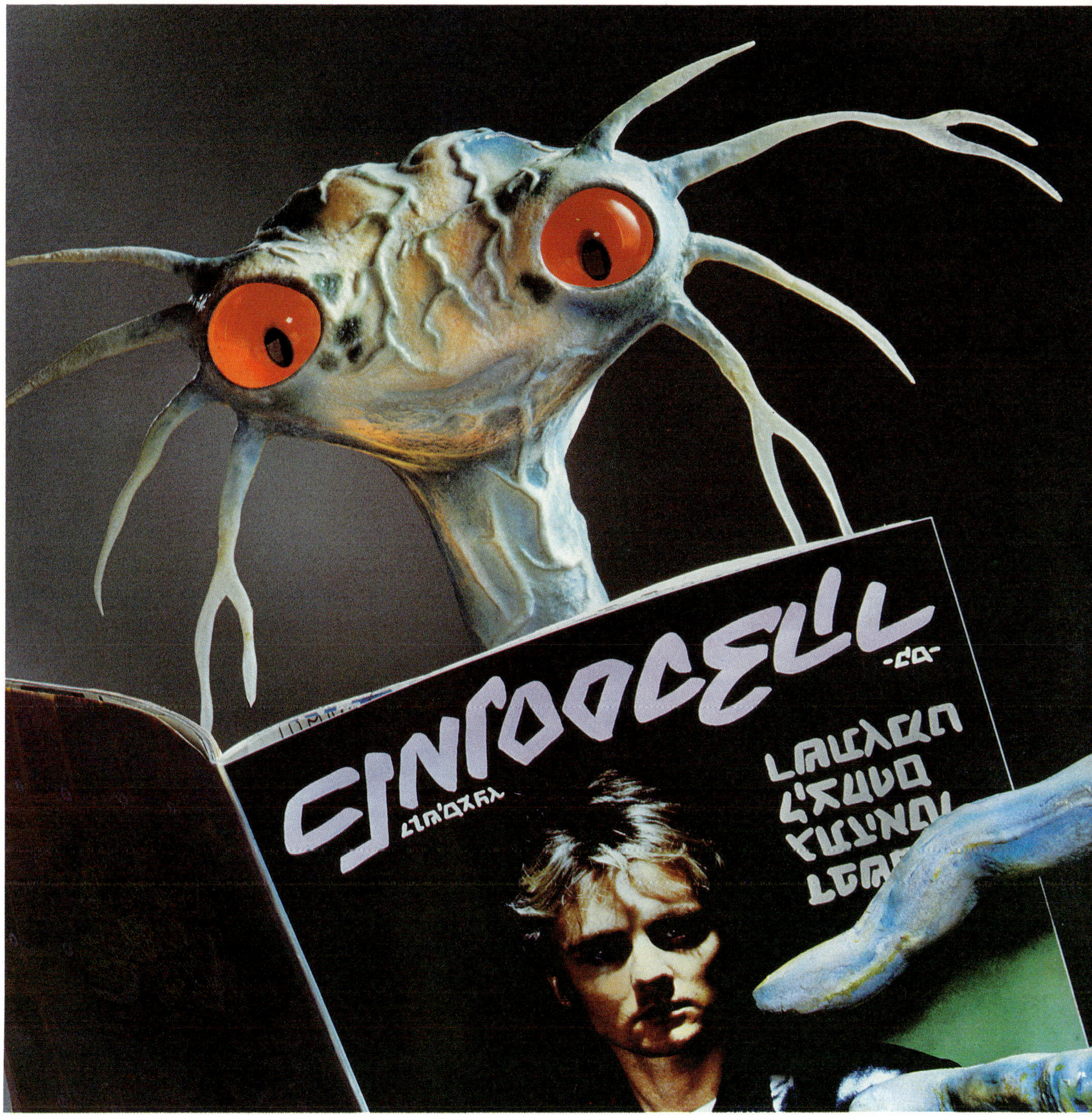

⊕ Simple R-type colour prints. The cover of the magazine which Creepy is reading was photographed and printed in advance. A mock-up was made and thrust into Creepy's hands.

⌑ This was used in 1981 for the cover of Roger Taylor's solo album 'Fun in Space'. Roger is the drummer with Queen. He felt that the cover should basically reflect the title, and that it should have some reference to space and science fiction without being the almost predictable air brush illustration of starships or bizarre interstellar wastes. A touch of humour was a prerequisite. One of my other suggestions was a collection of covers for sci-fi books, full of strange people, enigmatic creatures and haunting landscapes. I like to look at them in the front of the bookshop, but only en masse, never individually. Roger decided to use this on the inner bag. Each cover referred obliquely to songs on the album. They were illustrated by George Hardie, Ian Wright, Colin Chambers, Colin Elgie, Jeff Cummins, Paul Maxon and Jill Furmanovsky. Ian Wright was responsible for all the graphics on the actual album package.

○ The album title seemed rich enough in possibilities. I read the lyrics and listened to the music, but, in truth, was inspired by the title. Don't know where the idea came from. I remember it came to me as a complete vision, while I was sitting in my

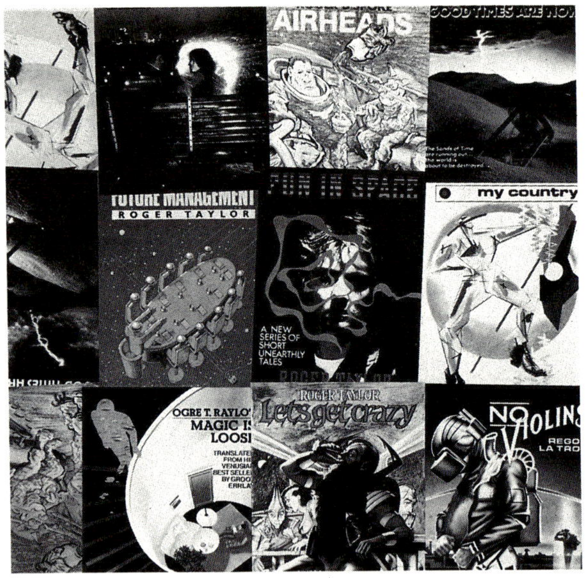

motor caught in a traffic jam on my way to work. Sounds pompous and pretentious, I know, but that feels the best way to express it. Sometimes when one is thinking idly an image just comes to mind. It often arrives during states of reverie or sleepiness. Fine for creating, not much good for driving.

Chauvinism is, I suppose, the main theme in this piece. The idea that beings shaped differently from us either look weird or are going to behave weirdly seems narrow-minded. Perhaps we would seem odd to visitors from space. Weirdness is like beauty: it exists only in the eye of the beholder. Difference is no valid reason for distrust. Whilst we on earth read about extraterrestrials, albeit only in fantasy at the moment, perhaps they in turn read about us. Creepy thinks it's make-believe as much as Roger does. At least they both seem enthralled. Fun in space. And so on.

'Pretty forgettable. I had to look at it for quite a while before I saw what it was.' (Phil Stoker – Manager, Virgin Megastore, London)

'Hated it! Looks amateurish. The writing is vague and as the monster is reading on the front, it doesn't attract people's attention. I don't see the point of it.' (Keith Johnson – Manager, HMV, London)

'When I first saw this sleeve, I thought at last Storm has recorded an album, the photograph on the front was so lifelike – warts and all. But then I saw the picture of Sting on the comic and realized that it was for Roger Taylor!

'Though I think that Hipgnosis have been responsible for some of the most memorable images during the last decade, their strike rate of good, average and duff is inconsistent. Their best is better than anyone else's, and when you are the best you are judged by your own standards and not by the industry norm.

'So I particularly liked this sleeve because it ended what I thought was an unusually barren period for them. At first glance the appeal is in the typically unique Hipgnosis humour and the strong visual impact. But like all good sleeves there is more depth to it, drawing the reader into the fun, excellent design and rich variety of illustration on the liner bag. Continued interest is guaranteed as many facets emerge later, especially when listening to the music. Its not forgettable like a lot of sleeves, or a home game at Arsenal.' (Peter Wagg – Chrysalis Records)

XTC Go 2

One typewriter
Lots of paper
An obliging secretary

It looks like an easy one, doesn't it? Well it wasn't – it took ages. I wrote it first in long-hand, then we typed it and tried to fit it into an approximate square. We enlarged it by PMT and made it negative. It didn't fit. I rewrote it and we tried again. Didn't like the degree of enlargement and still didn't like some of the line lengths. Tried again. It was OK, but we weren't sure about the white out of black. So we experimented with different colours, sometimes in positive, sometimes in negative. Eventually we came back to our first combination, and the client agreed.

It was finally submitted for publication as a one-piece flat A/W.

XTC used this for their album 'Go 2' in 1978. I can't remember what their actual brief was, but I remember they rejected our specific designs. Then they noticed a rough for this one lying on the floor. A member of the band picked it up and, dusting off the odd footprint, said, 'This looks interesting, what's it for?'

It was an idea I'd first submitted to Pink Floyd some years previously, but they didn't like it. Then I showed it to 10cc, thinking that they at least would respond to its inherent contradictions. Not so. XTC wanted to use it even more when they heard its history. Perhaps if it was too near the bone for the other bands, then so much the better for the brave new world of which XTC were a part.

We'd done a lot of record sleeves, even by 1974, and part of me was sick to death of what they were supposed to do. All those record companies, managers and bands (no, not *all* the bands) keen to use the sleeve to *sell* the record, and therefore wanting the cover to by eye-catching, tasteful (or tasteless – is it any different?), stimulating, full of intrigue and impact. Anything, so long as it would fulfil the main aim of getting the public to notice. In my naiveté perhaps, I thought that anyone who bought a record for its packaging was crazy. But . . . CBS, I hear, conducted a secret survey and concluded that packaging could affect sales 20 per cent *either* way. Bands in the years leading up to 1982 have been very image and merchandising conscious. It doesn't matter what I think. Covers will seldom be areas of pure aesthetic delight. Nor will they ever be entirely removed from their commercial purpose. Yet here was a chance to say my piece and do a sleeve at the same time. Its root is in the work of R. D. Laing, perhaps badly assimilated by me, and reworked as a design. However, it was artfully 'non'-designed: ordinary typewriting, not too accurately spaced. Didn't want the message overembroidered. It's complicated enough anyway as an example of doublethink and honest hypocrisy. Here in the book, of

This is a RECORD COVER. This writing is the DESIGN upon the record cover. The DESIGN is to help SELL the record. We hope to draw your attention to it and encourage you to pick it up. When you have done that maybe you'll be persuaded to listen to the music - in this case XTC's Go 2 album. Then we want you to BUY it. The idea being that the more of you that buy this record the more money Virgin Records, the manager Ian Reid and XTC themselves will make. To the aforementioned this is known as PLEASURE. A good cover DESIGN is one that attracts more buyers and gives more pleasure. This writing is trying to pull you in much like an eye-catching picture. It is designed to get you to READ IT. This is called luring the VICTIM, and you are the VICTIM. But if you have a free mind you should STOP READING NOW! because all we are attempting to do is to get you to read on. Yet this is a DOUBLE BIND because if you indeed stop you'll be doing what we tell you, and if you read on you'll be doing what we've wanted all along. And the more you read on the more you're falling for this simple device of telling you exactly how a good commercial design works. They're TRICKS and this is the worst TRICK of all since it's describing the TRICK whilst trying to TRICK you, and if you've read this far then you're TRICKED but you wouldn't have known this unless you'd read this far. At least we're telling you directly instead of seducing you with a beautiful or haunting visual that may never tell you. We're letting you know that you ought to buy this record because in essence it's a PRODUCT and PRODUCTS are to be consumed and you are a consumer and this is a good PRODUCT. We could have written the band's name in special lettering so that it stood out and you'd see it before you'd read any of this writing and possibly have bought it anyway. What we are really suggesting is that you are FOOLISH to buy or not buy an album merely as a consequence of the design on its cover. This is a con because if you agree then you'll probably like this writing - which is the cover design - and hence the album inside. But we've just warned you against that. The con is a con. A good cover design could be considered as one that gets you to buy the record, but that never actually happens to YOU because YOU know it's just a design for the cover. And this is the RECORD COVER.

course, it should have begun: 'This is a page in a book . . .'

I swear by all that's sacred I never knew the predecessor of this piece. Neville Brody pointed out that there is a pop art painting called 'This Is a Painting' using the dictionary definition. This piece was also set white on black and typewritten. I nearly died when I saw it.

'I wouldn't bother to read it.' (Steve Kincaid – Our Price Records)

'I thought it quite memorable and, yes, I did bother to read what it said. I think other people did too.' (Phil Stoker – Virgin Megastore)

'Offbeat. I think the script made tedious reading. It isn't going to draw people to the sleeve initially. It doesn't even mention XTC until the fifth line. Not a good way to sell a band.' (Nick Turnbull – HMV, London)

'Conceptual packaging! This is the epitome of the literal idea: it really does speak for itself. Being such an overstatement, its cleverness may become tiresome halfway through (one gets the message after a line or two). But, unlike many other ideas, the textural quality of the type makes this graphically very effective – it really stands out.

'It also seems quite suitable for the band (ecstasy). Presumably they have a liking of wordplay and it's a pleasant alternative to something pictorial – especially coming when it did.' (Bush Hollyhead – Illustrator/designer)

'Although I think it was an interesting idea, and we carried it right through our marketing campaign: casette insert, posters, T-shirts, etc., it just didn't work for a number of reasons. What was actually written was gobbledegook, and it wasn't exciting enough visually – people just aren't interested, when going through a rack of records, to read all that. I personally didn't particularly like it, and perhaps the public didn't either – it's still the worst selling XTC album.' (Simon Valley – Virgin Records)

'In their desperation to please us, they pulled out the office "joke". A sleeve, the design of which was purely an explanation of what the perfect album sleeve should be. We said it was excellent. They coughed nervously and, blushing a little, said that this "joke" had been previously refused by many major groups on the grounds of it being too heavy, too blatant, etc. This made us want it even more. This, I suppose, made us the foster parents to the antichrist of all album covers. Porno/typographically perfect. Obscenely obvious.' (Andy Partridge – XTC)

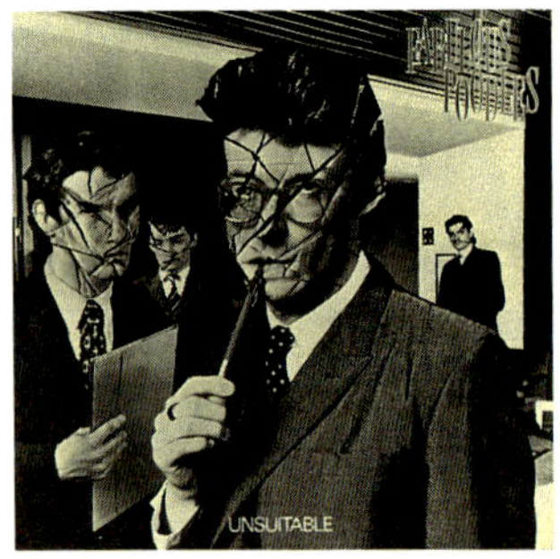

Face Crumpling

B/W photographic collage. Hasselblad with normal lens, using Tri-X, flashlit foreground figure, f11 at 1/60th. The office location is shot in daylight. Copy neg taken on large-format copy camera and tungsten lights either side.

Three separate pictures montaged together, copied, with the final reprint retouched. The face distortion consists of cutting out the head and crumpling it up and then flattening it out again. The creases and ridges are left there as three-dimensional things. The crumpled head (that is, the crumpled-up photo of the head) is collaged back onto the mangled neck and rephotographed. Since the ridges, etc., protrude from the surface, they cast shadows. This effect has its own depth and reality. It looks as if the man's face is actually pulled over his bone structure (cranium) like an ill-fitting jersey (or glove). And it was weird to discover the crumpled-head photo had to be made larger than the real photo head so when we squashed and then unravelled it, it came out at a size compatible with his body.

This is, in fact, the roughs we did for the Fabulous Poodles. They used the idea for an album called 'Unsuitable' in 1979.

This is one result of endless fiddling with photographs. It wasn't dreamed up for anyone specific, just an idea that emerged from the general morass of work going through the studio. It is related to games played with the surface of things, like 'Wish You Were Here' or the 'Forks' picture (page 17). Another device for trying to escape the inherent inhibitions of 2-D photography. Trying to create the illusion of depth on the paper.

We see it as both gruesome and humorous. Perhaps it's some dreadful disease, like elephantiasis, which horribly affects the boat race. Or perhaps he's developed it through years of working long hours at the office. But the lab coat gives it away: he's really a young scientist working hard on his research project (the resilience of the modern prophylactic?). He's been working late, trying to think it through. He chews his pencil. He is worried. His brow wrinkles as he wrestles with mighty concepts. But it wrinkles so much it spreads across the entire face, and remains. Was the research project really about how to reduce stress in everyday life? Or how to avoid the ageing process?

'A cut here
And a cut there,
Here a cut
There a cut
But not everywhere a cut cut.'
(Ian Plimsoll – Young & Rubicam)

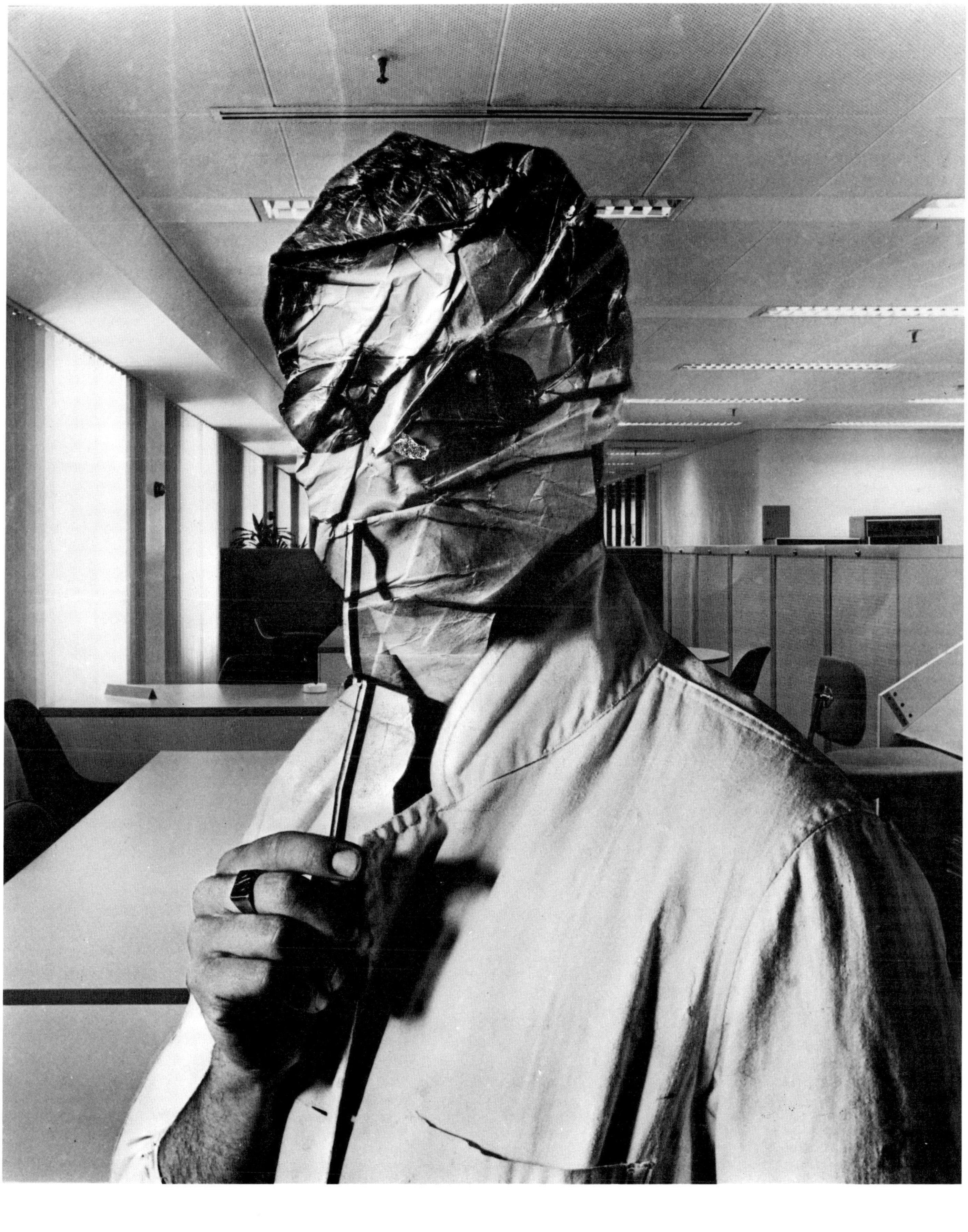

GGK America

Photographed with Hasselblad and W/A lens (50-mm). Daylight Ektachrome, f16 at 1/250th, using available daylight.

The location is an isolated farmstead in Amarillo, Texas, which in February is one of the few places in America not covered in snow. The original idea was set somewhere on the great plains, Nebraska, for example, but the weather there prevented any shooting. The cars were hired from a local town. The picture is taken from a helicopter, late in the afternoon.

In order to organize the shoot, a short-wave radio was used between the chopper and our assistants Peter Moon and Paul Maxon on the ground. The cars were stationary, since it proved impossible to coordinate them actually racing down the road. There was also the danger of a real accident, considering the kind of locals who were doing the driving. The specific angle and position of the chopper itself would also have been difficult to synchronize. Po was playing the part of Biggles, which was jolly brave since he gets vertigo standing on a railway platform.

A dye transfer print to allow rendition of autumnal colours and facilitate the retouching for the speeding cars. Their colours are red, yellow, blue and black because of an in-joke about the four-colour printing process, not that it strikes me now as very funny.

This is another in the series for 'A World Atlas of Music' for Polygram and it is supposed to illustrate America and how Polygram saw themselves as a centre for all influences that congregate in US music, whether it be the West Coast sound or Delta blues. I think they saw themselves at a crossroads – a young foreign business in America which had yet to establish itself.

This was derived from the brief. The advertising agency had requested that if any location work was to be done, it should look appropriate to the country being illustrated. So Po flew off to Texas to take the picture. And meet Miss Ellie.

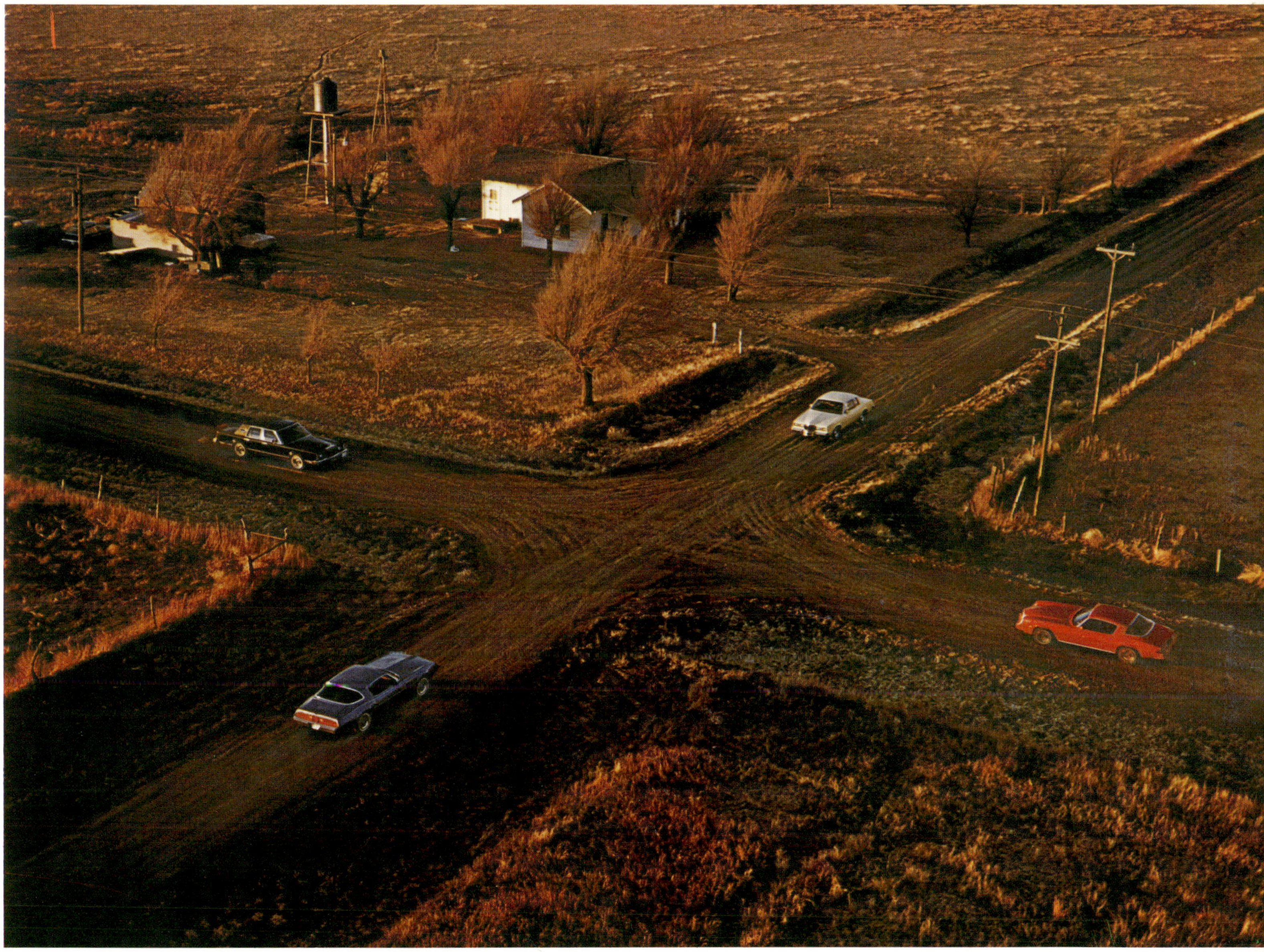

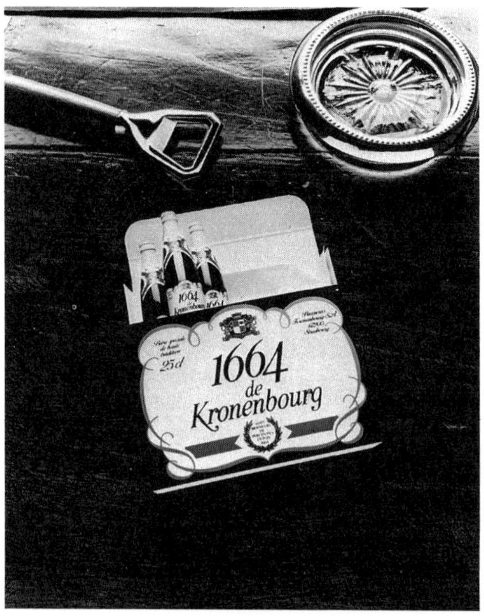

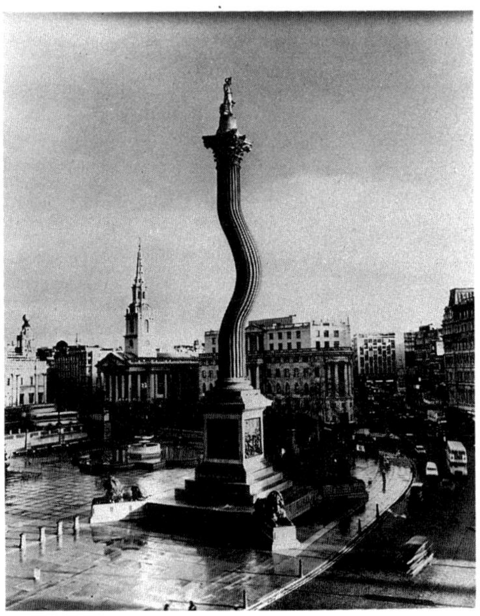

Advertising

We've included six pieces of advertising, more for their curiosity value than for their intrinsic worth.

(a) Volvo shot with 10/8 camera and daylight Ektachrome slide, plus masses of lights, reflector strips, polystyrene fills, glare removers, etc.

(b) Colman's, photographed with 5/4 camera. Background on 10/8.

(c) Talbot is an amalgamation of 2¼-inch Hasselblad, shooting by flashlight.

(d) Stella Artois is a combination of Hasselblad and flashlight with back lighting and rim fills, etc., for the beer, and 35-mm W/A, daylight Kodachrome for the background.

(e) Rank Xerox is daylight shooting with Hasselblad plus 50-mm W/A, Plus-X, and a variety of exposures.

(f) The bottles shot by 2¼-inch and the cigarette pack by 5/4 camera.

(a) Sweden (naturally enough) and a studio in Gothenburg. No A/W.

(b) Background is a shot taken in Texas, the Panhandle area. The doll is a specially built model shot in a studio along with the Rolls-Royce and models from an agency. Artwork is three-part dye transfer strip-in.

(c) Model aeroplane, boat, train shot in B/W then collaged, photocopied and lastly hand-coloured.

(d) Stella Artois is Belgian beer so the canal barges are Belgian. The beer is shot in our studio. Three-part dye transfer strip-in. The real problem was shooting the beer from a sympathetic angle and then doing a number of B/W negative compositional prints to see what the size and the position looked like before spending a lot of money on dye transfer prints.

(e) Nelson's column in Trafalgar Square, London. Early morning, thus no traffic or people. The A/W is B/W collage of three prints. The twist of the column is painted in by our retoucher Richard Manning.

(f) This is a two-part dye transfer strip-in. (e) and (f) were photographed in association with Robert Brimson.

There are no specific origins for these pieces. They are based on a set of instructions and on fairly precise drawings and roughs that had been prepared by the agency and, more particularly, by the client. The odd thing is that there is an inherent paradox in the making of all these pictures. Without wishing to be grossly egocentric, I think many of the approaches and devices used in advertising in the last ten years have come from general record cover design, if not specifically from some of our own. We know that a few, perhaps many, agencies hold our previous books in their offices. A French agency once rang us and said, 'We've designed six ads based directly on covers in your book. Would you like to photograph them?' And then when they got round to commissioning us, they proceeded to tell *us* what to do. The ad agencies must fulfil what their clients ask. But since a client may well have no idea how a picture works, the demands he makes often hinder the eventual success of the picture. So we, the 'artists', argue and disagree and try to persuade the agency to concentrate on what's going to work visually. But the agency is trying to keep the peace with the client and, in the end, after a lot of aggravation, they probably wish they had never approached us in the first place!

There is, in addition, a clash between us as designers (as well as photographers) and the agencies, who often see themselves as the designers. But photo design is what *we* do; there is no other ostensible reason to employ us. It's as if the agencies want to employ us but dare not, or only wish to pick our brains for a few of the tricks we've learned over the years. Perhaps it's because we're spoilt: our clients, musicians by and large, demand artistic excellence rather than a set of very specific renditions. And they *have* used us for our invention and imagination, not as technicians to pull together someone else's ideas. Well, that's what we like to think.

Unfortunately, these advertising attempts have usually ended in expensive failure. Volvo decided that our shots were fine but that there was something wrong with the car itself. Or so they told us. Either way, the job was killed.

The same was true for the Colman's job. They spent £8000 to see a photographic version of the design, rather than make a decision from the drawings, which were perfectly clear. Stella Artois was used successfully and even won some awards in Paris, although I'm not entirely sure why. I did this job very diligently because the art director, Marie V, was so damned attractive. If you can't do it for money, you might as well do it for love. Or lust.

Talbot was used for a car catalogue. We thought it was fairly successfully realized within the limitations which applied. The same goes for the advertisement for Rank Xerox, which was successful in so much as it was used in the national press, but a failure for us as the agency went bankrupt and we didn't get paid.

Kronenbourg was art-directed by Giles Soulier, who was very conscientious and attentive, but the campaign didn't get off the ground. Although they were our designs, they were *definitely not* the ones we wanted the client to accept.

There's a moral in all this somewhere. But what it is, or precisely where it's located, I've simply no idea.

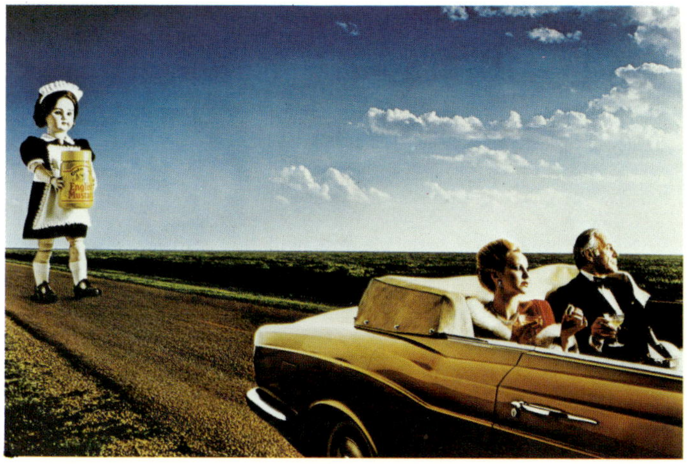

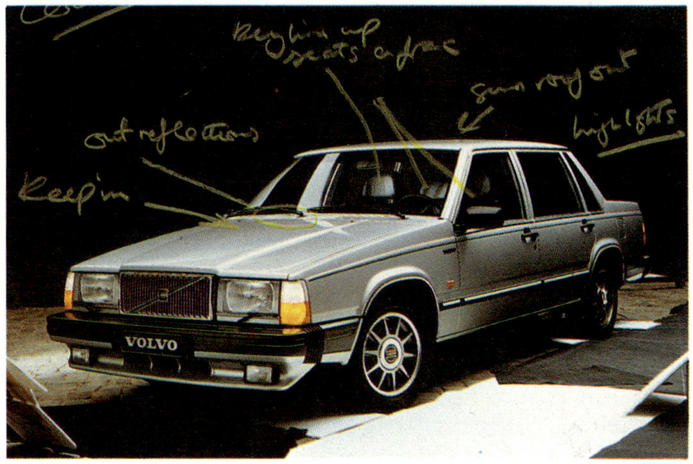
cut reflections
Keep in
highlights
VOLVO

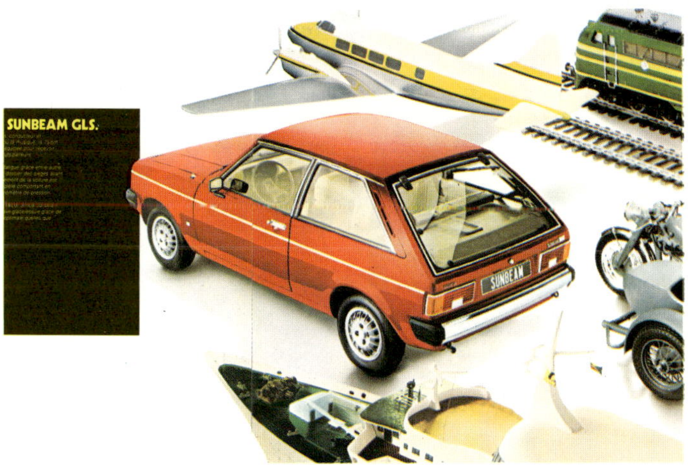
SUNBEAM GLS.
SUNBEAM

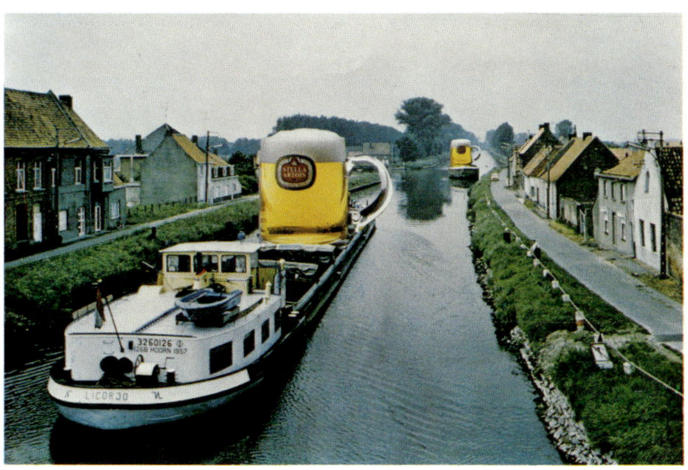

Desolation Angels

Shot on Hasselblad in three parts. Background, and guy and car with W/A lens in California. The girl on a standard lens in our studio. Soft side flashlighting. All Ektachrome 64. All exposures about f16 at 1/60th. The transparencies were made into R-type prints and montaged together in the right positions as A/W with an overlay to indicate to the printer of the sleeve which areas were to be left white.

The background was shot near a place called Death Valley Junction on the California–Nevada border. We searched for several days for a suitably desolate spot, and shot other photos that appear elsewhere on the package. On the way back to Los Angeles, in a red Mercedes coupé, doing about 120 m.p.h., Po was stopped by a police roadblock. The scene was potentially very ugly (well, he was doing sixty-five m.p.h. *over* the limit!) and he had visions of weeks spent languishing in a red-neck jail. Then the officers saw Po's Pink Floyd tour T-shirt and he hurriedly explained in his best David Niven English accent that, yes, he really did do all those covers and he definitely could get them tickets for the next concert! A few words with the hanging judge in the next town and a small fine later, and he was on his way. Thank God, they didn't look in the boot.

This was shot for Bad Company's 'Desolation Angels' album. We can't remember any specific brief. We had already worked several times for this band and their management, and we knew the kind of thing they liked. We presented a whole bunch of ideas, but were still pleasantly surprised when they chose this, since it was our favourite too.

The idea of leaving bits out of a picture was not really ours. Some months before we did this, we saw a rather rude picture by a friend of ours, Geoff Halpin, which had certain parts left out (and a good thing too, considering the subject). In fact, the idea has been used lots of times in many different ways: from Beardsley to 'Meccano Magazine'. Anyway, we liked it, and developed it to produce this design. It might be possible to find some intellectual meaning in the missing bits, but my mind is a blank.

'Typical Hipgnosis sleeve! To me it conveys the same sort of mood as "Presence" by Led Zeppelin which came out around the same time. It typified the band's change in style and audience.' (Keith Johnson – HMV, London)

'I like the way this picture works by bringing the white border into the picture. Removing various objects and interrupting the framing makes the picture and border work as a whole, instead of two separate entities. It also enhances the composition and emphasizes focal points by removing unnecessary visual information, thus making the picture work in two ways: either as a continuous photograph or as a balanced arrangement of white shapes.' (Geoff Halpin – Designer)

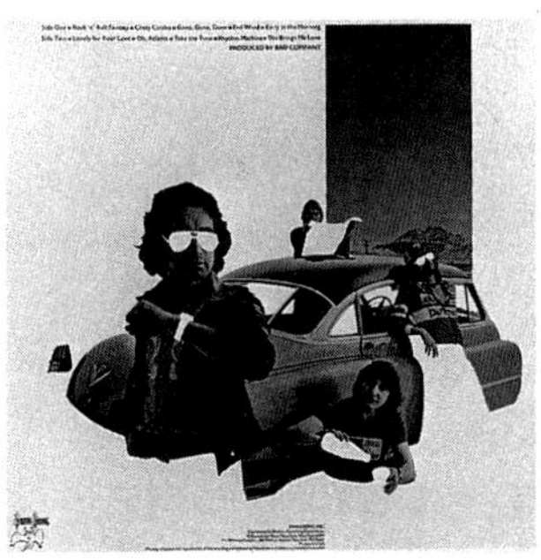

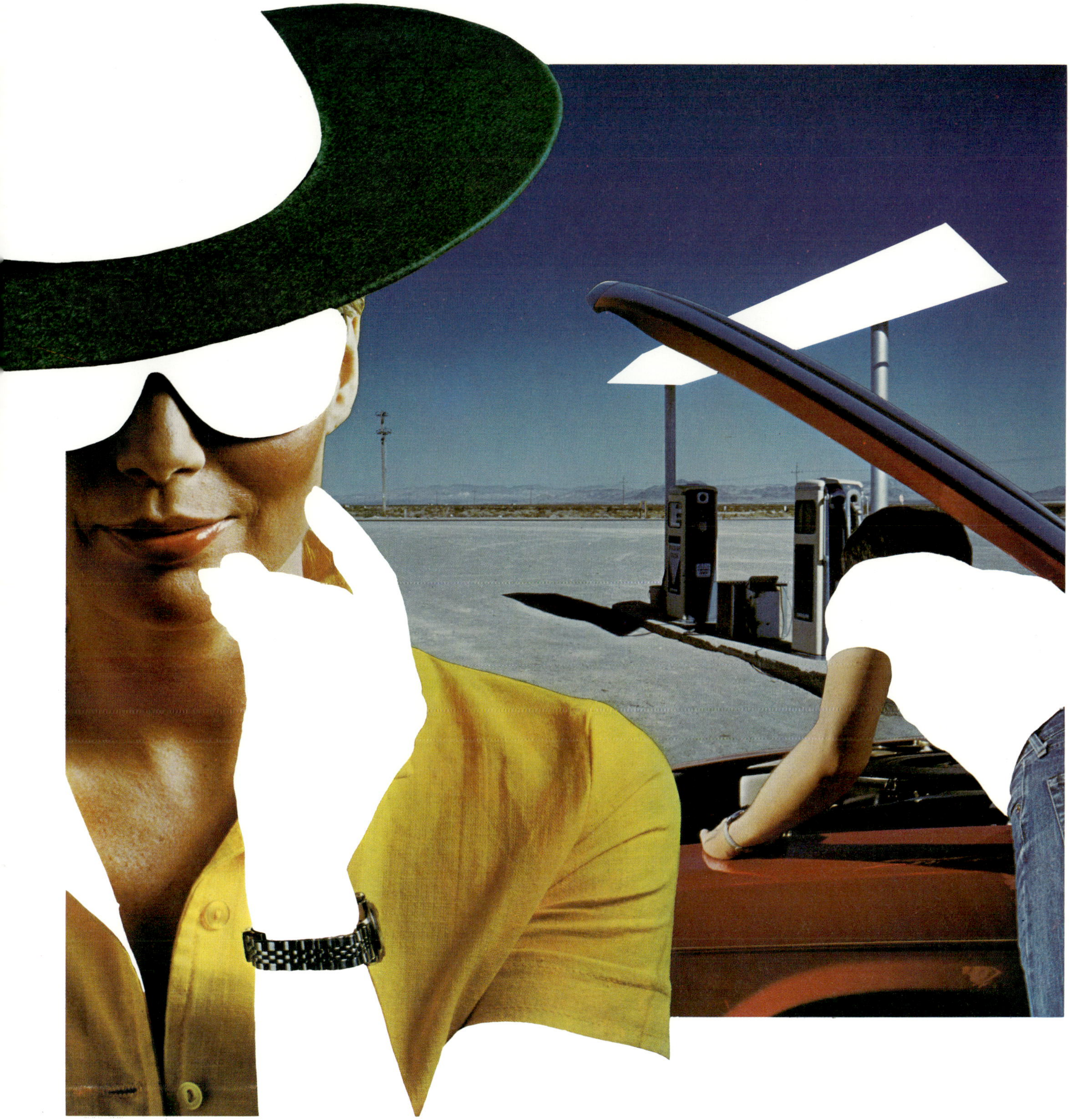

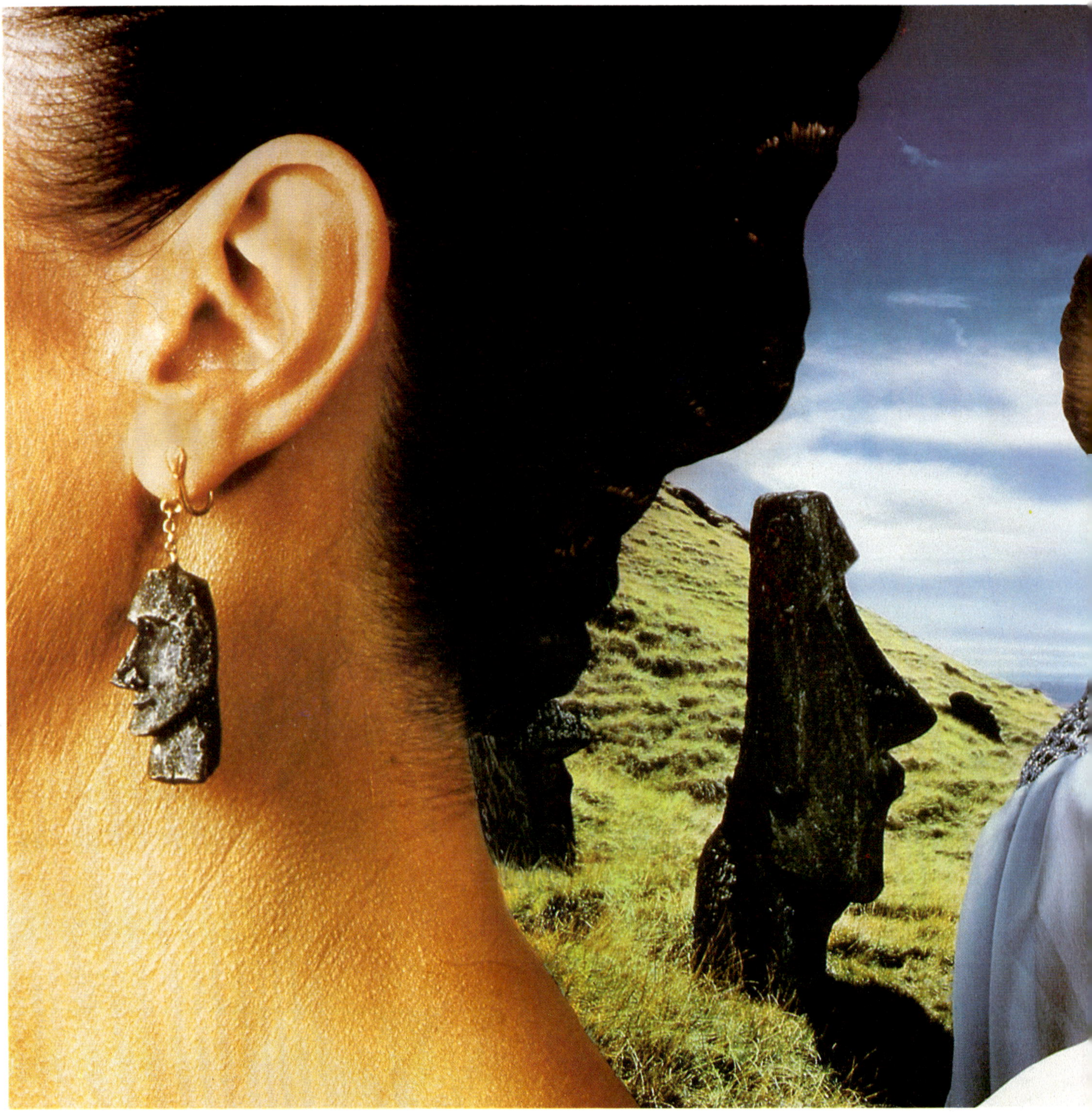

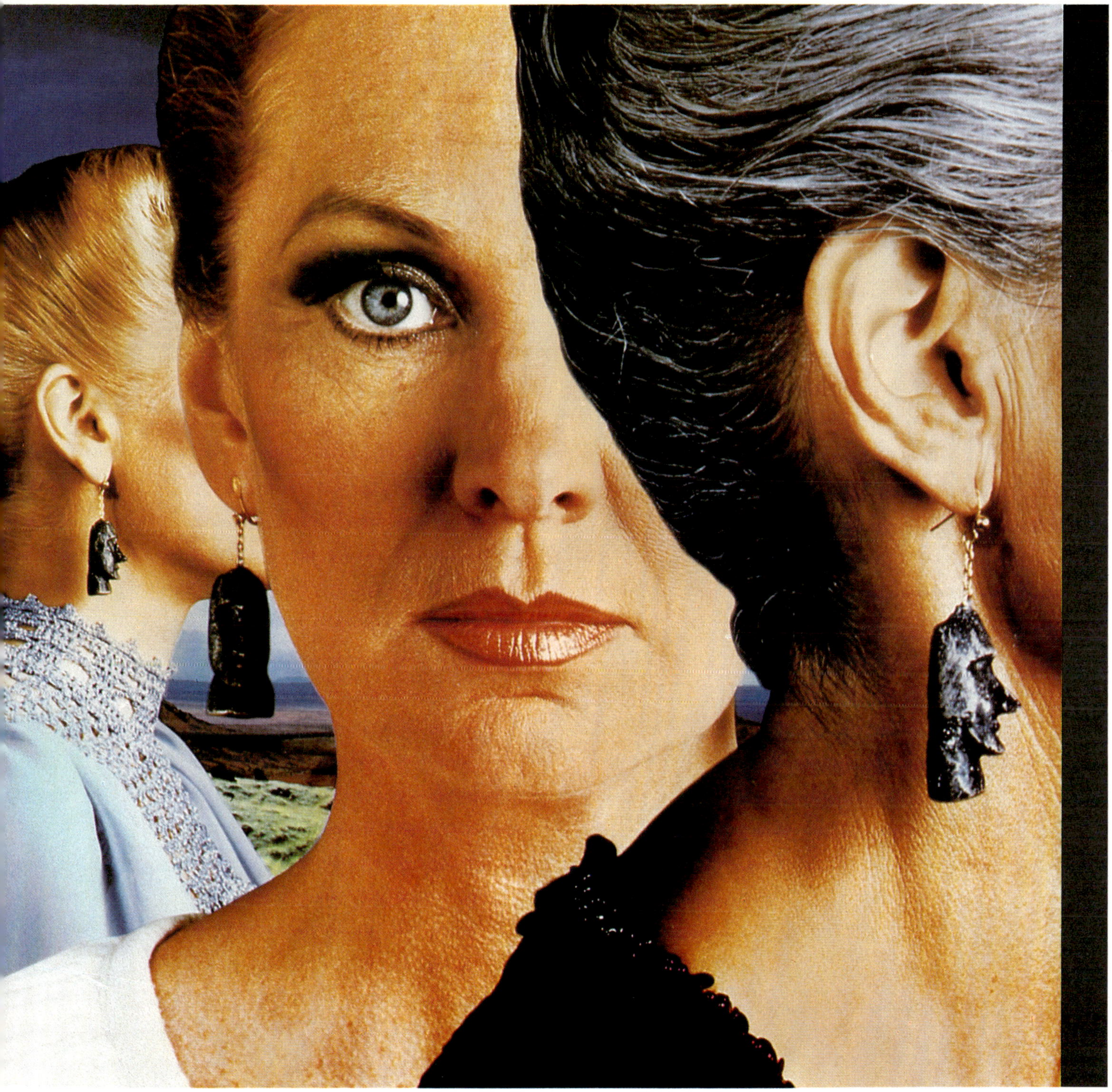

Styx

Trusty Hasselblad plus 120-mm lens. Daylight Ektachrome exposed normally in the studio using flash. One head and large umbrella, 2000 joules to right-hand side and reflector board on the other side to bring out shadow detail.

This was really one occasion when we wanted the clients to insist on reality in design, thus requiring a quick trip to Polynesia, but they wouldn't wear it. The women are models, photographed individually in our studio. The Aku Aku earrings were specially made for the picture.

This is precise collage based on a black and white drawing of the idea. The prints are all R-types made directly from the selected transparencies. The background is made up of two library shots of Easter Island. Their arrangement, in relation to the foreground faces, was extremely awkward – the most difficult part of the whole job. The women were easy, especially as we had already photographed them according to our drawn-up plan.

Several little devices and tricks were used to enhance the 'presence' of the picture. The faces are all shot on a 120 lens (a slight telephoto instead of a normal), so that the consequent foreshortening makes them *feel* closer. Their hair styles are smoothed back and severe, partly to ease cutting them out for montage, and partly because of the type of women they are supposed to represent. Daylight and flashlight are mixed on purpose so that the women are slightly unrealistic in relation to the background – the idea is not that they are literally on Easter Island, so much as connected to it in some way. The sense is more important than the physical reality. The light coming from different directions is a device to reinforce the non-physicality of it all, as well as to accentuate greatly the edges of the faces – the lightness behind the darker edges. The choice of forty-year-old women, as opposed to nymphets for example, is to take the mind away from obvious sensuality and keep it on the idea and visual content. (I know, some forty-year-old look great. I mean, I'm nearly forty.) Finally, the one visible eye has had its cornea cleaned up and bleached whiter than normal.

The American band Styx used this on the front of a gatefold album called 'Pieces of Eight' in 1978.

Something in Styx's lyrics made me think of obsession, and of Easter Island. I decided to adapt an idea I'd once had about pyramids. Images of pyramids have been used for everything from paper money to record covers. For me they also became a symbol of woolly post-hippie thinking. The belief was that they had hidden powers. They could aid meditation or sharpen razors. The pyramids became a repository for all the semi-cosmic theories that were current at the time. The same was true of those phenomenal statues on Easter Island. How did they get there? Were alien species responsible for their existence? I was doubtful both of the speculation and of the kind of people who indulged in it. Most of them knew nothing about these haunting statues (or the pyramids) and consequently ended up reducing human appreciation of their significant presence to an automatic response. The women in the picture are, as I see them, the epitome of this reductionist syndrome.

'The Strange Adventures of Menopause Island'

'There is a fascination in the mind with the ageing process, and what could be more tantalizingly perverse than the mystical image of fading beauty. This album cover is one of my personal favourites because of the controversy it caused. No one at the home office understood what was going on, or why this was the image for an album called "Pieces of Eight". Quite frankly, neither do I, but I don't care.

'The cover was a perfect vehicle for the "gadget mania" that was rampant in the record industry when we released the album . . . there were Easter Island ashtrays, picture discs with the centre hole in the women's nostril, earrings, badges, posters, and more mysterious memorabilia than I can remember. This cover is an art director's dream. On reflection, I would have liked the Easter Island image to have been a fridge, but after all, hindsight is 20/20 vision.' (Jeff Ayeroff – A&M Records, Los Angeles)

Heathen Earth

This isn't exactly a Hipgnosis design, but Peter did it and we liked it, so here it is.

The teeth are hand-drawn on Kodatrace. The background glow was achieved by exposing photographic paper in the enlarger and carefully holding back the central area. I suppose we could have airbrushed this, but we wanted a luminous sort of feeling, so we didn't.

This was for a group Peter was in, called Throbbing Gristle. In general, their sleeves were intended to differ from both the current popular styles (at that time, derivative, busy images were in vogue), and the style of whatever the group's previous album sleeve had been. In this instance, the last one was a photo of the band smiling benignly at the edge of Beachy Head. Probably also intended to look nice, neat and new. It was released in 1980.

All the TG sleeves were designed by the group themselves, and put together by Peter. For this one somebody suggested a medical or veterinary-type drawing of a dog's jaw bone. Peter found some in a library book and this one looked the most promising and was duly drawn up to size. The numbers were added for personal reasons. The line of type was inserted at the top because TG wanted the only type on the front to be different from the name of the group and from the title. Although it was never stated at the time, the line is a quote from a surprisingly sweet song by Charles Manson.

As with most aspects of the group, this design was arrived at mainly by instinct. This is different from the way Hipgnosis operates, where intuition may play its part in the conception, but where analytical thought is necessary for the final realization of a design. Strange but true.

'As with all natural processes, a non-human image implies a heathen celebration and the teeth of danger. Applying the laws of magic and will, an image of a dog produces a dog. The dog appeared on the 23rd of the month. Time is both a trap and a revelation.

'It took one hour to record the album and six weeks to decide on its title and cover. What difference does that make, you might ask? Forty-one days and twenty three hours!' (Genesis P. Orridge)

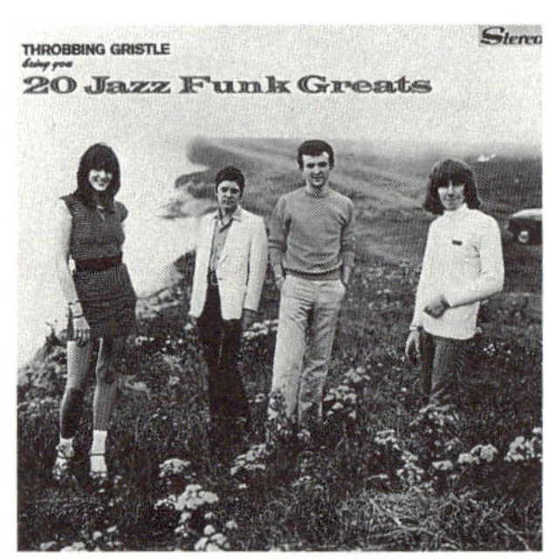

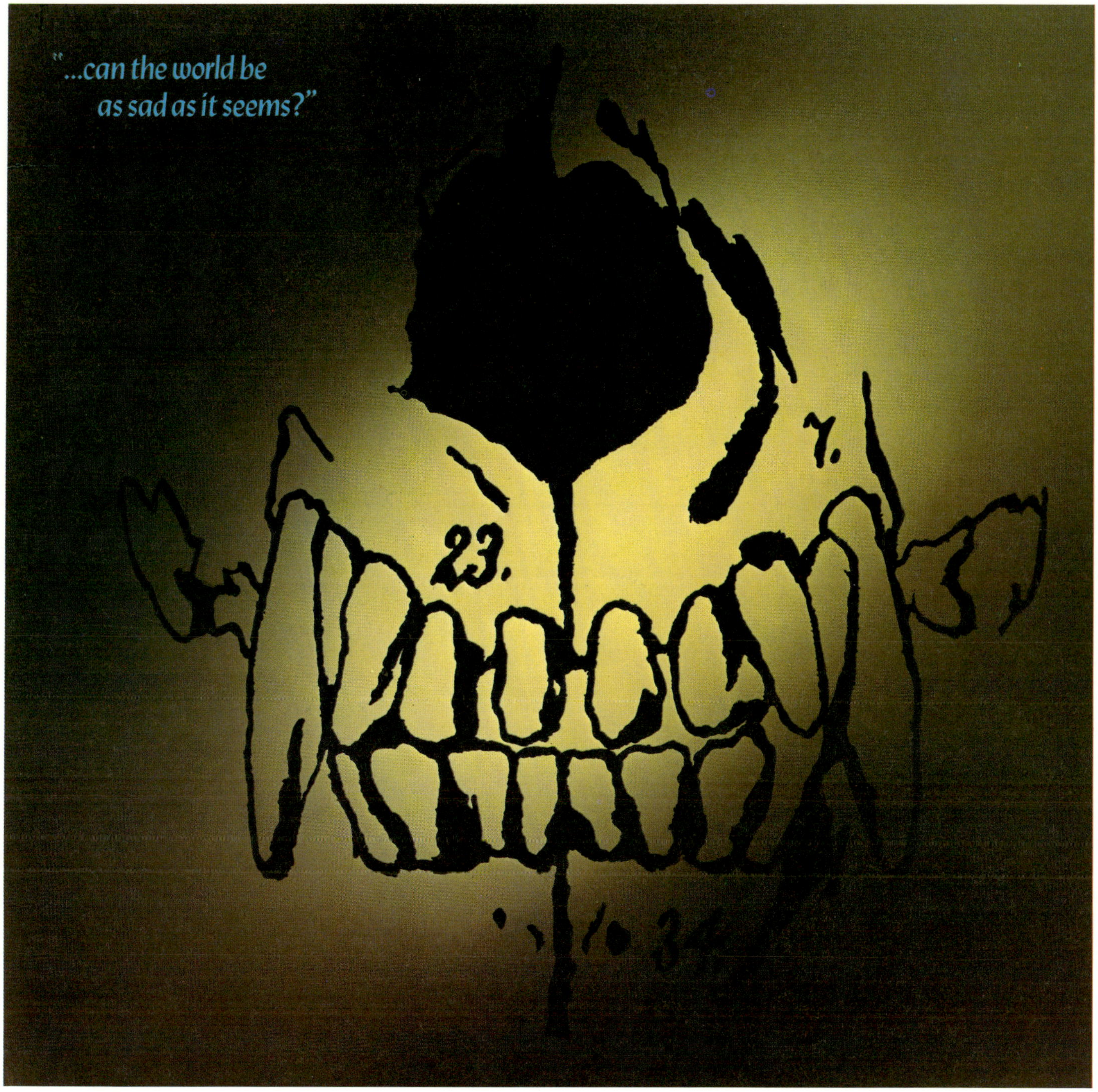
"...can the world be
as sad as it seems?"
23.
7.

Biko

All the shots taken with Hasselblad using normal and W/A lenses, except the eating picture which was taken with 35-mm. (A 35-mm camera is more portable and more discreet. Since the eating shot was taken in a public place, we did not want to be discovered and thrown out. It would have been a difficult job explaining what the picture was for.)

Other material was photographed in our studio using a backdrop made of ordinary bath tiles. The A/Ws are straightforward B/W prints, plus a couple of keylines.

Peter Gabriel wrote a song called 'Biko', released in 1980. This material was used on the picture bag. This is what Peter wrote at the time: 'Bantu Stephen Biko was a young South African leader who died in 1977 as a result of injuries received during interrogation by the South African security police.

'I believe Steve Biko was very important. He could have been a very positive force in Africa, and a leader that young people all over the world would have identified with (ref. "Biko" by Donald Woods).

'When I heard, on the radio, of Steve Biko's detention, I was sure that publicity would protect him. World attention had been attracted to the large number of prison suicides: slipping in showers, jumping from windows, and hanging . . . I was shocked one breakfast time to hear of his death, and wrote down some thoughts in my diary which were to be the start of the lyrics two years later.'

Proceeds from the sale of the record were donated to the Steve Biko Black Consciousness Movement.

Even though these photos do scant justice to the song and to the brief, they *do* constitute a stab at it. Communicating political or social ideas is morally and emotionally complicated for an artist, especially a commercial one. When you are not a political activist there is a temptation to steer clear of complex issues. We are private politicians, if you like, living our lives as best we can. This is hard enough in itself, and I'm sure we often fall short of our own limited ideals. Nevertheless, that's as far as our aspirations go: active politicians we are not. Our knowledge is not extensive, and our motives are open to question. We can attempt a visual comment, but what do we actually do in terms of clear political or moral acts? Do we stop eating South African peaches? Do you?

It struck us that the evidence overwhelmingly suggested that a grave injustice had been done. What happened to Biko was a part of the wider issue of South African apartheid policy and all its ugly manifestations. It became relevant to extract one particular theme before we got lost in the multitude of possibilities. We focused on indifference. South Africa displays an awful indifference to the basic dignity of man, in order to operate an apartheid system. It has no belief in a common humanity, or in the principle of the equality of men, whatever their colour. This indifference is matched by the apparent indifference of the rest of the world.

At the same time, we had a conscious desire to avoid overtly gratuitous images of gruesome violence, such as decrepit and mutilated corpses. We decided instead that the limb and its single wound would be more powerful. And the people eating are *only* eating. They are indifferent to the problems of racial discrimination. They are out to lunch. Along with the rest of the world. Everybody washes their hands of it and the parade of unforgiveable mistreatment continues unabated, especially in South Africa.

Peter Gabriel decided that this set of pictures would be too busy for the front cover of his single bag, preferring instead the photograph of the black man amidst the columns. A lone figure set against the entrenched structures of a cold and insensitive authority.

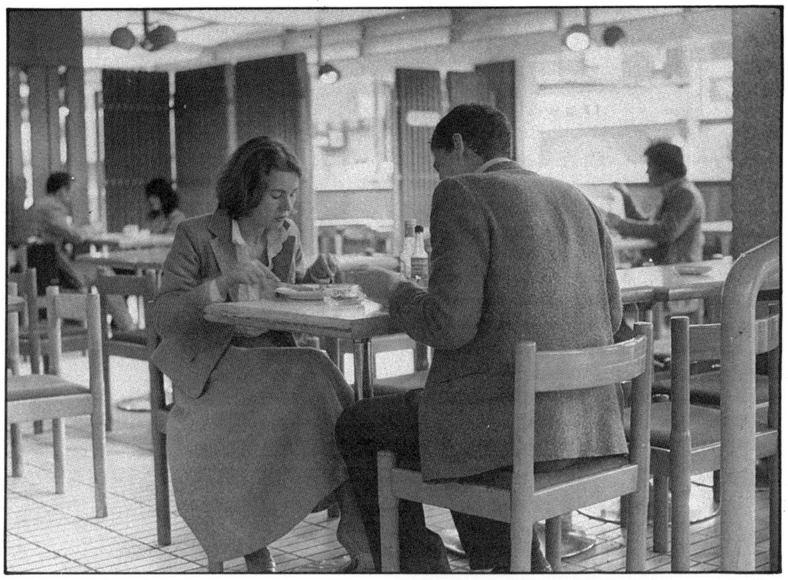

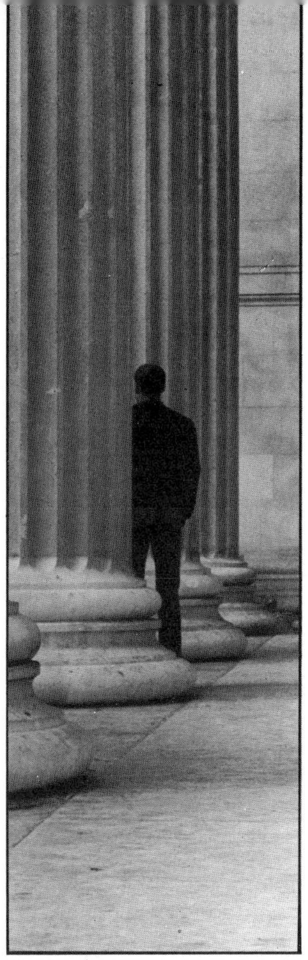

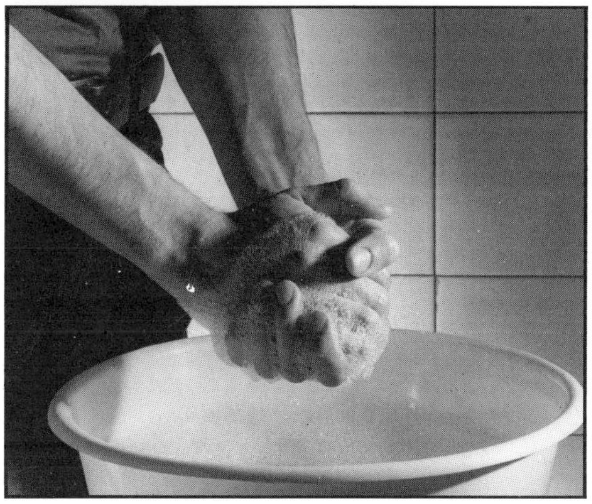

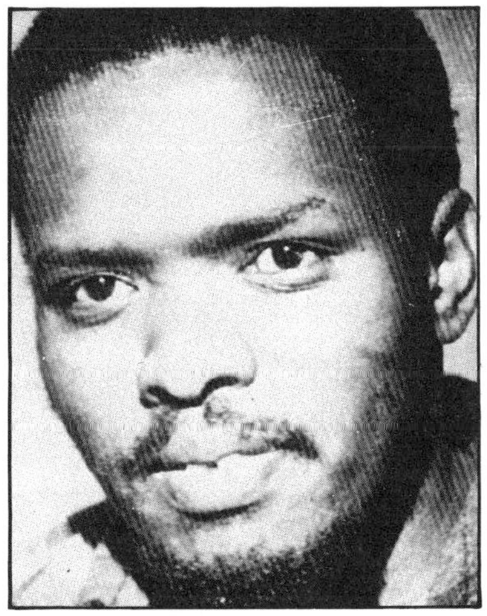

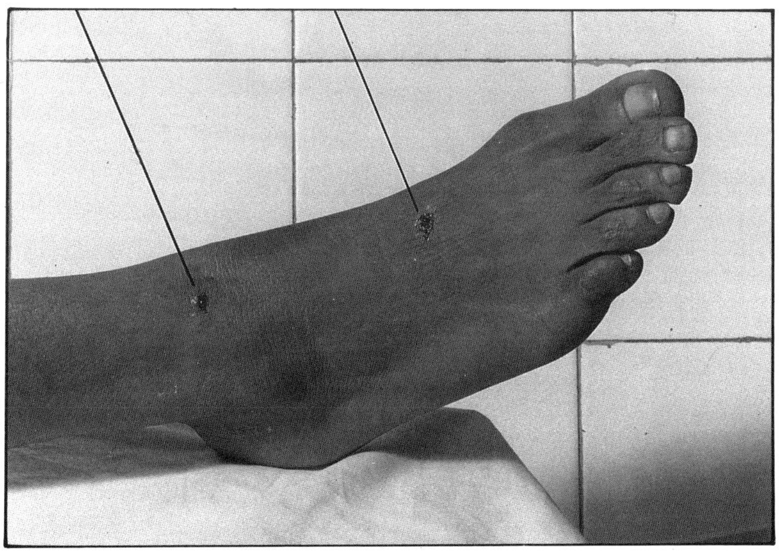

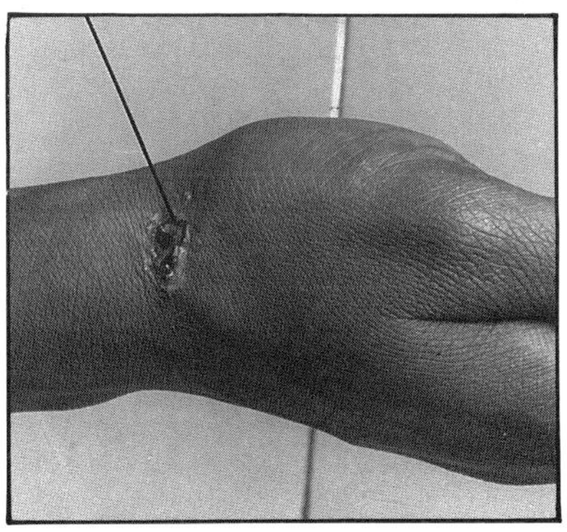

4

Communicate
She said, as he boarded the train,
Off on his holiday caper.
Write to me . . . phone,
I'll feel so alone,
And anyway, who'll get my paper?

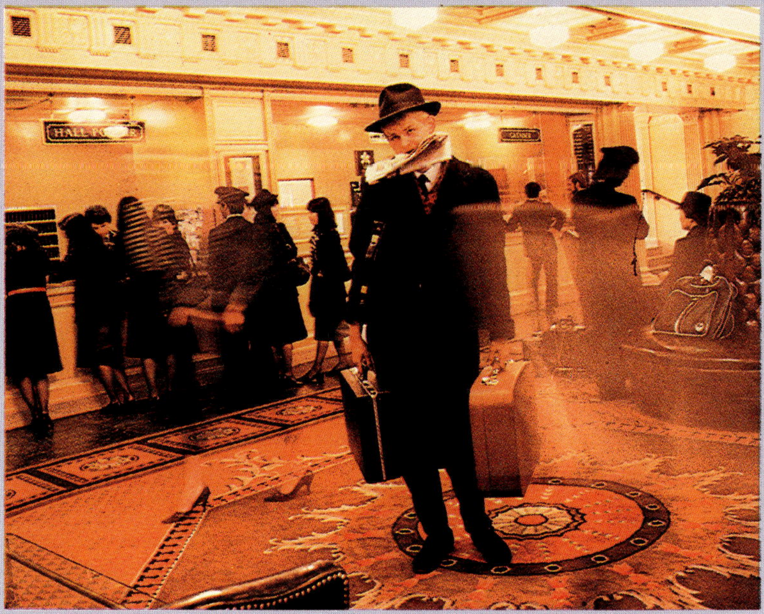

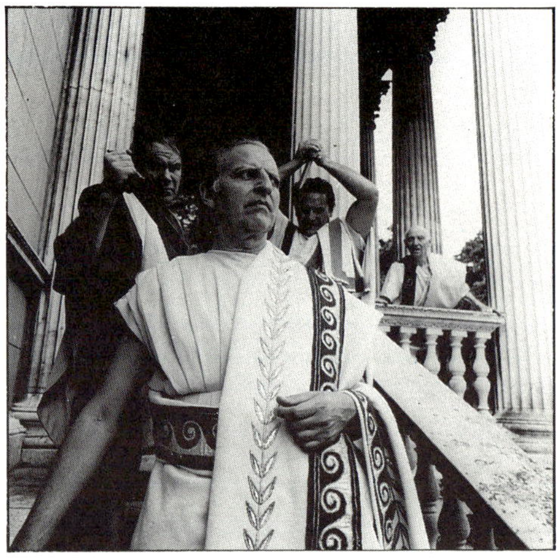

10cc Greatest Hits

Background: photographic copy of an old Victorian print, hand-coloured in the bottom right-hand corner, and doctored to give us the royal smack.
Top left square: line drawing printed in specified colours, same for shot man.
Top right square: 35-mm photo taken by Nikomat with W/A lens, and hand-coloured green.
Bottom left square: $2\frac{1}{4}$-inch Ektachrome, Hasselblad 500C plus 50 W/A, flashlit.

The boxing glove is a line drawing, as is the bent poker, and colour designated where printed. The arrow and apple is a full-coloured acrylic painting. Boxers and billiard balls are mechancials, and Babe Ruth is a torn-out print from a magazine.

The 'Titanic' was shot in a water tank at Shepperton, where they made 'The Cruel Sea' with Jack Hawkins and the stiff upper lip. The icebergs are polystyrene. The Victorian print is of the state opening of Parliament. Top right is a bank in Mayfair, London. The rest is drawn.

Very complicated drop-in artwork. The base picture is marked up to indicate where the illustrations and photographs are to appear. Keylines were drawn to make it easier for the positioning of the corner squares. The remaining items were left to the printer. He had to make negative masks of these pieces and then burn a hole in the films of the base art that he had previously processed. He then physically cut in the films of the new ingredients, performing a preliminary test to check if he had got all of this right. He had, but he wasn't very friendly about it.

The paintings were done by George Hardie, Jeff Cummins and Mick Brownfield.

Lp cover for 10cc's 'Greatest Hits', 1979. The manager, Rick Dixon, actually gave me the job over the phone. The lads, he said, were too busy to get involved. After all, it was a repackage, so it didn't warrant the same care and enthusiasm that a new album with new songs would. 'Do whatever you like and then convince the band that it's OK,' he said. More difficult than I thought, at least politically, since 10cc had just got divorced. Lol and Kev had gone off to seek their fortunes.

I had only the one idea and that was to take the brief literally. The songs were too diverse to pick a particular theme, and a band photo would be boring and inappropriate in view of the matrimonial circumstances. So I thought about a collection of great hits, displayed visually. The word 'hit' is nice and flexible. So we dreamed up the following Big Hits: mafioso shooting; boxing (twice); Babe Ruth; a billiard break; the largest bank hit in the UK; a royal hit in the Victorian kisser; the 'Titanic' and iceberg; a poker used by Tom to whop Jerry; and William Tell's archery. On the back cover are Julius Caesar's murder and a couple of oddities: a statue of a swallow hit by a cricket ball at Lords and, of course, the biggest hit of all – a camel trying to get through the eye of a needle.

There were plenty of other suggestions, but they were rejected as inferior. George Hardie then submitted some ideas for the mixed media layout, and between us we chose this one. He also designed and illustrated some of the ingredients, and looked after the illustrations. We stayed home and copped the money.

'Being involved in this experiment, I feel free to say that it was a brave, but not an unqualified success. It looks very finished rather than a try-out and this, for me, is the problem. The cost of reproduction prohibited making changes and an experiment to which you can't react is only half done. There are some nice ideas involved.' (George Hardie – Designer)

'Happy with it. Interesting examples of physical hits. Speaks for itself. We usually have one main idea but this appealed to us because the ideas reflected the songs and ideas within songs. I like the swallow at Lords – a sad hit.' (Graham Gouldman – 10cc)

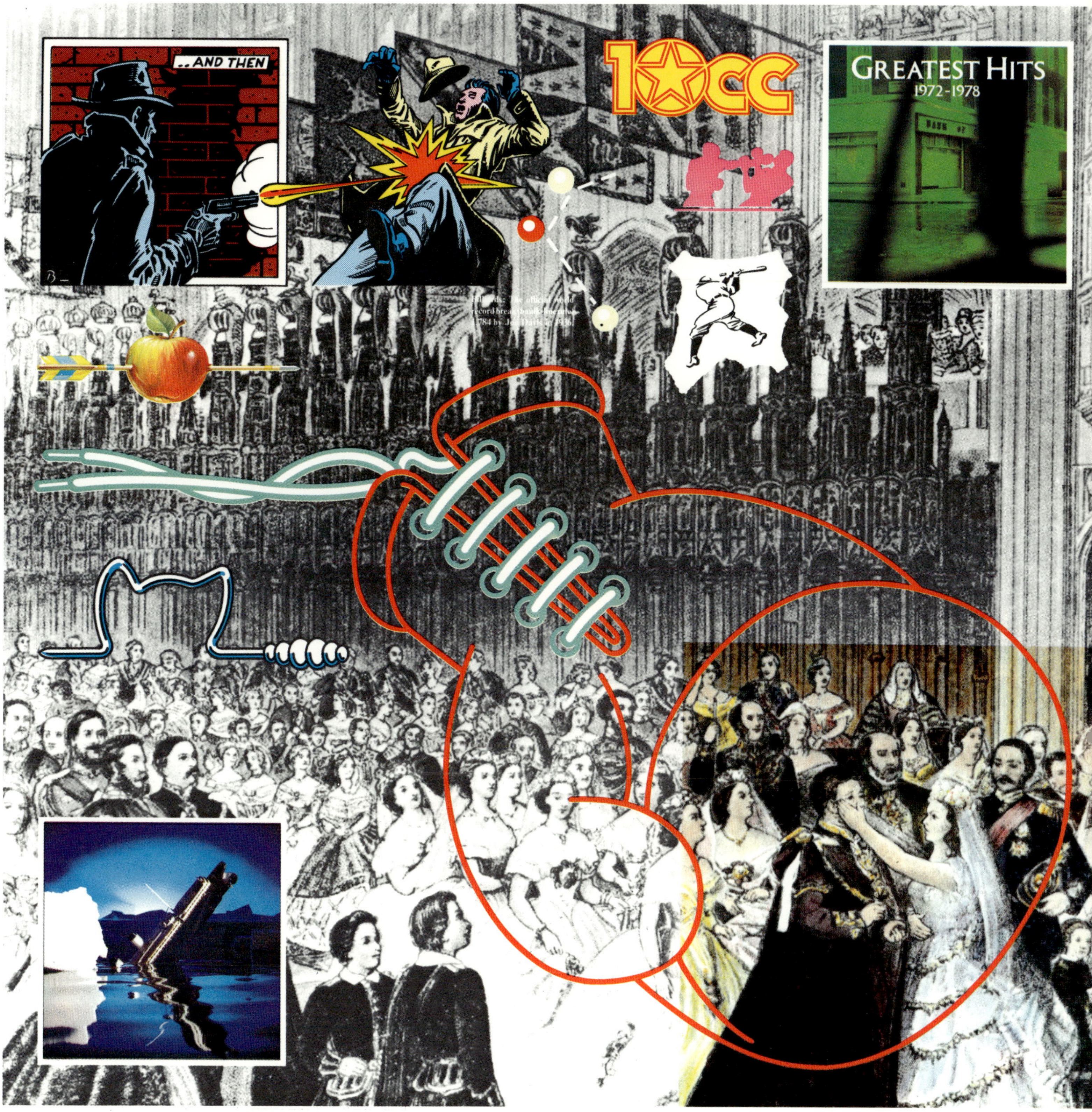
..AND THEN
10CC
GREATEST HITS
1972-1978

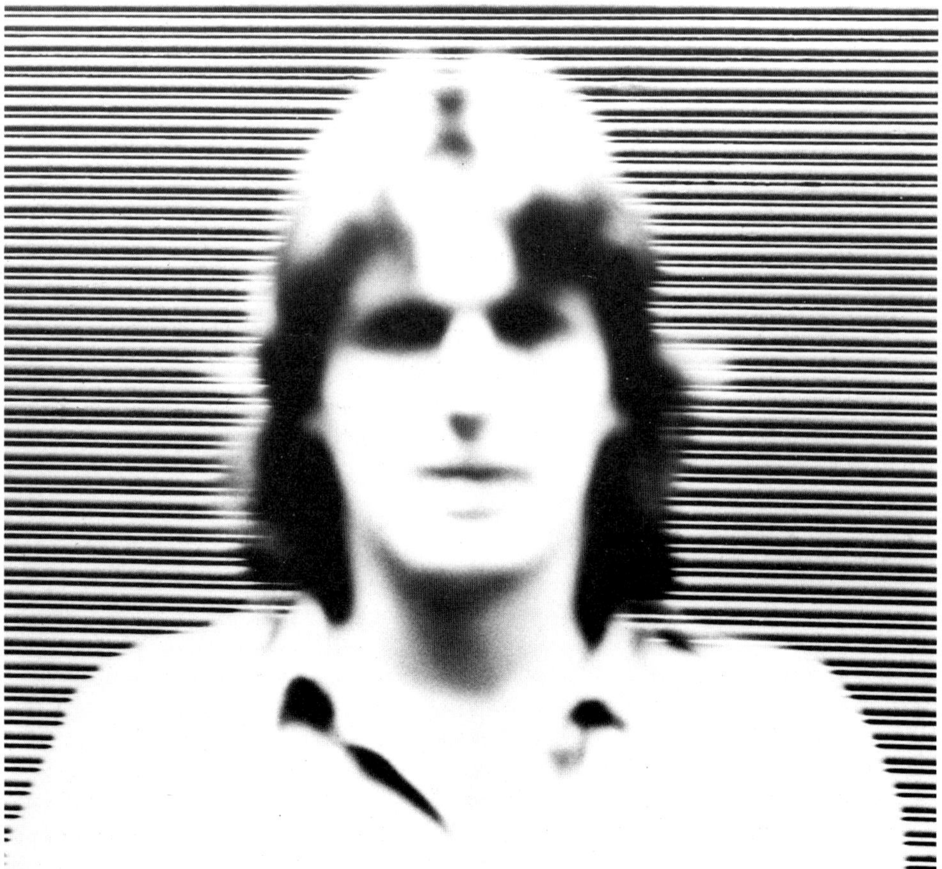

John Whetton Morning Routine

A little policy statement. We decided to let the pictures in this book breathe freely, to let them speak for themselves in an uncluttered way. Each page, or spread, was to have its own picture, just the one.

It seemed like a good idea until we got down to selecting the material. We wanted to include these two pieces, but without giving each a page to itself. So here they are, sharing the same spread, although they hardly know each other.

The photo of John Whetton was used for a single-record sleeve in 1981. It is an attempt to redefine portraiture, an attempt to find a different way of giving emphasis and character to the shape of a face. The rigid lines behind were chosen to accentuate the out-of-focus quality. I think the face belongs to John Whetton, but it's difficult to tell. I like the sunken pits that are his eyes, suggestive of character yet totally unclear. The black hole, in which everything disappears.

The breakfast routine speaks for itself. It was designed as part of a set of greeting cards which were supposed to explore the men-versus-women syndrome and to examine role-playing and stereotyped attitudes. The client, Ruby Street Graphics of New York, wanted us to make it amusing, but also accurate and just a little accusing. In this picture, designed by Po, and written by Peter and me, the relationship between the couple has deteriorated into a set of automatic cues and responses. Neither can face the other, nor face themselves. The bitter dialogue, largely unspoken, has reverberated round the room for so long that it has etched itself into the wall, like weird wallpaper. In fact, that's just the way we did it: we hired a sign-writer to paint the wall of a set in our studio.

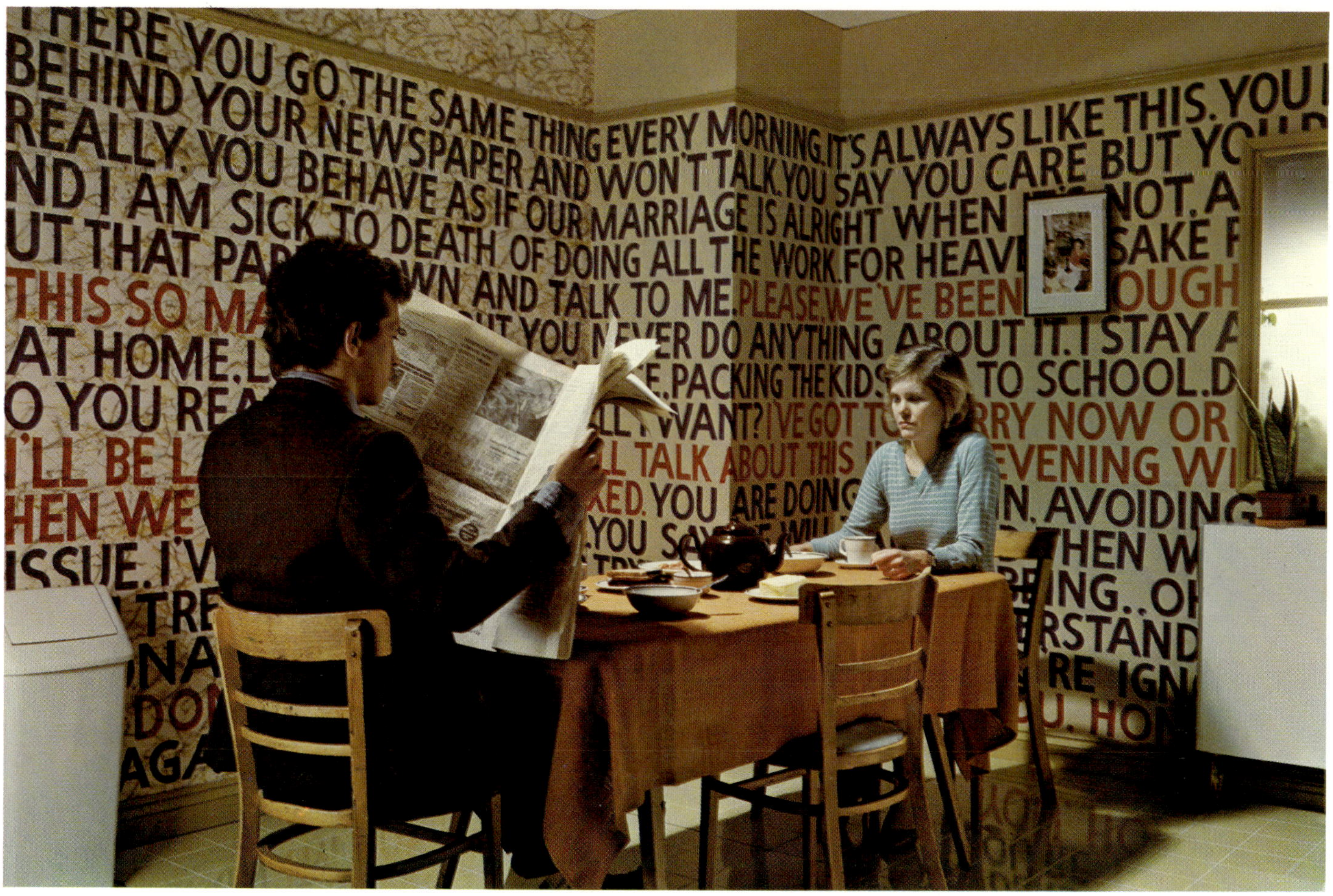
HERE YOU GO, THE SAME THING EVERY MORNING. IT'S ALWAYS LIKE THIS.
BEHIND YOUR NEWSPAPER AND WON'T TALK. YOU SAY YOU CARE BUT
REALLY. YOU BEHAVE AS IF OUR MARRIAGE IS ALRIGHT WHEN
I AM SICK TO DEATH OF DOING ALL THE WORK. FOR HEAV
SAKE
UT THAT PA
WN AND TALK TO ME. PLEASE, WE'VE BEEN
THIS SO MA
AT HOME.
YOU NEVER DO ANYTHING ABOUT IT. I STAY
PACKING THE KIDS
TO SCHOOL.
O YOU REA
I'VE GOT TO
RRY NOW OR
I'LL BE L
LL TALK ABOUT THIS
EVENING WI
HEN WE
YOU ARE DOING
AVOIDING
ISSUE. I'V
YOU SAY
HEN W
ING.. O
ERSTAND
RE IGN
U. HO
AGA

Led Zeppelin In Thru the Out Door

We decided to shoot flash and not tungsten to freeze the models. They might have tried too hard to keep still with the much longer exposures needed for tungsten. The bar is lit with approximately fourteen flash heads, each with separate pack – 28,000 joules in all. Hasselblad plus 50-mm lens, Plus-X, f22 at 1/60th.

This is a set. Po went to New Orleans to gather references for a bayou bar. The set was designed from these. It was built as a complete room so that we could shoot in any direction. We had one central figure, surrounded by six other people, and we photographed from each of their viewpoints. We chose to use a set rather than shoot on location because the lighting, the decor and the models could be better controlled. The relative costs seemed to be the same.

The entire contents are hired props. These were gathered over three weeks by Camilla Garret-Jones, and the set was designed in conjunction with Colin Andrews and Nick Pemberton. It took four weeks to design and one week to build. Lighting took a day and a half and the shooting took two solid days. A real back-breaker. It took just one day to strike. What a pity. Such a beautiful set. Downtown New Orleans to rubble and sawdust in twenty-four hours.

Careful B/W printing by Peter. Six angles, six prints to standardize. Then they were sepia toned. The brush stroke is obtained by using a clear acetate mask with a solid black brush stroke across it. Peter printed through this, removing the mask during exposure. The brush stroke therefore received less exposure and was paler than the rest. The exposure relationship between surround and brush stroke was the subject of many tests and arguments. We wanted the stroke to stand out, but not be so weak as to lose detail, nor the surround to go so dark that you couldn't see anything. Finally, the area in the brush stroke was hand-coloured with dyes. Mostly, of course, with a brush.

Led Zeppelin commissioned this piece for the cover of their LP 'In Thru the Out Door', released in 1980. Their brief was simple: they felt the album to be new, fresh and direct. They wanted the sleeve to indicate just this, nothing else.

This piece was specifically designed to the brief. The music had a barrel house, bayou-bar feeling to it: late-night blues laced with rock 'n' roll. Much more direct than some of their previous material. This gave us the location: Deep South, trailer park or bar. Atmospheric, yet real and intense. None of the cosmic inclinations suggested by the covers of 'Houses of the Holy' and 'Presence'. The downbeat bar, night people loitering, aimlessly drifting through the twilight. But Zeppelin had emphasized freshness, a positive approach like, say, a new lick of paint. So, over this sweaty old bar scene is an area wiped clean, like a duster across a neglected window, or a sweep of colour across a white wall. Remember the beginning of Disney's 'True-Life Adventures', where an enormous brush paints in the world, stroke by stroke?

The central figure burns a message from a friend. The others watch, but without any great interest. The drunk fumbles for his wallet, the piano player plays on. We purposely concentrated on the atmosphere. No single dramatic event or hint of unreality. Just people in a bar.

The actual packaging of this sleeve comprised six variations from the six viewpoints. The liner bag had a B/W design which carried coloured ink that could be released by applying water, or even spittle. The idea was from Jimmy Page. He said the brush stroke on the front reminded him of those children's books where this effect was produced. The whole cover was wrapped in an ordinary brown bag, suggested by Peter Grant in accordance with an old record company executive's maxim: 'If the group is big, it don't matter what the cover is. You can wrap it in a brown paper bag! It makes no difference to sales.' So we did. And it didn't.

'It doesn't matter what this sleeve was as it was hidden by a brown paper bag. As a result it didn't sell particularly well because the punters are so dumb they don't realize what the album is.' (Keith Johnson – HMV, London)

'A multi-layered atmosphere of seedy gloom and despondency, resembling the art of a Kienholz construction. Beautifully styled, cast, constructed and photographed, containing a story line one can only wonder at. The main character, low on spirit, is locked elsewhere, hopelessly oblivious to all. He is pulled out of the visual commotion by use of the pale smear across that area of the photograph – or is that meant to say something? A clean start? Washed out? Wiped out? Perhaps simply to add a strong graphic element. Either way, the whole thing is a real feast – the business cards and photos on the wall, the bottles, radio, lighting, characters, etc. What is he burning, and why?' (Bush Hollyhead – Illustrator/designer)

'I didn't like the brown paper bag, and thought at first that the six angles on the bar were a touch of insanity. But in the end it worked a treat – all power to pomp.' (Robert Plant – Led Zeppelin)

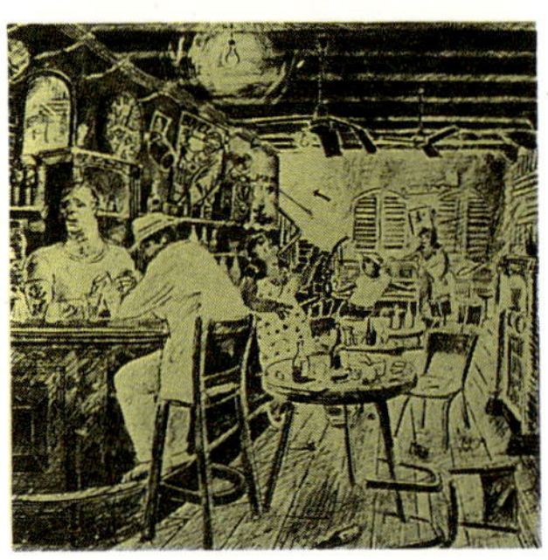

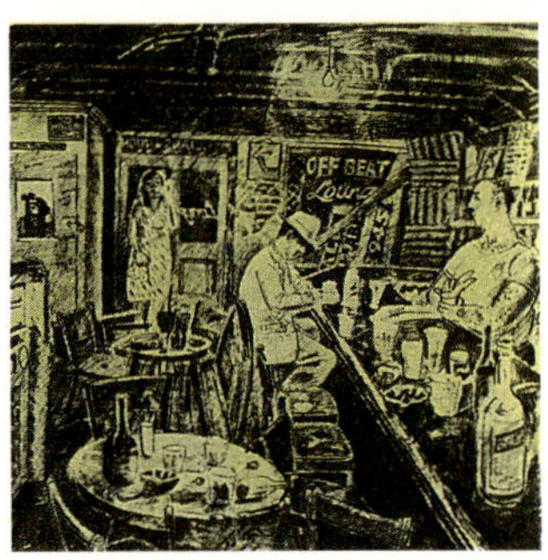

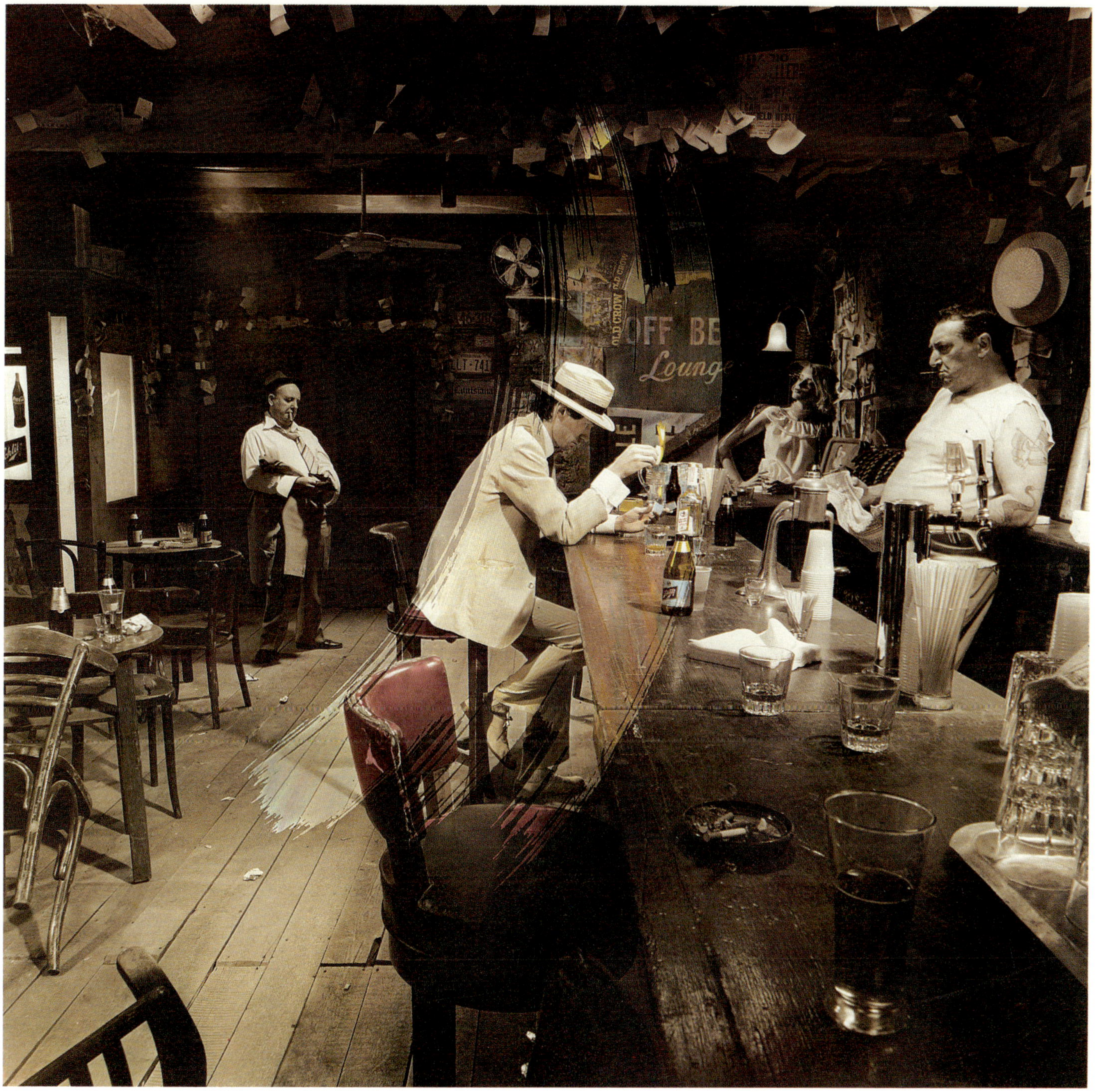
OLD CROW
OFF BE
Lounge

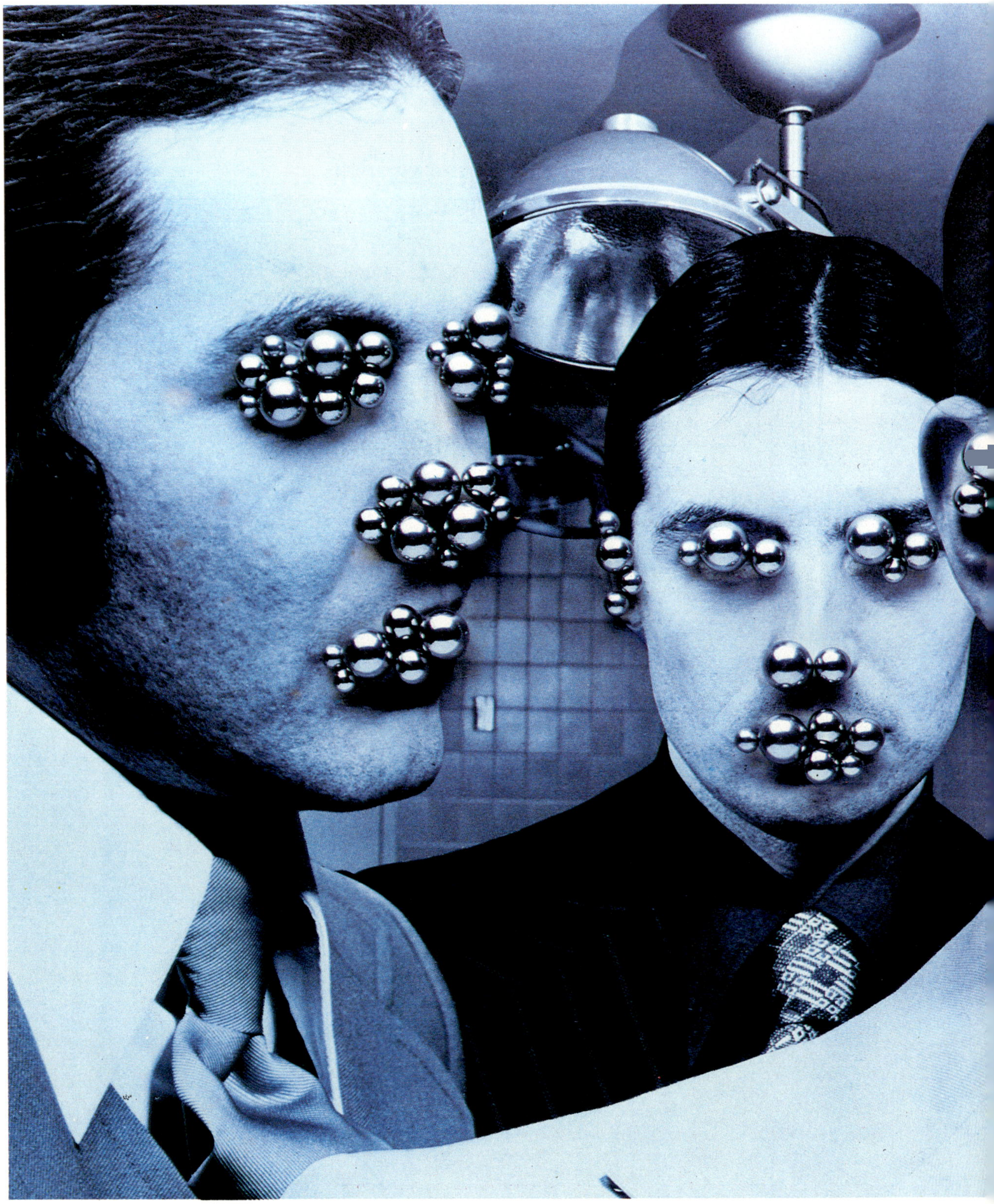

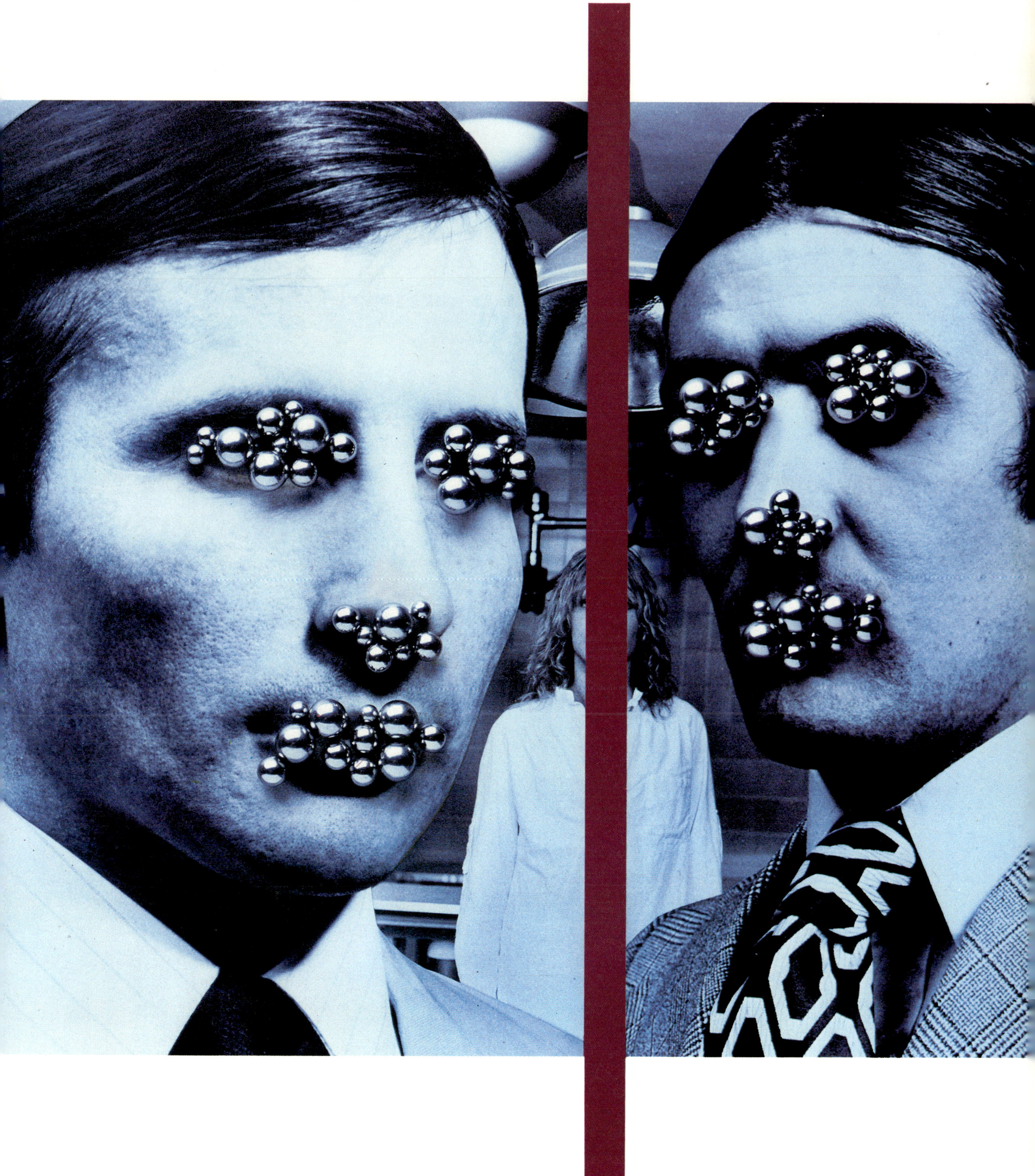

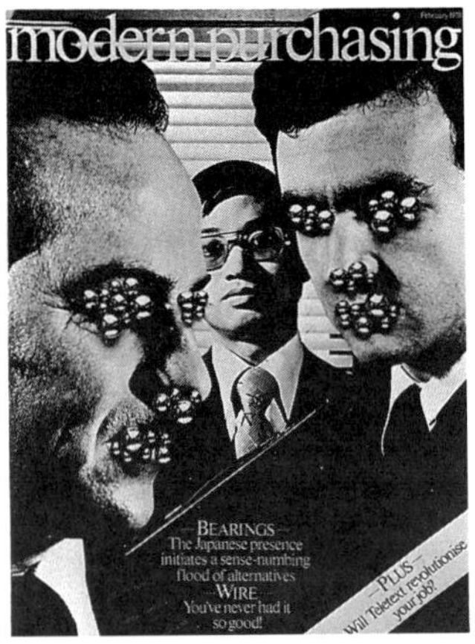

UFO Obsession

We used a Hasselblad with portrait lens, panning across the figures and taking two shots. It is lit with a fish-fry as top light and suitable reflector fill-in. The original is in B/W Tri-X, f16 at 1/60th. The copyprint is on 5/4 Sinar, using colour Ektachrome 64 ASA.

Po shot this picture in a Los Angeles hospital. The people are a heavy rock band called UFO. The suits were specially chosen as versions of those vulgar numbers American businessmen seem to favour. I sometimes feel that the entire American condition is illustrated by their sense of dress. There's a view that says you can learn all you need to know about America by sitting in a variety of hotel lobbies right across the land. That, and a weekend in Montana.

The clusters of ballbearings are arranged with great care on a B/W print of the band, and held in position by judicious use of double-sided Sellotape. A copy transparency is taken, lighting it so that the bearings show up clearly and cast very little in the way of shadows. The blue tint in the A/W is obtained by using colour film to copy B/W material, but the degree of colour is uncontrollable. We tried repeating the process but could never achieve the same steely-blue result. Some imponderable question about the mixture of daylight flash, exposure time and film development, which we didn't have the patience to solve. Techniques interest us in so far as they are aids to the successful realization of our designs and no more. What do you think we are, dilettantes?

UFO were well known to us, and their manager gave us the brief over the phone from Los Angeles. He wanted the band featured on the cover this time, but he said he wanted them to look bizarre. The band used it for an album called 'Obsession' in 1979.

We revamped an idea I'd had for the front of a marketing magazine. The magazine's lead story concerned the flooding of the European ballbearing market by the Japanese. UFO did not object to the previous usage so long as it looked all right. 'I mean,' said the manager wisely, 'how many fucking people are going to read "Marketing Today"?'

We left Michael Schenker without bearings as if the rest of the band were consultants at some very sinister hospital, discussing why Michael was not afflicted as they were.

The other idea expressed here is concerned with lack of communication and a blocking of all the senses. The nose, eyes, ears and mouth are submerged below what looks like metal fungi. Perhaps an alien strain that seeks out the atmospheric waves that flow to and from the sense organs. On the other hand, these fungi could be aids to good communication, heightening the reception of incoming stimuli, like the Babel fish in 'The Hitch-Hiker's Guide to the Galaxy'.

'Lovely sleeve. Reflects the band's image, and at least someone bothered to put the name and title in clearly. Looks wonderful in displays.' (Keith Johnson – HMV, London)

'This was one of the first album covers where we desperately wanted the group on the front, and when Storm and Po actually agreed, little did we know what form it was to take. Entering the rear door to the University of Los Angeles and being directed to the Animal Surgery (dissecting, of course), we knew somehow it would be very different from the teen idol picture we had envisaged. So, with our hair slicked back, and rented suits, we had one of the funniest photo sessions of our career. With the finished work which was completed after the session, we managed to produce one of the most strikingly different album covers we have ever had and, to this day, it remains one of my favourites. I can still remember Michael Schenker asking, very innocently, why he had no balls.' (Phil Mogg – UFO)

Nightfall

Hasselblad 500C, 120-mm lens, f11 at 1/60th, flashlit one head through slatted mask to give shadowing on background. Plus-X treated normally. Or tungsten lit with three pups: one for source light, one for background, and one for fill with heavy trace and set farther back. Some things wo don't remember.

The doll and the toys are from junk shops. The eyes belong to our ex-secretary Judy. Our studio doubles as a Victorian attic. The place looks pretty cluttered anyway. In fact, Susan Hill, who is responsible for Vermilion and for the publishing of this book, didn't actually believe that Hipgnosis could work in such decrepit surroundings. She went away and rang back to verify. When she returned she spent most of the first interview eyeing the peeling decor. She later called it 'recession chic'. We meet at the publisher's place now. But she's a girl in Vermilion.

This is another theatre poster designed for Lumiere & Son to publicize a particular production of theirs. It was a play called 'Nightfall'. It's in B/W because of the economics of a fringe theatre troupe. Dave said the play concerned a gaggle of bizarre characters who live in beach huts. Every so often, a plane flies overhead at night and drops dolls on them. The characters think the dolls are very special and they decide to show their respect by performing strange rituals. These gradually become emptier and emptier, the communication between the characters becomes more and more brittle. A climax is reached amid a frenzied ritual, ending in a violent stripping away of illusion and the veneer of pretence.

This was designed in sympathy with the gist of the play as far as we were able to understand it. There is the nighttime mood, the attic and lengthening shadows, the aeroplane and the toy doll. This discarded plaything, sitting eerily in the half light, looks wide awake as though a human nature were trapped inside the inanimate shell. Things are not what they seem, and in fact very few people, when asked, know what is odd about the picture.

'Couldn't work out why this image had the haunting effect it did. Maybe it seemed refreshing in the context of Hipgnosis's work to encounter a straightforward image. No tricks, simply a medium interesting mix of airplane and doll. Whilst wondering how and why they had been so restrained with the plane, I saw it! They'd done it again: those blinking eyes! And is that another eye in the background, to the right of the ear, or is it a happy accident?' (Bush Hollyhead – Illustrator/designer)

'A brief brief. Aeroplanes drop rag dolls on an isolated community – adults infantilized by aviators. I admired the *limpid* eyes peering from the porcelain but what of the darker one glimpsed gazing from the gloom beneath? Is it meant or figment? Is it cement or froment?' (Dave Gale)

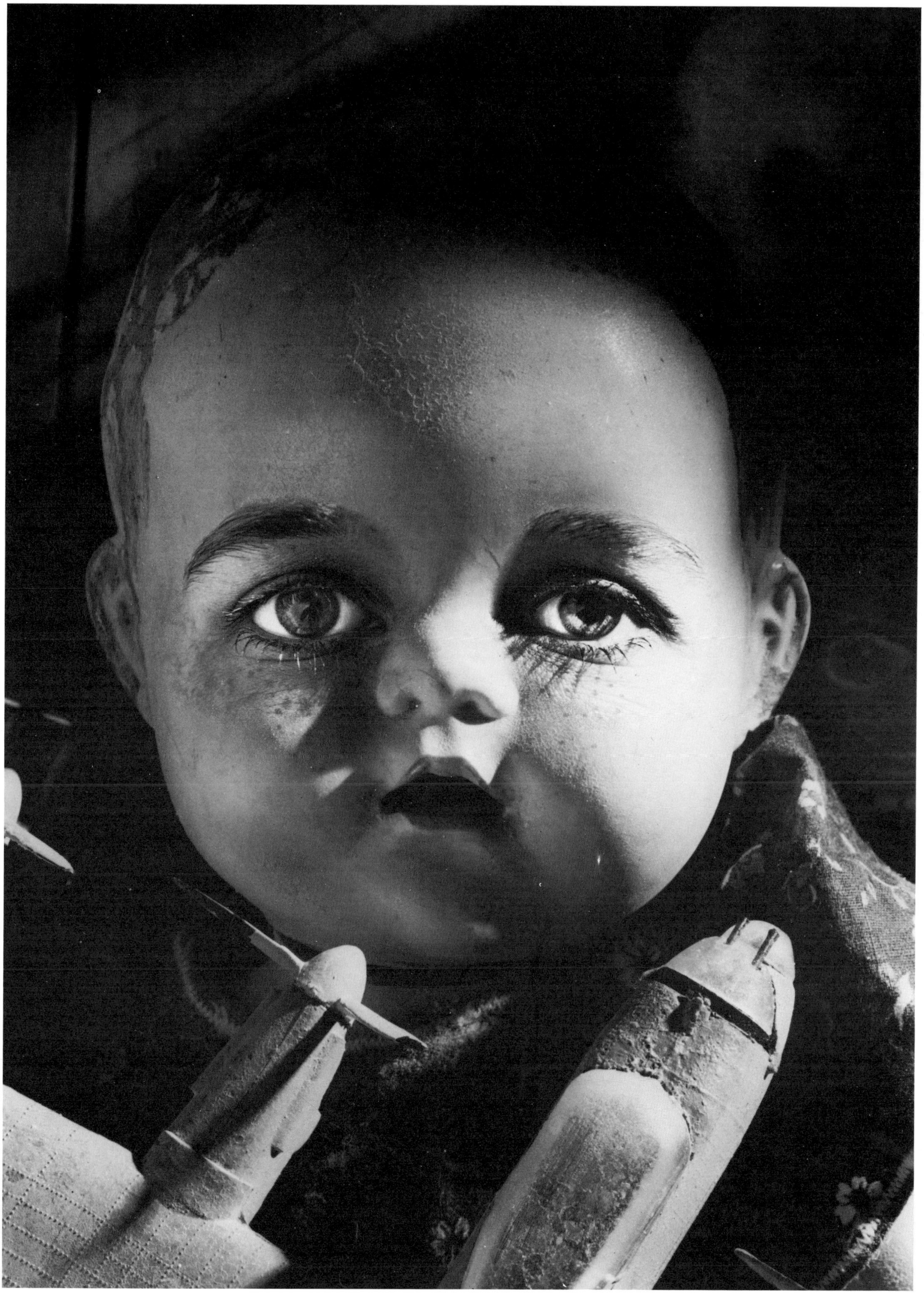

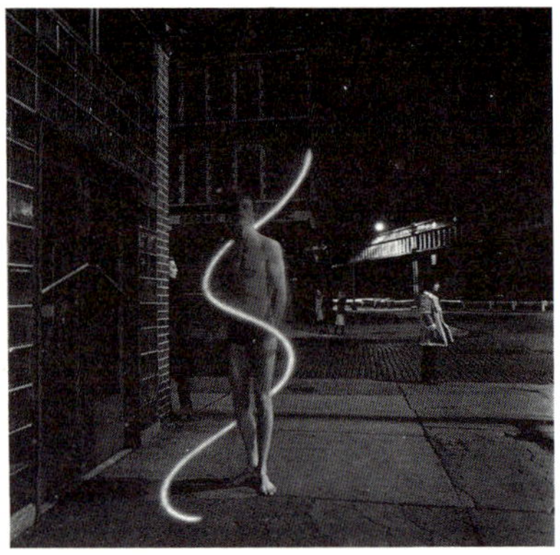

GGK Austria

Photographed on Hasselblad with W/A 50-mm lens and daylight Ektachrome uprated half a stop. Shot by available light and Chromafilter. The location is in Austria. The people are musicians from a Viennese musicians' agency and the instruments are their own. The time was 4 p.m. and the weather was dreadful.

A dye transfer print was produced from the selected 2¼-inch transparency and Richard Manning retouched the neon shapes. First he bleached away the background and then sprayed on the dye of the preferred colour. Finally, he bleached 'light' shadows on the ground and gave the neon shapes a brighter vignetted edge to achieve luminosity.

This picture was for 'A World Atlas of Music', and represents Austria, which Polygram recognized as a place with a great heritage of classical music. Although this 'classicism' was extended and updated to meet the demands of the present era, Polygram felt that it was never entirely abandoned.

I think the design was chosen by the client because he felt it was panoramic, very elegant and had the right blend of tradition and contemporary invention. The musicians are making beautiful music and the neon flourishes are an attempt to represent these sounds visually. The shapes relate to the instruments and the shape of their respective sounds. We thought they worked for the composition as a whole, as well as for the individual instruments and the postures of the various musicians. The setting is an Austrian country palace. It reminds me of 'Last Year in Marienbad', when the guests, dressed in tuxedos and evening gowns, stood motionless along the great path in front of the hotel, casting shadows in different directions.

Po once had an idea for a room in which all of the furniture was edged in neon: the chairs, the table, even the skirting board and picture rail had neon strips defining their shapes. When you turned off the main light but left the neon on, your room turned into a Hipgnosis photodesign. Quel horreur!

Our first experiment with neon was a recent sleeve for an electronic band called Synergy, fronted by Larry Fast, wizard of the synthesizer and occasional musician with Peter Gabriel. We imagined an article of clothing for humans in the distant future, which comprised a simple band of energy. It could hover close to the person 'wearing' it, warming and protecting him. Its shape and length could be altered, controlled by his amazing telepathic powers. It could also be an indicator of his state of mind or his feelings. It could be a means of communication. It could also be a weapon. We called it the Stym.

'I'm usually bored by lines on photos because they tend to be used for decoration and fashion rather than meaning. These lines, although they've no literary meaning, seem to express the abstract and emotional qualities of classical music rather well.' (George Hardie – Designer)

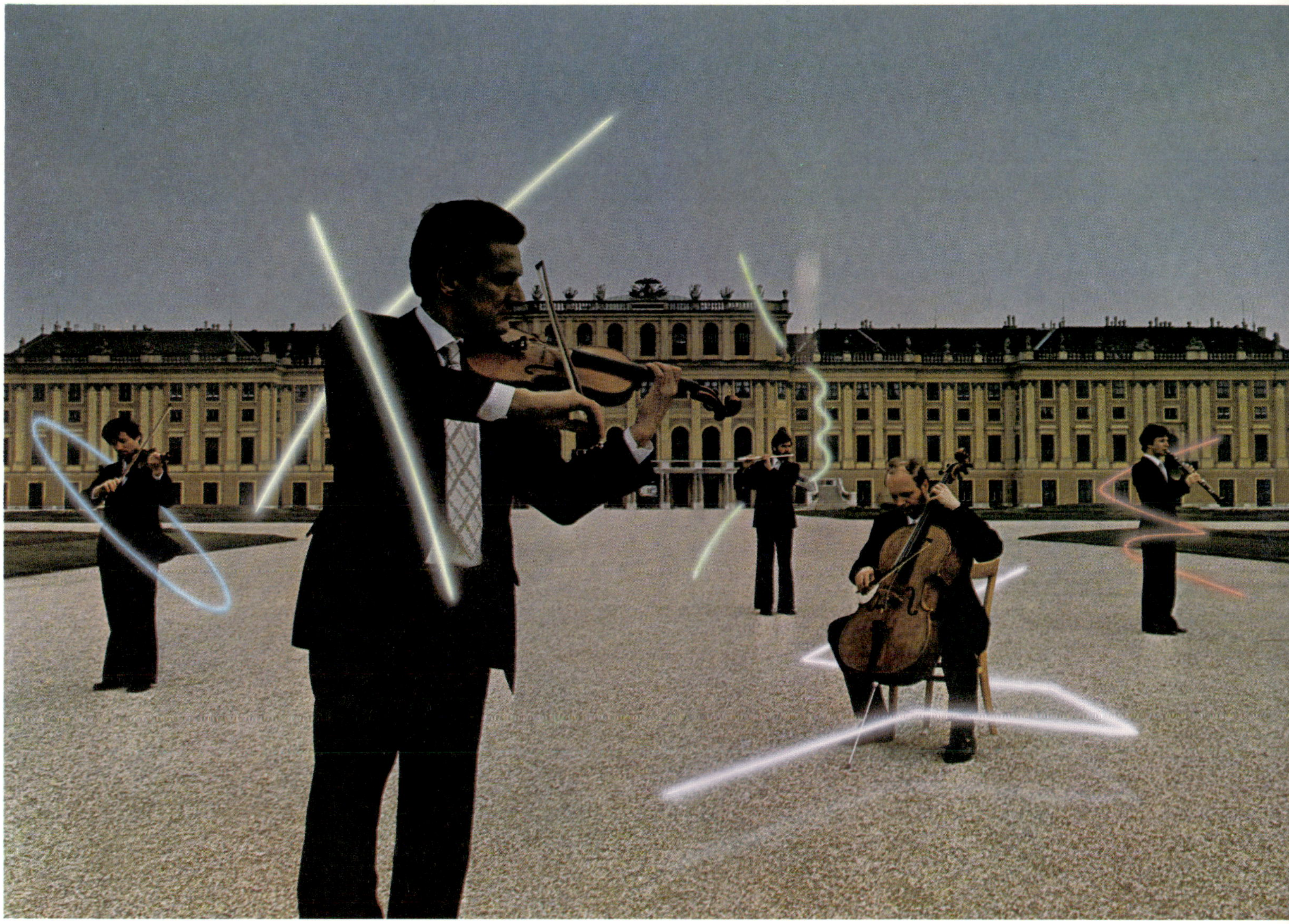

Jean Pool and Tilt

A nighttime shoot with the Hasselblad (they should pay *us* for all this plugging!), 50-mm W/A, Tri-X, and one handflash directed at the pool. It bounced off and lit the bushes beyond. The man with sextant is taken in the studio against a window with flash, which meant balancing the exposure between this and daylight.

Cozy Powell is a straight B/W photoprint. The poster on the opposite page is a collage of two prints, the sextant photo cut into strips and stuck down. If it was not immediately apparent, you will now understand that these pictures are testament to the wisdom of shooting a variety of alternatives when on location, either in the wilds of the British countryside or in the Mojave Desert.

The collage is a poster for the theatre group Lumiere & Son. It was used to advertise a play called 'Jean Pool' in 1980. David Gale of Lumiere & Son described the play over the phone as a bizarre detective story. 'You know me,' he said, 'it ain't a straight narrative thing. More a trail of unconscious clues into the psyche. The detective is trying to locate his position, charting unknown seas, searching for signposts.' The sextant is a water instrument, relating to the pool. This is the Pool of the title and the jeans are the Jean of the title. Jean Pool. Sounds silly. It *is* silly, but still gives the image a thriller flavour. Who has been killed and left floating in the pool?

Cozy Powell wanted something unfussy, and our only instructions were to avoid anything overmeaningful: 'Don't want any of that old complicated Hipgnosis stuff.' I'm not sure, but I think he liked the starkness of the image and its rock 'n' roll connotations: stoned nights by the hotel swimming pool, and too much of absolutely everything.

The 'Jean Pool' poster is a re-exploration of a theme: the dual-image statement (cf. Voyager, page 37). It sometimes seems necessary to express a narrative idea with two pictures: in this case, the protagonist observing the clues, and the crime itself. The cut strips were a way of suggesting that one image emerges from the other. It is, in effect, a hard-edged version of a superimposition. We estimated that the viewer's eyes would wander in and out of the two photographs, which is why one is framed by the other, and why one becomes dominant at the top (of the strips), only to be superseded by the 'border' of the other. I think we expected that it might have that dreamlike quality of images continually drifting in and out of each other. The strips were thought to be a graphic presentation attractive in itself, somewhat like the slats in a blind through which the scene outside is only vaguely glimpsed. Clues to a picture which can take shape if you change your focus. Blinds and slatted light also felt relevant to the detective genre.

The Cozy Powell cover is presented like a piece of magazine journalism, where a startling picture is punctuated by a piece of very strong type. We envisaged it as an exposé. There should be, in fact, an accompanying text on the opposite page, telling you how and why a figure was found floating, perhaps dead, in the pool at night. The directness of the picture and the words together are designed to pull you into the text to read the story. There is a tale to tell, but in this instance you'll have to make it up for yourself.

'Jean Pool is a woman detective of elegance and enigma. Imagine my surprise when he produced a snap of a pair of jeans in a pool.

' "Do you see what it is?" he inquired.

' "I'm afraid I do," I replied.

' "What do you think?" he sought.

' "It is daring. It is modern. For me that is enough," I returned.' (Dave Gale)

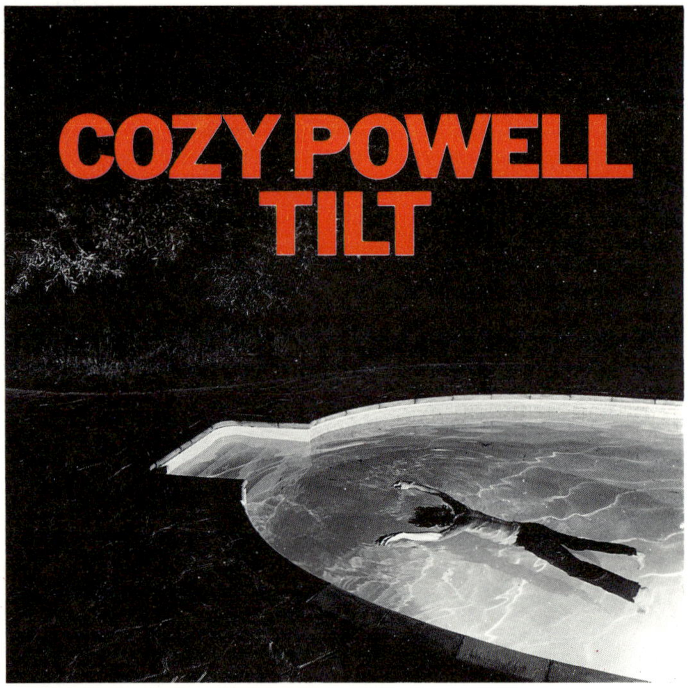

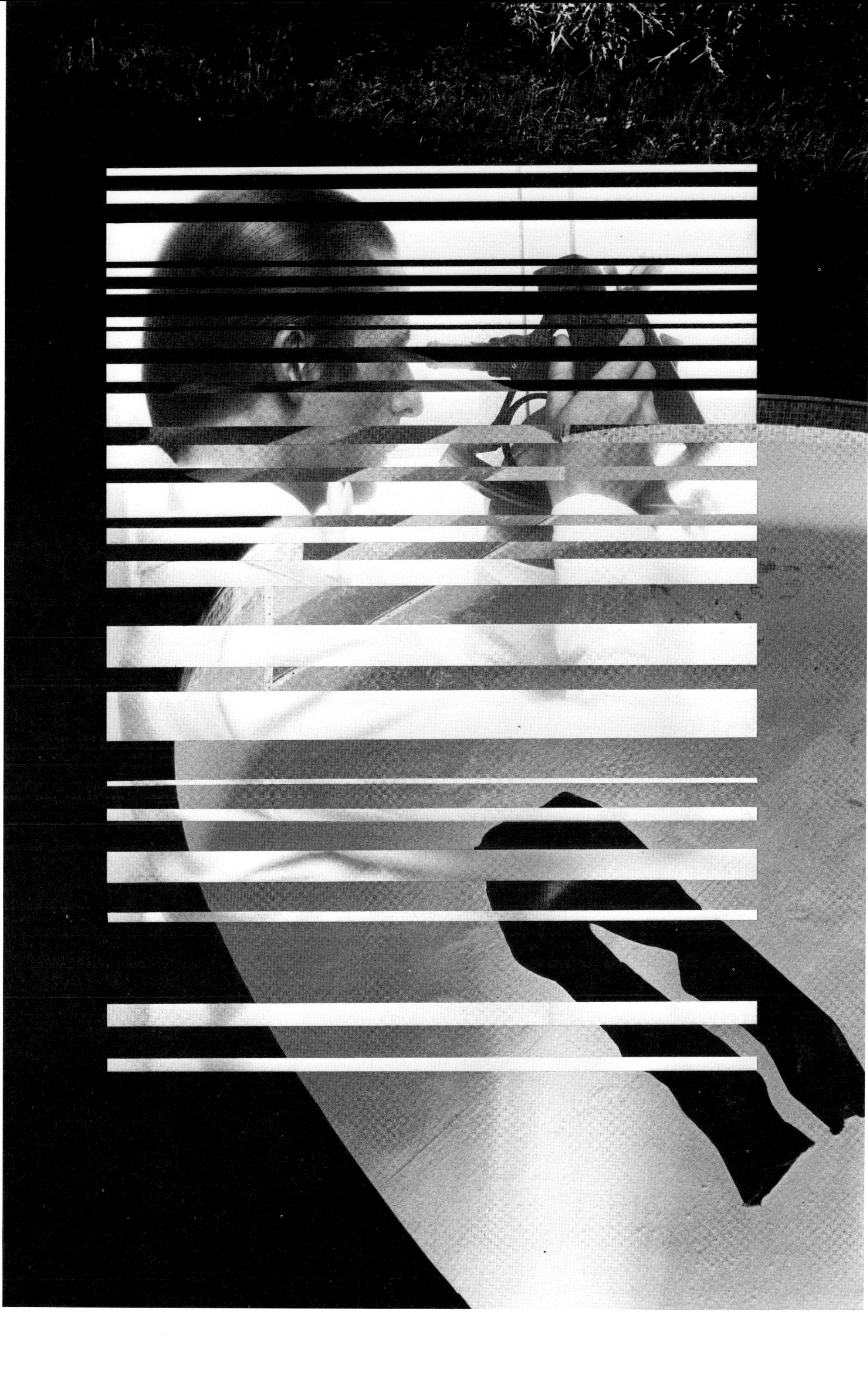

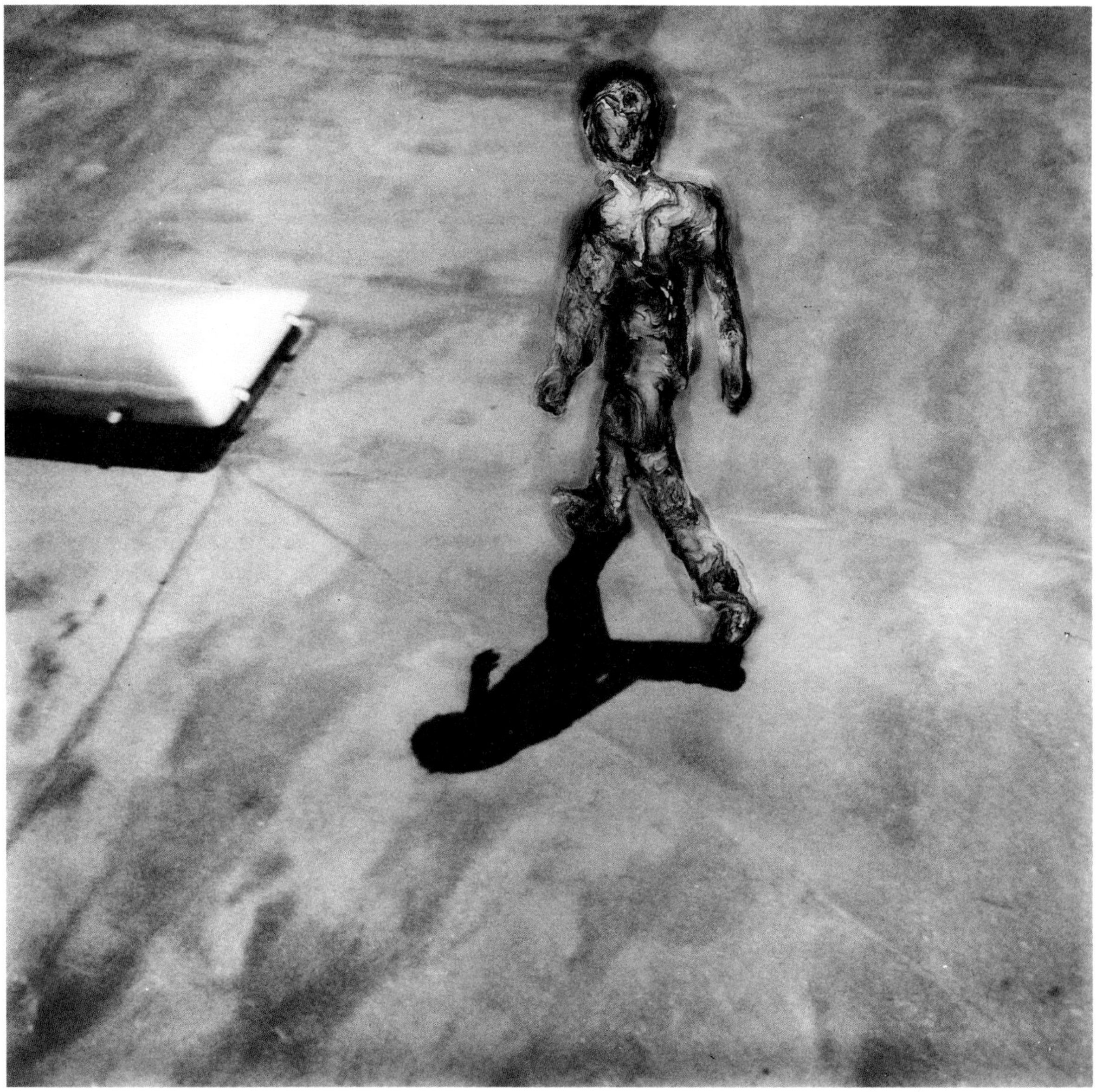

Peter Gabriel Charismagraph

Initial pictures were taken with Polaroid camera using SX70 film. The developing film is then disturbed and rephotographed using a copy camera. On page 116 is a B/W copy. On the subsequent page is a direct enlargement of the original colour Polaroid.

Peter Gabriel, one-time singer of Genesis, is the figure in the close-ups, but not in the midshot. The locations are in the Hipgnosis studio stairwell and on a local rooftop.

The disturbance of SX70 is possible because the developing chemicals are sandwiched between an opaque backing and a transparent front. As the Polaroid develops, you can apply pressure to the transparent front covering and shift the chemical reaction going on underneath. Different degrees of pressure and different instruments (pen, pencil tip, fingernail, old screw, edge of coin, etc.) will give different effects. The extent of disturbance is dependent on how long pressure is applied during development. There comes a moment when the chemical reactions are over and the positive image is fixed and further changes are hard to achieve. Variations in temperature also affect the process, specifically in colour formation. In fact, anything from spilled alcohol to electric sparks may disturb a developing Polaroid and produce unexpected results.

This Polaroid technique is quite widely known and was pioneered by Les Krims. Our attempts were geared to taking it out of the Polaroid context – by gross enlargement

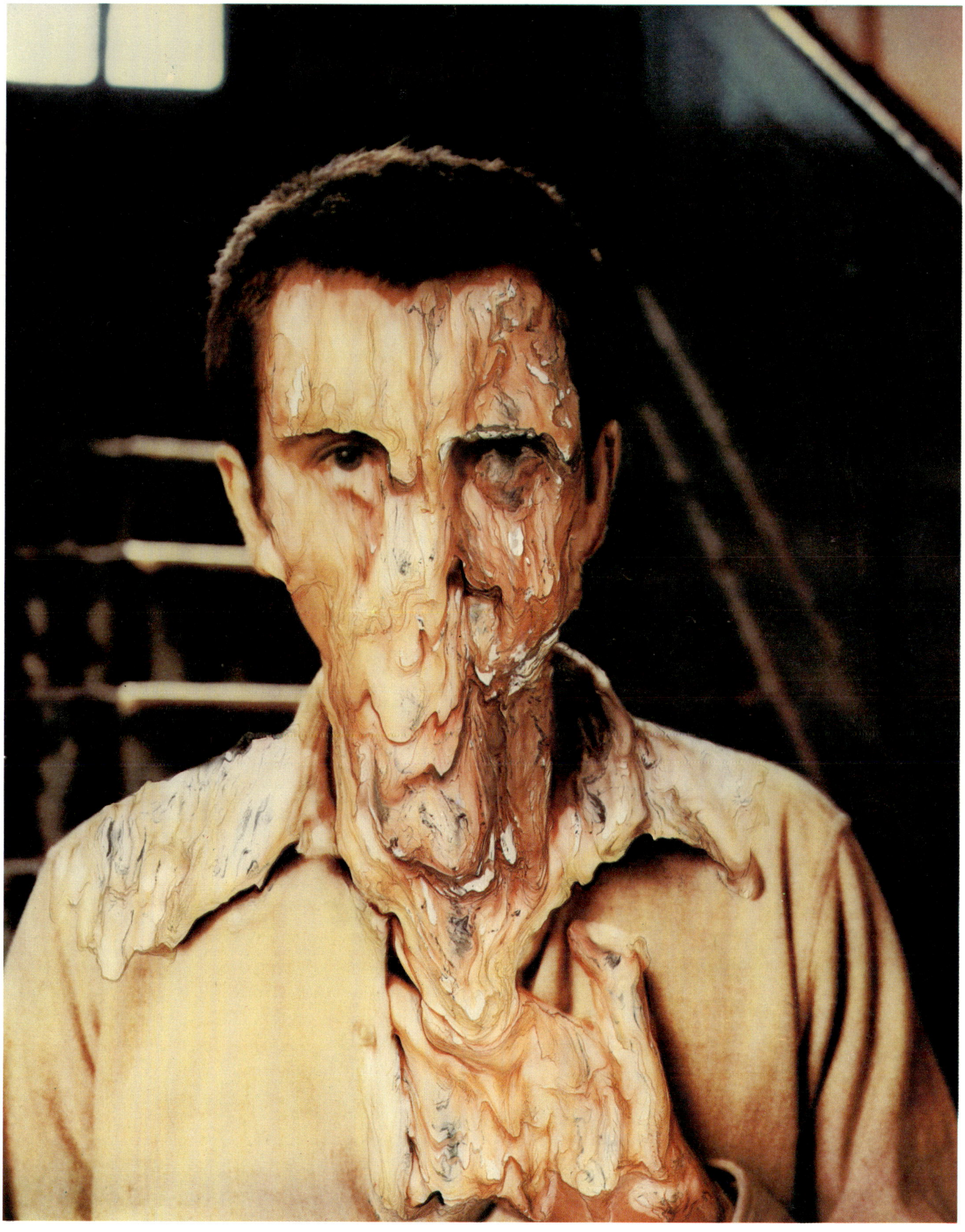

and changing to B/W – and to making it fit a specific idea.

⌧ Peter Gabriel used this material for his third album, released in 1980. He came to see us but I don't remember what he said. I think we discussed the deeper meaning of life or the design of the gas cooker, and referred only obliquely to his album cover.

○ Many years ago we tried to simulate movement in the photographic emulsion in an effort to suggest that the image had melted and begun to slip down the print. We tried heating a glass plate negative but it failed miserably. Les Krims's experiments with SX70 gave us a simple method of arriving at our melted look.

These pictures were inspired by a dream. I saw Peter as a character from a horror/psychological movie, his face dripping as if it were made of wax. I had him encased in a fragile bamboo cage. I also saw a set of superimposed images to his right, in some way representing his thoughts.

We kept the main part of this nightmare (would *you* like to dream about your clients?) and dispensed with the peripheral bits.

The central motif, the liquid face, is very like the paintings by Francis Bacon. The SX70 seemed a good way of arriving at a particular approach to photography. In addition, Peter Gabriel was one of the few rock 'n' roll luminaries who would put up with such disfigurement. And bless his cotton socks for that.

< 'In the third album, when it came out, Peter's "melted" face was everywhere: on the buses, huge posters in the street, etc., and I think that this very strong image, combined with his music, helped it to sell so well. The music is the most important ingredient, but a strong sleeve is also important. If I saw an interesting sleeve in a pile of records, I'd put it on to hear what it was like. I wouldn't buy it because I never buy records anyway.' (Gail Colson – Manager of Peter Gabriel)

'I think of all the things that Hipgnosis have done for me, these images are the best. Storm rang up to announce he'd had a dream and I feared this might confirm his reputation as an acid casualty. As he spoke of dripping flesh and the meaning of his mission in life, I became captivated and another great piece of merchandising material found the mark.

'Playing with all the Polaroids was FUN, FUN, FUN. Everyone involved in the shooting was having a go at messing up the pictures. I remember long arguments about which of the many distorted faces to use. The poster with all the outtakes and Storm's rude comments is still my favourite. Some of the images for ads use distortions in much the same way as Francis Bacon does in paint.' (Peter Gabriel)

Polaroid Containment

⌧ This is shot with Hasselblad and W/A using Tri-X, on location in London. And, of course, Polaroid. The A/W is a complex mixture of collage – girl and Polaroid on background – and doubleprinting – ghosted man in background.

○ Wipe away a tear, for this is another rejected design. We decided to include more unpublished material in this book than we did in the last. *The client is not always right.* **Call me irresponsible, but I'd love to have this inscribed on the front door of every advertising agency in town.**

Yuming, the Japanese singer, called her album something like 'Meet You Last Evening' (see pages 34–5). Future and past tenses are at odds, but the Japanese frequently use this phrase when considering the ambiguity and paradox of life. We mulled this over. Contradiction and conundrum. Plenty of scope here. But we decided to restrict ourselves to photographs and two dimensions only.

I was reminded of an episode of 'Sapphire and Steel' that I'd liked. In the series, a couple of aliens (in human form, of course) had been dispatched to earth in order to report any other alien phenomena. They had extraterrestrial powers. In one story they became heavily involved with a mysterious twilight figure who existed only in the world of photography. He could pass from photograph to photograph, reappearing within the 2-D world, visible to us only when he was 'occupying' an actual photograph. In between the photos was a dangerous, uncharted region through which he travelled at great speed. The character was intent on sucking victims into his 2-D existence and freezing them in photographs. He would add them to photographs that already existed and from which, once included, they could not escape. Very sinister stuff! I was enthralled. I wish I'd thought of it. A 2-D world that an entity could glide around in. I think of all the many photos of the world he could explore. Is he in this book?

Peter took the idea of being trapped in a 2-D world and married it with a belief expressed in some cultures that the camera steals souls. Tribes, as far apart as New Guinea and the American West, who had seen cameras or photographs only briefly, were sometimes very distrustful, if not terrified. So, the woman takes a photo of her friend, and unexpectedly he is sucked from our 3-D world into the 2-D world of the Polaroid. He reacts as if suddenly entrapped, pushing frantically against the sides, trying to break out. He didn't know it was coming, for he had been standing in a quite relaxed pose. His soul has been stolen.

Either it will teach him not to trust his girlfriend or to remember that they don't make Polaroids like they used to.

< 'Soul stealers for the stars? Deep in the vaults of 6 Denmark Street is the Hipgnosis collection of nail parings and hair clippings.' (George Hardie – Designer)

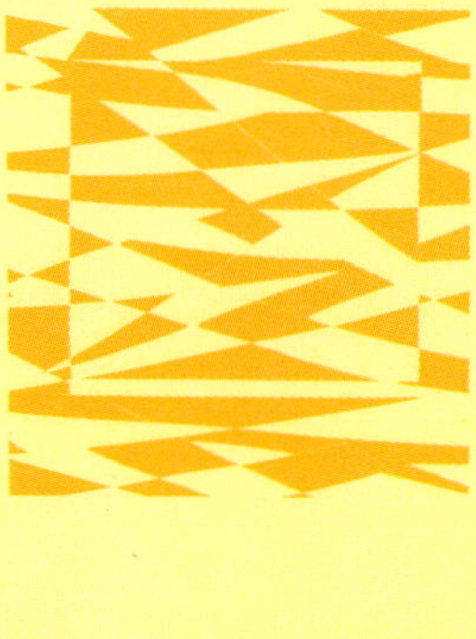

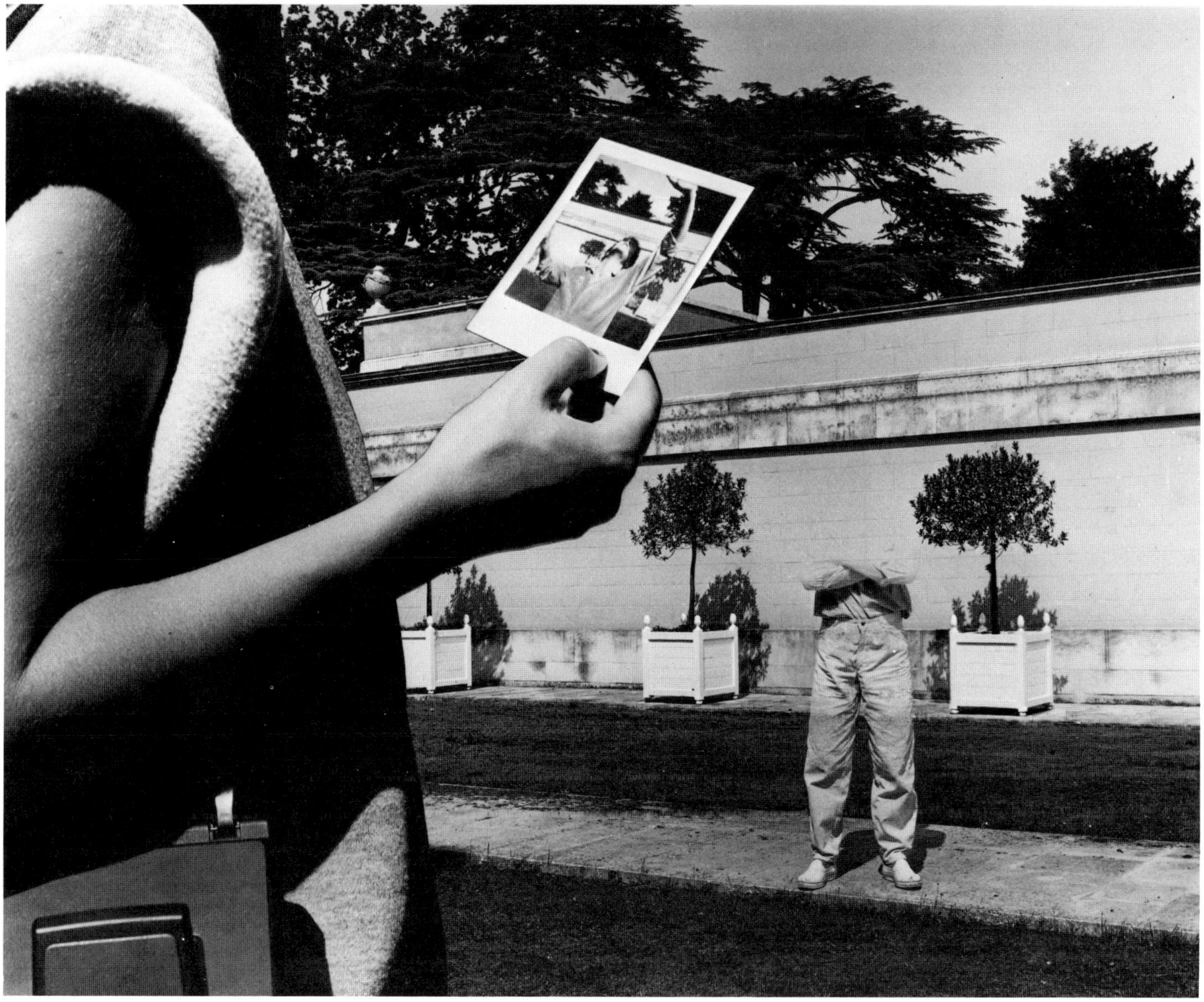

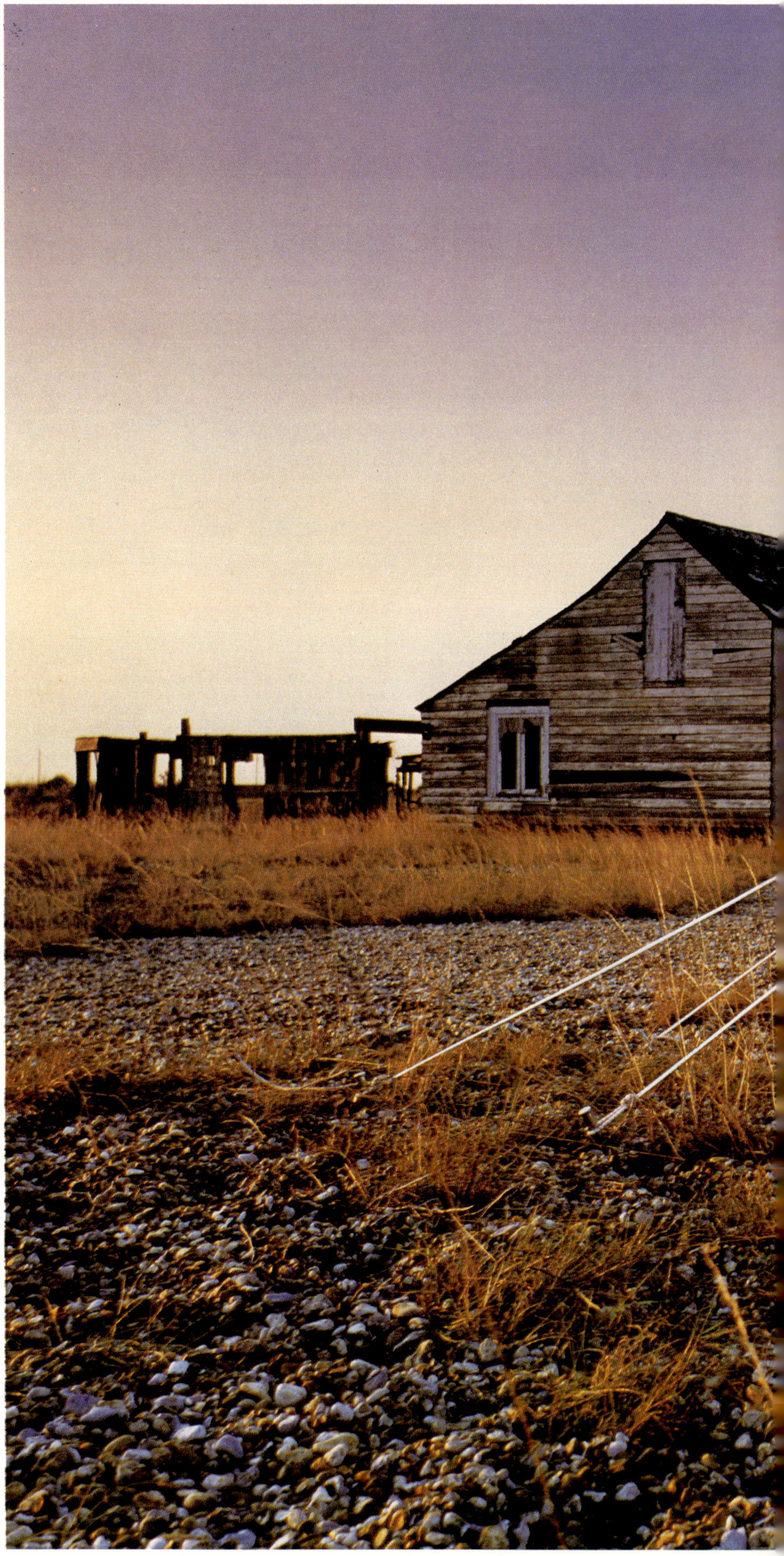

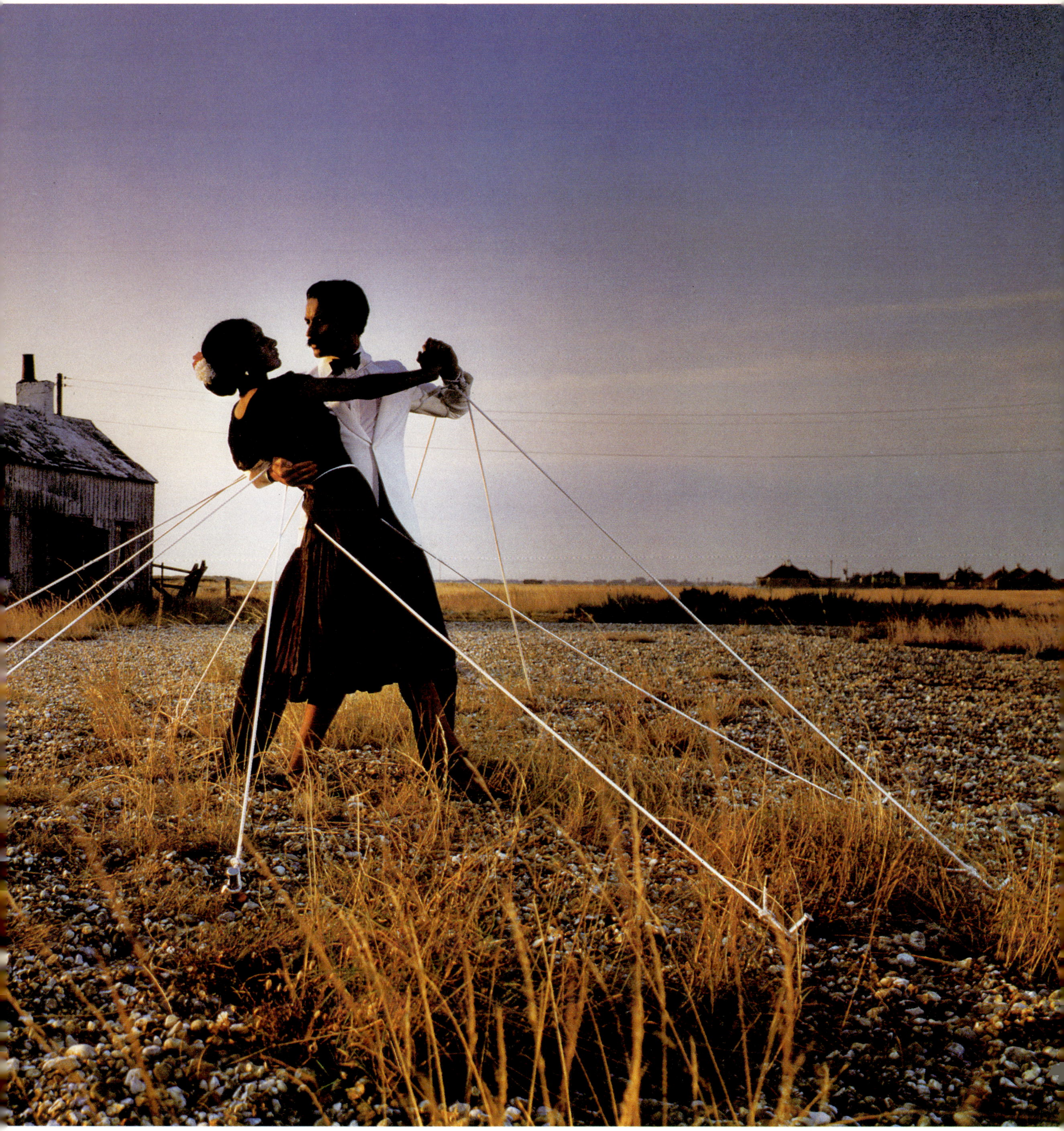

Pink Floyd A Collection of Great Dance Songs

The photograph is taken with Pentax 6/7, using daylight Ektachrome uprated half a stop, f16 at ⅛th. Available light plus Chromafilter to add colour to the sky. Evening time.

The location is a favourite of ours and it's in England. At Dungeness, on the south coast, there are the remains of a deserted shanty town of wooden fishing huts and dilapidated boat sheds.

We did tests for this in a park in London, which turned out to be crucial since we used ordinary white rope. This proved impossible to keep taut when the couple adopted a flowing dance pose. It was the male model, Peter Jessup, who suggested that we use elastic rope. As they turned in their tango, they pulled the ropes tight.

The Pink Floyd used this for the cover of their compilation album in 1981. Nick Mason told me Columbia Records may have seen the Floyd's 'better output' as 'dancing material'. Another brick in the disco wall. But does anybody else agree? I doubt it, and so we introduced a touch of sarcasm and came up with 'A Collection of Great Dance Songs'. It was accepted by the Floyd, as much for its irrelevance as anything. What meaning has the cow on 'Atom Heart Mother'?

This piece was originally designed to illustrate the music of Argentina. Did I say Argentina. . .? At the time of writing (April 1982), a recent opinion poll has shown 82 per cent of the British public in favour of dispatching Britain's massive fleet to oust the Argentinian intruders from the Falkland Islands. The Empire Strikes Back. Teach Argentina a lesson or they will invade Anglesey. Britain will never allow armed aggression to succeed: that's the stated principle. And how, might our children ask, did we get the Empire in the first place? But as to the real reason for the Falklands conflict cynical thinking might suggest a diverting of attention from home affairs, or a foreign plot about wheat; slick thinking would suggest oil.

The brief mentioned the restrained passion in Argentinian music, unlike their football. Hence the dancers, full of movement, restrained by the ropes. It takes two to tango. It takes two to fight.

'As a sleeve it's OK, but a lot of people didn't associate it with Pink Floyd, especially mums and dads who were buying it as a Christmas present the time when it came out.' (Nick Turnbull – HMV, London)

'This is a picture of a Spanish salesman and his wife getting away from it all at their ethnic Sierra cottage. They are rehearsing their ballroom dancing for the company dinner whilst practising on a new Californian exercise machine. Alternatively, I suppose it could be a wry comment on life as one knows it, but then, who knows it?' (Jill Furmanovsky – Photographer)

'He was grovelling at my door and I felt that I just had to take his tatty old picture. Anyway it was so awful I thought I'd get it cheap. I've had a couple of beers . . . I remember now . . . I liked it because its funny and incongruous and because not many would, I think, see our music as dance songs. That sounds better, doesn't it?' (David Gilmour – Pink Floyd)

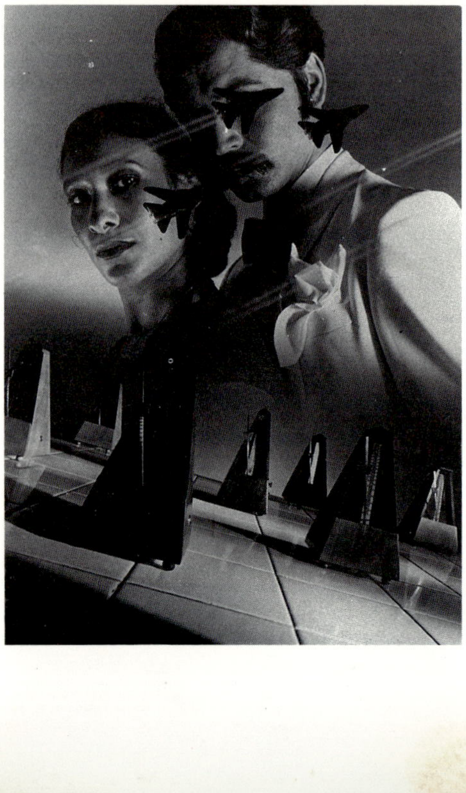

The Hanging

Photograph taken with Pentax 6/7, normal lens, daylight Ektachrome lit by hand flash. Gold surround done by John Harwood using something called schlaage which is like real gold leaf. Rope from Beales Yacht Chandlers.

The A/W begins with an R-type print made directly from the transparency. This print is then affixed to a piece of solid board. The area around the figure is prepared with a red base and the gold schlaage applied. This is executed (for want of a nicer expression) in sections. Sheets of gold are peeled off and then rolled down onto the background. The gold is reworked by rubbing it a varying number of times with different degrees of abrasiveness in order to give that roughened effect, where lots of red and other colours show through the uneven texture. The actual A/W looks really beautiful with that old burnished-gold surface done very delicately.

This was submitted to Paul McCartney for his album cover 'Tug of War', released in 1982. He said he wanted something that reflected the tug of war in life: the ups and downs, the good and bad, the fundamental polarity of all things. He didn't want anything domestically oriented like a Kramer *vs* Kramer situation. He wanted something about the eternal cut and thrust of things, the tug of war of existence. Not in quite so many words, of course.

There are times when we at Hipgnosis are individually keen on particular things. This was one of them. Peter said he was interested in icons – those gold-encrusted paintings from Russia. Saints surrounded by areas of gold. This expresses reverence, and the awe in which the saints are held by their devotees. Perhaps there was a desire to show respect by putting something of real material worth into the painting. Art for Art's sake. Money for God's sake.

This interest in icons coincided with an anti-image phase in Hipgnosis. A desire to get away from still pictures into either textural or abstract graphics, or into moving images. We liked the icon idea because we thought of icons as having an actual tactile quality. But we needed a picture that wasn't just a copy of a Russian icon or simply an image of a saint. Something which had some connection to the concept of tug of war. Since we were anti-image at the time, rather than drum up an appropriate metaphor, we worked on inventing something at odds with the origin of our idea, something, indeed, at odds with the purpose of an icon. Something irreligious. It occurred to us that just about the most irreligious thing a person can do is to commit suicide. Thus we decided on a man hanging himself to convey this irreverence. A tug of war in the mind, in the soul. But such an image would *never* grace an icon. A tug of war with itself. A self-contradiction.

Paul rejected the idea. He said that after John Lennon's death, this was too near the bone.

'Just not my image,' he said.

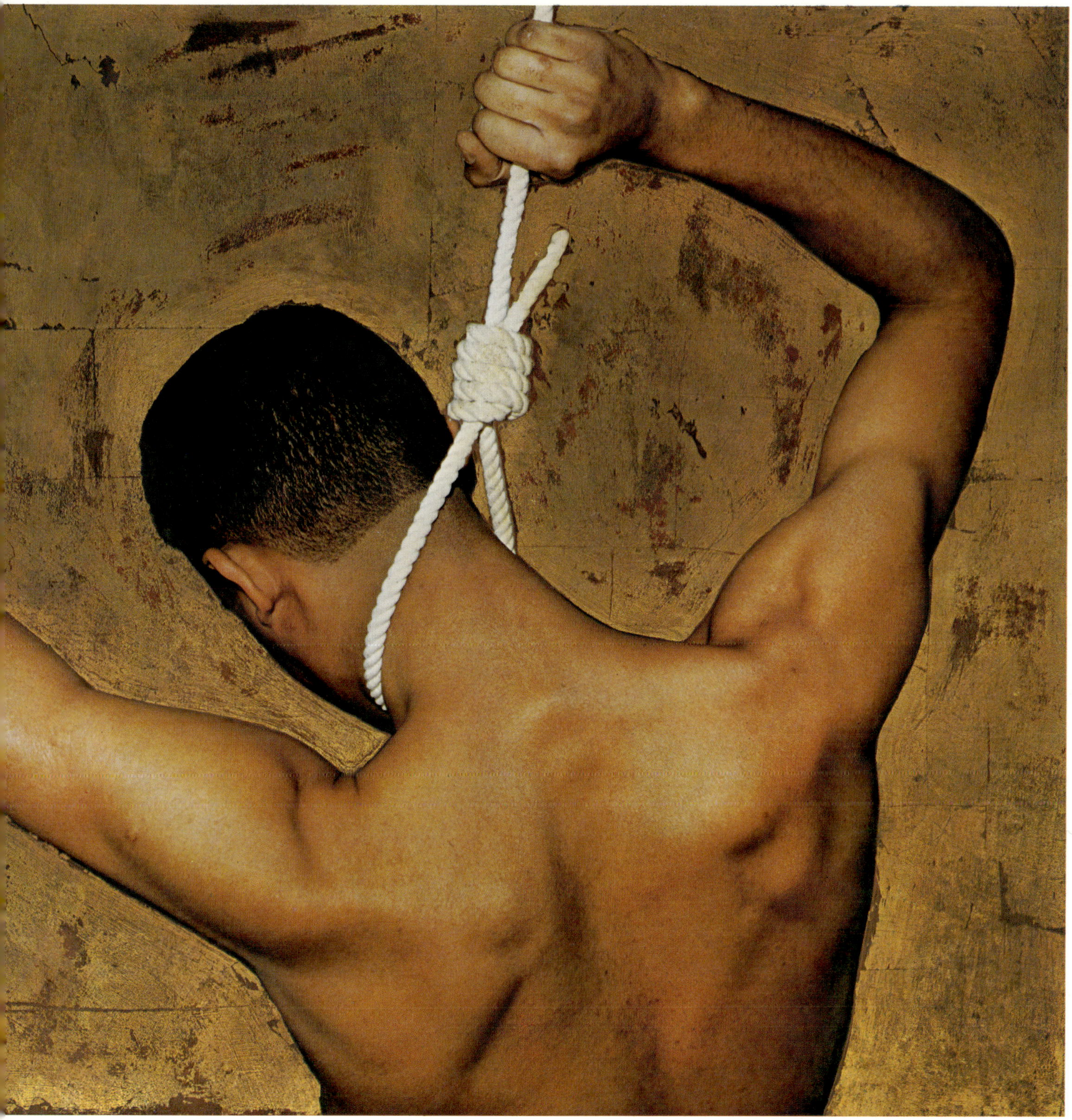

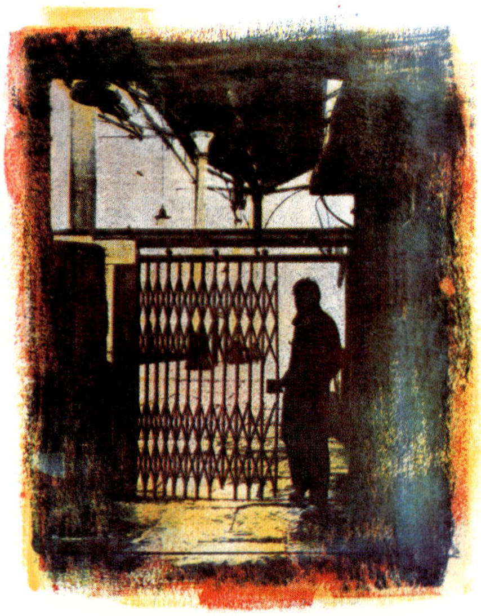

Glossary

Acetate mask Thin film of plastic with a photographic emulsion which can be developed to render some areas of the normally transparent film solid black.

ASA International standard system of measurement of film sensitivity.

Blueprint Graphic format used by architects, in which plans are printed in dark blue on a pale blue ground.

Bowens Quad flash Proprietary brand of mains-powered flash equipment.

Bromide Substance alleged to reduce the sexual prowess of the human soldier; also common name for silver bromide which is the main component of the dark bit in black and white prints.

Butting Positioning two photos or images together without any gap.

B/W Black and White.

Chromafilter Proprietary name for special kind of photographic filter which is graduated between a dark colour and clear. Placed in front of the camera lens, it is usually used to intensify the colour of the sky.

Colour bars Set of vertical coloured bars that are used in TV and broadcasting to align the level, phase, etc., of video signals; also a strip of repeated colour rectangles that indicate the density of the four colour solids in the standard printing process.

Cyclorama White curved background, used in photographic studios, to eliminate all sense of depth or perspective.

D-163 Brand of developer made by Kodak, normally used for the development of photographic paper.

Dye transfer System of colour printing (described more fully on page 44).

Exposure Term used for the amount of light allowed to strike the emulsion of the film.

F-stop Standard designation for the variations of aperture in lenses, which affect the degree of exposure and the depth of field of the lens.

Fills Small quantity of additional light used to illuminate the shadows left by the main light source when they are too dark.

Fish-fry Type of light source in which a number of flash heads are shone through a large sheet of white Perspex. The light from a fish-fry is diffuse, clean and modern-looking.

Flat art Artwork that is opaque and seen by reflected light, as opposed to a transparency, which is viewed by light coming through it. Normally two-dimensional.

Glare Effect which occurs, usually accidentally, when the light source strikes the lens directly, causing areas of the photo to be lighter and to lose detail.

Grant projector Apparatus used in graphic studios to enlarge or reduce artwork images and make tracings from them at different sizes.

Hasselblad Proprietary brand of camera that uses 2¼-inch square format film and features lens of exceptional quality. (And they are still not paying us.)

Joule Unit of energy usually used to measure light.

Keylines Single black lines used to indicate the extent of a picture to be reproduced.

Kodachrome Particularly fine-grain colour film.

Kodatrace Plastic film that you can write on like tracing paper, except that it won't tear or stretch.

Letraset Brand of transfer lettering with which words can be added very simply to prints or artwork one letter at a time.

Line artwork or line print Photo print or illustration consisting of only black and white and no greys.

Matts Our word for acetate masks (see above).

Mechanical An artwork made up of lines and instructions to indicate areas of colour and shading to be applied by the printer and not by the artist himself.

Negative Black and white film (well, usually) after it has been exposed and developed on which the scale from light to dark is reversed, and from which prints can be made.

Nikomat The 35-mm camera system that we use.

Old bogeys Solid material, originating in the nose, which accumulates in small round lumps and sticks to things that are important. Not to be confused with old fogeys.

Pentax 6/7 Camera system using 2¼-inch film but which, unlike the Hasselblad, produces pictures that are 6 × 7 cm in size.

Photoflood Light bulb similar to normal ones but of increased brightness.

Photographic emulsion Thin layer of chemical deposit on a plastic film base which reacts to light and developer to form an image.

Pin bar Small bar of metal with two individual pins on it such that sheets of film with holes in them corresponding to these pins will always fit on the bar in exactly the same place and in register.

Plus-X Relatively fine-grain black and white film made by Kodak.

PMT (photo mechanical transfer) Black and white printing system which produces line films or prints very simply and quickly.

Positive What Peter rarely is about Storm's ideas until they work out OK; also refers to pictures or transparencies that show the scale of light to dark the same way round as the original scene.

Proxar Additional lens for the Hasselblad system which allows focusing at extremely close range.

Pups Affectionate term for low-power spotlights usually used in the film industry.

R-type Colour printing system in which positive prints are made directly from positive transparencies.

Rim lighting When the light is placed behind the subject and pointing towards the camera so that it only strikes the subject's rim. Incredible, isn't it?

Sepia toning Method of chemically altering black and white prints from black to brown, giving them an old-fashioned appearance.

Shutter speed Literally, the speed with which the shutter of a camera opens and closes, affecting the exposure.

Sinar 10/8 Camera system which uses large 10 × 8-inch sheets of film, giving very fine quality at the expense of portability and convenience.

Snoot Metal tube placed on flash heads to produce a narrow spotlight effect.

Strip in Term used to describe the printing of two colour transparencies on the same piece of paper.

2k As in the metric system, k denotes 1000, 2k is therefore 2000, which in this case is a measurement of electrical power used by a particular spotlight.

Trace Tracing paper.

Travelling matte System used in the film business by which foreground objects or figures can be 'invisibly' inserted into a separate background scene.

Tri-X High-speed black and white film made by Kodak.

Tungsten Technical term for type of light source used in old-fashioned Hollywood movies and not so common now, except in films by us.

Umbrella In photography a term for something just like the meteorological kind but with the inner surface lined with reflective material. This is attached to a flash head so that the light bounces off the umbrella and onto the subject.

Vignette The printing of photographs with a soft graded edge.

Wide angle (W/A) Lens with a wide angle of view. Opposite of a telephoto.

Hipgnosis is Aubrey Powell, Peter Christopherson and Storm Thorgerson.

Aubrey 'Po' Powell

Born 23 September 1946 in Sussex. Educated at King's School, Ely, Cambridgeshire, then London School of Film Technique. Worked as a blue-button clerk in Stock Exchange, bus conductor, waiter, on the dole, window dresser and assistant scenic designer in films and television. Currently producer for Green Back Films and director of APP, both spin-offs from Hipgnosis. Still living life to the full and becoming larger on all fronts as a result.

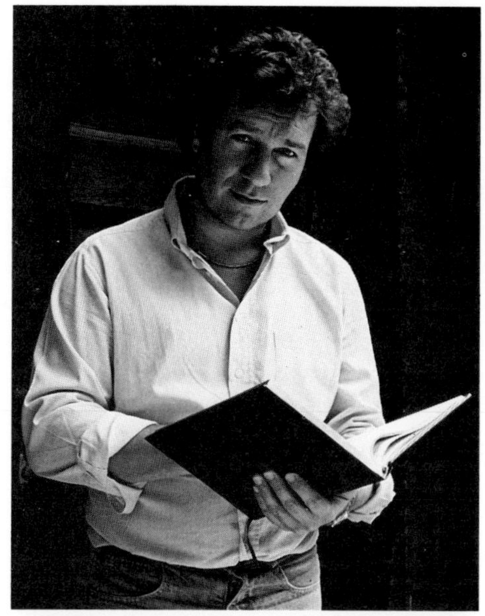

Peter Christopherson

Aged twenty-seven, 6 feet, short dark hair, brown eyes. Director of Psychic Television Ltd, a religious organization, and Green Back Films Ltd, an artistic and commercial organization. Partly educated, partly handsome, and partly hardworking. His whole is none the less greater than some of his parts. Still the youngest partner, even after all these years.

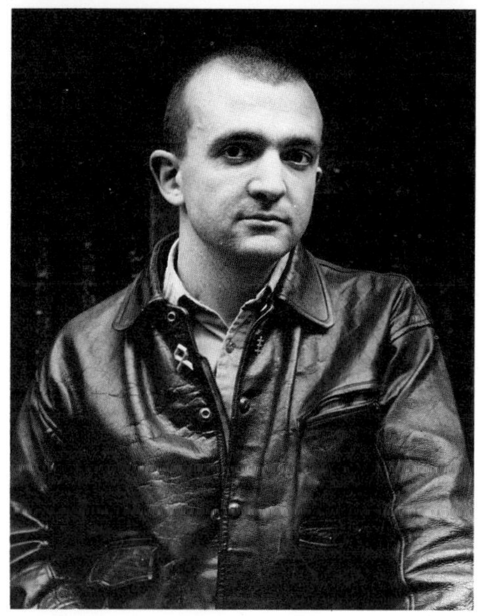

Storm Thorgerson

Born in 1944. Tortuous yet healthy youth in Potters Bar, Middlesex, and Whitely Bay, Northumberland. Educated at A. S. Neill's, Summerhill, Brunswick Primary, Cambridge, and Cambs High School. Various temporary and holiday employment before becoming a hard working full-time student for six years; BA Hons Leicester University, MA Royal College of Art (1966–69).

Stumbled upon Hipgnosis with Po in 1968 and had an immediate neural breakdown. Got shrunk, got sort of married, got a kid, got some more work, got unmarried, got upset, got a grip, got laid, got better.

Director of Green Back Films and STD, and occasionally Lumiere & Son.

Lives alone with his son, Bill, aged ten. Still keen on tennis, acupuncture and the deeper significance of life. Huh?

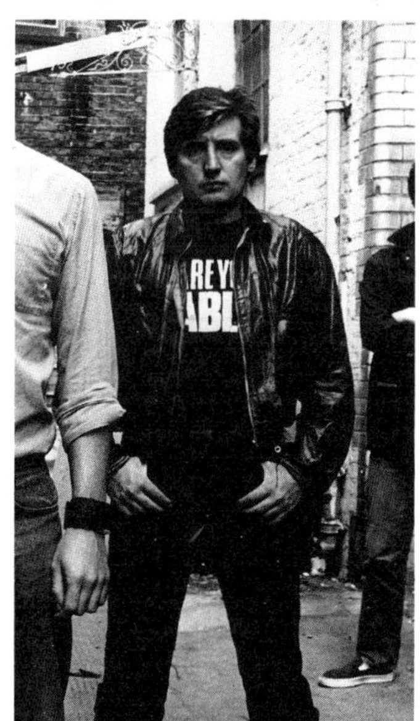

We would particularly like to thank the following studio assistants for their unbelievable devotion and unflagging enthusiasm during the design and production of all the work in this book:

Richard Draper
Paul Maxon
Colin Chambers
Marcus Bradbury
Andrew Ellis
Anthony Taylor

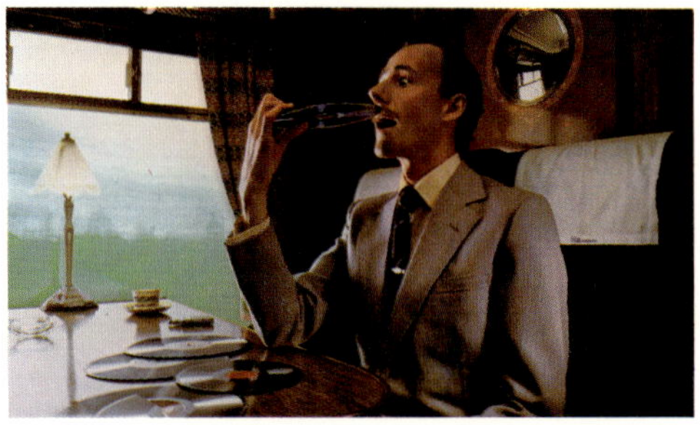

For 'The Goodbye Look'

Design by Neville Brody and Hipgnosis
Layout and artwork by Neville Brody and Colin Chambers
Text by Storm Thorgerson
Edited by Nick Sedgwick
Girl Tuesday and typing: Claire King
Material selected by Hipgnosis
Production assistants: Colin Chambers, Daniel Cohen, Chrisophe Brun
Break page photographs by Andrew Ellis
Main title with respect to R. M.

Retouching by Richard Manning
Photoprinting by Robin at Carl Henry Ltd and Simon at Simon Bell Assoc.

Finally, many thanks to George Hardie and to photographers, designers, bands, executives and friends who have kindly contributed to this tome